From Boys to Men

THE MIDDLE AGES SERIES

Ruth Mazo Karras, Series Editor
Edward Peters, Founding Editor

A complete list of books in the series
is available from the publisher.

From Boys to Men

Formations of Masculinity in Late Medieval Europe

Ruth Mazo Karras

PENN

UNIVERSITY OF PENNSYLVANIA PRESS

Philadelphia

10 9 8 7 6 5 4 3 2

Published by
University of Pennsylvania Press
Philadelphia, Pennsylvania 19104-4011

Library of Congress Cataloging-in-Publication Data
Karras, Ruth Mazo, 1957–
    From boys to men : formations of masculinity in late medieval Europe / Ruth Mazo Karras.
        p. cm. — (The Middle Ages series)
    Includes bibliographical references and index.
    ISBN 0-8122-3699-8 (cloth : alk. paper)—ISBN 0-8122-1834-5 (pbk. : alk. paper)
    1. Boys—Europe—History—To 1500. 2. Young men—Europe—History—To 1500.
3. Masculinity. 4. Men—Socialization. 5. Gender identity. 6. Maturation (Psychology)
I. Title. II. Series.
HQ775 .K373 2002
305.31'09'02—dc21   2002031965

For N.J.M.K. and E.R.M.K.

Contents

I

Masculinities, Youth, and the Late Middle Ages

MEDIEVAL EUROPE WAS A MAN'S WORLD. Recent scholarship has revealed that women in the Middle Ages could hold property, wield political and spiritual power, and make or influence crucial decisions. Yet these women still operated within constraints created by a patriarchal society. Within this patriarchy not all men were in the same position in terms of their power and influence, or in terms of the way society viewed them as gendered beings. Just as society shaped roles for women and defined norms for them (which many, of course, transgressed), it also shaped roles and defined norms for men. Different walks of life created different sets of expectations for men, and individuals did or did not live up to those expectations in a variety of ways.

University scholars, for example, enjoyed a privilege of learning that was inaccessible to women. They lacked some of the aspects of masculinity available to men in other segments of society—marriage and fatherhood, for example, or the wielding of military/political power. Young men who came to the university were initiated into an alternative masculine subculture based on ideals of rationality and moderation, but they not infrequently chose rather to imitate the aristocracy from whose ranks many of them came. Other young aristocrats chose another path with a different set of ideals: knighthood, with all the accompanying mythology of chivalry. Here the realities of late medieval warfare and the politics of marriage alliances clashed with the ideals of single combat and of love. Within the towns, many young men followed a path that traditionally led from apprenticeship in a craft to mastery and independence, but again things did not always work out that way in practice. In all three arenas, young men competed with each other and with their seniors to take their place within an elite. Like women, men lived complex lives that did not always mesh neatly with cultural expectations. This book is an attempt to investigate the complexities of those expectations and their impact on medieval understandings of gender.

Masculinity in the Middle Ages may seem relatively straightforward. This is the period, after all, that gave Western culture many of its conventions of heroism and chivalry. Surely the ideal man of the age was the Knight in Shining Armor. A recent Men's Studies textbook, in its brief historical introduction, defines medieval masculinity this way: the dominant medieval model of masculinity, the "chivalric male," stressed "self-sacrifice, courage, physical strength, honor and service to the lady, and primogeniture."[1] This simplified description fits well with an understanding of medieval masculinity as the opposite of femininity. Did the medieval church not teach that women were daughters of Eve and sources of evil? Women were weak, men strong; women were lustful, men continent; women were foolish, men wise; women were fearful, men brave; women were untrustworthy, men loyal; women were greedy, men generous; women were soft and devoted to luxury, men could endure hardship. Another textbook on masculinity suggests that ideals of manhood have oscillated over the centuries between the two poles of "Puritan" and "Playboy"—with the medieval knight, displaying the virtues prized by the church, serving as an example of the Puritan while the Renaissance courtier personifies the Playboy.[2]

Like many historical generalizations, these popular understandings of medieval manhood contain a grain of truth but fail to stand up to close examination. "The" medieval concept of masculinity resists definition even more than "the" medieval concept of femininity. Recent scholarship in women's history has chipped away at the idea of a monolithic medieval view of women, or a single status for women. Women's experiences varied significantly depending on their position in society, and medieval concepts of "woman" differed among different genres of writing and different authors.[3] Even amidst all of this variety, though, many medieval authors—whether preachers, doctors, or legislators—treated women as a group, regardless of differences among them. Much less commonly did they treat men as a single group. We cannot say that medieval texts as a corpus share any single model of masculinity; indeed there is little prescriptive writing about men as men.

So few medieval texts consider men as a class in part because medieval society was so hierarchical that few statements applied to all male humans. Plenty of religious texts speak of "men" generally, but in the sense of all humans, not just males.[4] Medical texts generalize about all

males, but other genres more commonly make distinctions b
gious status (clergy or laity, regular or secular), birth, or occ
less commonly ethnicity, age, or marital status. Differences among men
may have been no greater than differences among women, but medieval
authors paid more attention to those among men.

No single form of masculinity, then, characterized the Middle Ages,
even the later Middle Ages in Christian western Europe. Concepts of
what it meant to be a man not only changed over time, they also coex-
isted and competed within any given medieval culture or even subculture.
By examining three different social contexts in the later Middle Ages, this
book will explore three divergent models of masculinity. Indeed, it may
be more appropriate to speak of "masculinities" in the plural than the
singular.[5] The medieval cases demonstrate the wide range of meanings
masculinity could take within a given society and caution us against a tendency to generalize about a given era, though they also show us that
commonalities remain not only within the Middle Ages but across time.

This book focuses not just on medieval concepts of masculinity in
different walks of life, but particularly on how men learned to be men.
During young manhood, a time that could range from the teens through
the twenties, men began to assume the status they would hold in life.
Various institutions worked formally and informally to inculcate proper
masculine behavior. This book does not draw much on the literature of
child-rearing and the abundant scholarship on medieval childhood; rather,
it looks at how the institutions of the court, the university, and the workshop formed young men who were no longer children but not yet fully
adult. Because medieval authors said little explicitly about men as men,
the case studies that follow will look at views of masculinity that are implicit in the way people discussed or treated particular groups of men.
They will look at young men learning to play the game of manhood.

Meanings of "Masculinity"

"Masculinity" does not refer to the male body, whose biological and
anatomical features remain relatively constant among different men and
over time, but rather to the meanings that society puts on a person with a
male body, which do change over time. The notion that "masculine" and
"feminine" are not universal characteristics that each person throughout
history possesses to a greater or lesser degree, but are created differently

within each society, is called in scholarly shorthand "the social construction of gender."[6]

The idea that gender is socially constructed is related to, but not quite the same thing as, the idea that it is learned through childhood socialization. Many psychologists in the mid- to late twentieth century adopted a theory that posits gender identity as learned rather than inborn; once learned at an early age it remains fixed, and if inappropriately fixed creates all sorts of problems later in life. This "sex role theory" deeply influenced social psychology. For many psychologists, the sex role represented not society's stereotypes but norms to which men and women should conform for a well-adjusted personality. If a man does not conform to masculine norms, his role socialization in early childhood has failed.[7] A social constructionist viewpoint agrees that identity is not inborn, but argues that whether an individual has a certain gender identity does not depend only upon whether he or she internalizes it, but also—or even more—on the way the world outside the individual views or represents him or her. Identity does not remain stable once inculcated, but is constantly in process, and expresses itself differently under different sets of circumstances.

Various scholars have claimed some components of masculine identity as essential or universal. For example, Elizabeth Badinter argues that unlike feminine identity, which happens automatically to a girl, masculine identity always has to be acquired. It requires the crossing of a critical threshold, such as a specific initiation ritual that marks a boy as becoming a man. A man must test and win his masculinity in a combat.[8] Badinter's universalizing notion comes from the psychoanalytic premise that a boy's relationship with his mother is always, regardless of cultural difference, the most important factor in masculine identity. The formation of identity becomes more or less difficult depending on the closeness of that mother-son bond in a given culture. While in many cultures a break with the mother plays a crucial role in the development of manhood, however, it need not always be so.[9] Not all cultures speak of becoming a man in those terms. To argue that psychoanalytic truths apply even in cultures that do not recognize them is not especially helpful for a historian who wishes to understand a society on its own terms rather than, or in addition to, ours.

A similar understanding of masculinity as a break with the mother appeared in the mythopoetic men's movement of the 1990s, with its universalizing archetypes.[10] The leaders of this movement used ancient myths, or modern versions of them, to construct a masculine identity. Such a mythological approach focuses on what stories about the past mean today, rather than using the stories as a historian would, as evidence about the past. Some medieval texts do depict a boy's growing up as a process of escaping from his mother's influence—for example, the story of Perceval, discussed in Chapter 2. This book will use medieval narratives, but in their medieval context, rather than as examples of archetypes.

To argue that gender difference is socially constructed need not deny any biological component to that difference. To what extent the differences between male and female bodies go beyond reproductive anatomy and body shape to other areas—brain organization, for example—is still in dispute. Both feminists and anti-feminists have argued for the existence of innate or essential psychological differences between men and women. The media give much attention to any suggestion of evidence for a biological basis for gender difference, but such studies so far have been inconclusive scientifically. Animal behavior does not predict human behavior well; gender relations, and levels of aggression among males, differ significantly between the two species of chimpanzees, our nearest relatives, and cannot be extrapolated to humans.[11]

Even if scientists could locate biological bases for gender difference, this would not disprove the notion that gender is socially constructed. Whether a difference has its roots in biology or culture, society always interprets it in particular ways. To take a fairly innocuous example: men as a rule have more facial hair than women (some human populations have more facial hair than others, but within any given population men tend to have more). One can imagine a society in which this difference is totally meaningless because people of both sexes use depilatory creams as soon as any hair appears. One can also imagine a society where having facial hair is extremely important as a signifier of dominance: anyone who does not have it, whether a woman or an underage boy, is marked as subordinate. One can also imagine a society in which facial hair among men is a signifier of social class or ethnic origin or political or religious views rather than of gender, or one in which the appearance of facial hair is a sign of "testosterone poisoning" and leads to the exclusion of the bearded from civic dominance. Thus a biological fact could be given very different cultural meanings. Humans live in societies; if genes influence some human tendencies, the ways those tendencies work themselves out in individual people's lives depend entirely upon social circumstances. To study the different ways societies understand masculine aggression, for example, one need not separate the inborn and learned components of that aggression.

Since different societies across time have constructed masculinity in different ways, we cannot refer to particular traits or behaviors in the Middle Ages as masculine or feminine merely because people today consider them so. In contemporary North American society the habit of paying a great deal of attention to one's appearance is often gendered feminine: many people find it normal for women and somewhat suspicious for men. In some other historical contexts, ancient Rome for example, people similarly accepted women's concern with clothing and make-up as normal (since it was normal for women to be empty-headed wastrels), but accused similarly concerned men of effeminacy. In other societies, however, or in particular subcultures, men are expected to care for their appearance. We must be extremely careful about automatically labeling any concern with appearance on the part of medieval men—or other characteristics construed as feminine today—as effeminate.

We can see the differences in the construction of masculinity in different periods by looking at Robert Brannon's description of the various features of manhood in the United States in the 1970s, which influenced many scholars:

1. No Sissy Stuff: The stigma of all stereotyped feminine characteristics and qualities, including openness and vulnerability.
2. The Big Wheel: Success, status, and the need to be looked up to.
3. The Sturdy Oak: A manly air of toughness, confidence, and self-reliance.
4. Give 'Em Hell!: The aura of aggression, violence, and daring.[12]

Some of these elements can be found (in slightly different form) in medieval images of manhood, but some of them cannot. Medieval culture did not necessarily gender traits like openness and vulnerability as feminine. Men's relationships with God always put men in a subordinate and vulnerable position. To assume that this vulnerability is always feminine is to impose a modern standard. Even when a medieval text clearly presents subordination as feminine—for example, when a writer represents the soul as a bride of Christ—it does not use these feminine images and characteristics in a "sissy" or negative way. Medieval culture, or some segments of it, also placed a high importance on the rejection of worldly status, recognition of one's lack of self-reliance, and utter dependence on God in all things; one might be a "sturdy oak" in relation to other humans but not in relation to the divine. Some medieval texts address much more explicitly the "aggression, violence, and daring" aspect of manhood; this aspect remains more constant than some others, but the reasons behind it and its meanings for the society did not necessarily remain constant. Medieval society also placed a higher value on brotherhood and other bonds among men than contemporary culture; male bonding does not appear in Brannon's list.

Although gender is different in different societies, it can feel like a set of fixed rules real to the men and women who live it. The knowledge that other societies treat one's behavior or desires as normal may not alleviate the problems that arise when one does not conform to gender expectations in one's own society. Yet, while a given individual may feel his or her gender identity fixed, rather than fluid, the way power relations within society construct these categories broadly across time still varies.

Historians who study masculinity generally accept the view that it is socially constructed and changes over time. One example of a field where the study of masculinity has been active is U.S. history, which has seen some fine efforts to establish periodization schemes for American manhood by identifying the points at which new models of masculinity arose and old ones went into decline. Michael Kimmel discusses the competition during the early republic between the "Genteel Patriarch" model, marked by landownership and a connection with British aristocratic lifestyles, and the "Heroic Artisan" model, which valorized the independent craftsman. Over the course of the nineteenth century the "Self-Made Man" supplanted both models.[13] Anthony Rotundo also presents three models: in chronological order, communal manhood, self-made manhood, and passionate manhood.[14]

As Kimmel, Rotundo, and others recognize, ideals of manhood may vary among different segments of society and may change at different rates, so that any periodization relies heavily on generalization. Rotundo's nuanced study, for example, focuses only on middle-class men in the northeastern United States; the picture would no doubt have been different had he looked at other regions and other social groups. Elliott Gorn's work on bare-knuckle prizefighting notes significant differences in ideals of masculinity between middle-class and working-class men. The former derived a masculine identity from their work and from being good providers; the latter held "a more elemental concept of manhood" involving toughness, ferocity, prowess, and honor. For one group, masculinity was responsibility and rectitude; for the other, it was sensitivity to insult and ability to give and take punishment.[15]

While noting that the societies they discuss did not adhere to a single model of masculinity, some scholars introduce the notion of "hegemonic masculinities," privileged forms of masculinity that make a claim to universal applicability. Some segments of a society may be powerful enough to impose their ideal as that to which men of all social groups should aspire. However, it would be far too simplistic to suggest that a hegemonic class unanimously holds a model of masculinity that expresses its class interests. Nor do different models of masculinity simply represent the ideological superstructure of different class positions. People of the same social group can have conflicting ideas about what a man should be—indeed, one individual can have conflicting ideas. Not only do societies adopt particular models and ideals of manhood under particular historical conditions, but individual men may also adopt them in particular situations in everyday life.[16]

Many studies of men focus on "crises of masculinity." Scholars tend to identify the period of their own focus as the important turning point, the period of crisis and resolution, of revolutionary change. The crisis of masculinity may be like the rise of the middle class, something that seems to happen at all historical periods. Indeed, the literature gives the impression that masculinity is an extremely vulnerable state, much more fragile than femininity, always threatened by any encroachment by women or anything remotely connected with the feminine. Whenever social and economic change affects the family, especially when women gain more power, masculinity goes into crisis.[17] Elizabeth Badinter identifies crises of masculinity in seventeenth- to eighteenth-century England and France, and again at the turn of the nineteenth to twentieth centuries, both due to changes in the nature of womanhood. Michael Kimmel reviews a number of crisis points in the modern history of masculinity.[18] John MacInnes argues that the whole idea of masculinity arises out of a crisis, the need to reconcile a belief in human equality with a belief in patriarchy.[19] Medieval Europe, however, did not espouse an ideal of human equality (except before God) so no such conflict of ideals threatened medieval men.

Men's History and Medieval History

Medieval historians, too, have identified various periods of crisis for masculinity based on specific historical circumstances. Jo Ann McNamara discusses a "masculine identity crisis" between 1050 and 1150, which she calls the *Herrenfrage* ("The Man Question," a play on medieval scholarship's old *Frauenfrage*, "woman question," which asked "what is society to do with surplus women?"). It arose because celibate men in this period came to monopolize many positions of authority. As long as lineages had defined and transmitted power dynastically, women constituted important links in that transmission and participated in the exercise of that power. With the church wielding more power and clerical celibacy enforced, the clergy—men who in some ways came close to traditional definitions of femininity—had to distinguish themselves clearly from women in order to maintain their power. They did so by claiming feminine incapacity.[20] While the notion of a crisis is useful when tied to specific changes in culture and society, as in McNamara's work, it becomes less so when applied to broad and vague social changes.

The period I examine in this book saw no "crisis of masculinity" in the sense of broad social trends that threatened all men. Most scholars take the later Middle Ages as a period in which the status of women eroded rather than improved, so no new feminine power arose to trouble the world of men. Rather, in this period various social changes, including an increasing stratification of society in which status at birth made a critical difference in a man's life, affected the masculine identities of particular groups.

Historians often—and properly—choose to focus on change over time, on significant turning points, or on cross-national or cross-cultural comparison. In this book, however, I have chosen to stress contrasts among different groups within late medieval European society rather than across time or place. The different forms masculinity takes even in a single society in the same time period confirm dramatically that it is not a single entity. Looked at on the micro level, Europe—even northwestern Europe— was not a single society, nor were the later Middle Ages—the fourteenth and fifteenth centuries—a single time period. Nevertheless, when we step back and look at the larger picture, both period and region form a coherent enough unit to treat them together.

A number of differences between the medieval and the modern era affect the ways ideas about masculinity were and are created, disseminated, and changed. First of all, medieval society had no mass media; printing did not exist until the very end of the period and pamphlets and broadsheets did not appear until even later. The sermons people heard in church every week provided some mass dissemination of ideas, but although based on a relatively coherent body of doctrine and a group of common preaching aids, these sermons were hardly uniform. No centralized authority dictated what question sermons would address each Sunday. Second, medieval Europe had no broad-based educational system, public or private. Noble boys mostly studied at home with tutors, although some cathedrals, chantries, or even parish churches ran schools. Third, it had no ideology of equality. In contemporary society, although we may never have achieved equality of opportunity or equality under the law, most people believe it a worthy goal, and this affects how they view differences among groups of people. In the Middle Ages, equality was for Heaven perhaps, but not for this earth. Medieval people had little sense that what applied to one man ought to apply to another (except for moral or theological precepts that applied to all humans).

The biggest difference between medieval and modern society that affected ideas about masculinity, however, is that a very large fraction of everything written in the period—and an even larger fraction of what has survived—was written by vowed celibate men. Much of what medieval people thought a man should be comes to us filtered through the eyes of men who had (officially at least) rejected sexual activity as a means of demonstrating manhood. This selection bias creates problems for modern historians searching for sources, and also affected the spread of ideas in the medieval period. Not all the sources for this study were written by churchmen, but some ideologies dominated medieval society more than others and influenced the views of a wide range of people. To understand masculinities in the Middle Ages, we need to remember that many other views go undocumented.

We need also to consider the hierarchical nature of medieval society. Contemporary society is by no means free of gradations of social status or power differentials among men, which have a significant impact on masculine identities. Michael Kaufman argues that "the common feature of the dominant forms of contemporary masculinity is that manhood is equated with having some sort of power." Men internalize a conception of power that implies domination and control.[21] In the Middle Ages, however, political and cultural power were so narrowly held, and control of lords and masters over workers and other subordinates so extensive, that to claim power as the significant feature of masculinity would make many if not most males non-men. This may indeed have been the case: one core feature of medieval masculinity, shared by the three different models discussed in this book, is the need to prove oneself in competition with other men and to dominate others.

Medieval masculinity involved proving oneself superior to other men. This cannot be separated from the understanding of masculinity as the opposite of femininity, for one could be superior to other men by being less feminine, or by dominating women more effectively. In different subcultures, however, the idea of being a man by not being a woman received greater or lesser emphasis. The sheer insignificance that women held for men struggling over their masculinity in some cultural contexts forms as much a part of the complex history of medieval misogyny as do discourses that overtly critique women. Women might threaten men or the social order if they moved beyond their rightful place, but most medieval men took the naturalness of women's rightful place for granted. The assumed privileges of manhood that men claimed in competition against each other relegated women to subordinate roles. The subjection of women was always a part of masculinity, but not always its purpose or its central feature.

In the later Middle Ages the primary way by which a boy established his adult masculinity was by testing himself and proving himself against other men. Women were often tools used in that demonstration. Women not only measured men's competition with each other; they also mediated men's love for each other. The exchange of women could be a measure of male bonding; so could love for the same woman. Men might demonstrate their gender conformity by ostentatiously pursuing women and declaring love for them, as well as by oppressing them. But they did not define themselves by their relation to women as much as by their relation to other men.

Both medieval and modern people tend to understand categories with reference to their opposites. In these terms masculinity is not-femininity and femininity is not-masculinity. We must be careful, however, not to move from this tautology about categories to a conclusion about individual persons. In some cultures when a man thinks of being a man, he thinks of not being womanish; in others, however, he may think first of not being childish. In a culture where men perceive a threat from women, it may be most crucial for men not to behave like them, but other cultures may treat it as equally important for a man to prove his maturity and readiness to assume the adult role.

In the late Middle Ages, different segments of society adopted different understandings of what it meant to be a man. The same elements were present in all the cases, but the emphases were different. In the case of the knight, as discussed in Chapter 2, masculinity was understood as the opposite of femininity, and dominance over other men was achieved through violence and through control of women. For the university scholar, who forms the focus of Chapter 3, a man was not only the opposite of a woman but also, and more explicitly, the opposite of a beast, and dominance over other men came through rationality. For the craft worker of Chapter 4, manhood was, centrally, the opposite of boyhood, and control over other men came via economic means in a paternalistic system. In all three cases these models were cultural constructs that bore a complicated relation to how men lived their lives, but these constructs were what boys learned when they learned how to be men.

The Ages of Men

Even when "man" primarily means "not-woman," masculinity takes on different configurations and meanings depending on position in the life cycle. Different societies define stages of the life cycle in different ways, just as they define gender in different ways. The question of what constituted childhood, adolescence, and adulthood in the Middle Ages is easily as complicated as the question of what constituted masculinity and femininity.

Since this book is concerned with the formation of masculinity at the life stage of young manhood, we need to look at how medieval people understood that stage. Some scholars, citing psychological theories of child development, have argued that people in all societies experience adolescence.[22] Others have argued that while many societies recognize a period of youth or adolescence in between childhood and adulthood, different cultures conceptualize this period in very different ways. Although medieval people recognized many of the same age categories as do moderns, they understood them to refer to quite different chronological ages, and expected people at a given stage of life to feel and behave quite differently from what we expect today.

A large body of medieval literature focuses on the theme of the "Ages of Man," which we might call the stages of life. (The term "Man" here translates the Latin *homo* or human being, but the texts almost invariably describe only the lives of men and boys at each stage.) These stages vary substantially from text to text. The most common age schemata, deriving from different classical Greek, Roman, and Arabic traditions, divide human life into four or seven ages, although some texts use three or six. Young manhood appears in different guises in these texts, sometimes lumped together with childhood. Dante, in his *Convivio*, followed a common four-age tradition that considered *adolescenza* the first age, going up to age twenty-five and characterized by submissiveness, agreeableness, shame, and bodily beauty.[23] Avicenna (Ibn Sina), the great eleventh-century philosopher and doctor, followed an Arabic tradition taking the first stage up to thirty.[24] A competing scheme divided young manhood more sharply from childhood: Philippe de Novare, in his 1265 text *Les quatre âges de l'homme*, made *jovens* (youth) the second age, lasting from around age twenty to forty, and Gervais du Bus's *Roman de Fauvel*, ca. 1314, also made youth the second of four, from fifteen to thirty. A different humor controlled each of the four ages; youth was sanguine.[25] Isidore of Seville's early medieval encyclopedia, widely used in the later Middle Ages, divided life into six ages, with *adolescentia* (defined as "mature enough for generation") from fourteen to twenty-eight, and *iuventus* (youth) from twenty-eight to fifty.[26]

These ages-of-man schemata did not reflect social practices or the ages at which boys took on adult status. The fact that vernacular poetic texts also adopted them, however, means that they went beyond a small scholarly circle.[27] The scheme of the Seven Ages also appeared prominently in art, including wall painting and stained glass as well as manuscript illumination. A wide audience thus had access to the representations of life stages, even if the artists intended them primarily for monastic viewers already familiar with the scholarly conventions involved.[28]

In the modern scheme of childhood/adolescence/adulthood, the adult is fully mature. When one becomes old enough to work for a living and to marry—in contemporary North American society often connected with a rite of passage, graduation from high school or university—one becomes an adult. People recognize a number of gradations—middle age, old age—but do not tend to make a sharp distinction between young and old adults. For most people in the Middle Ages, however, the transition from childhood to a working career did not imply maturity in other ways. Work—whether agricultural, artisanal, or intellectual labor—began at an early age, usually what we would consider today early adolescence. For aristocratic and some urban girls, marriage might come at a similar age, but for all but a few men, and for many women (especially in northern Europe), marriage came much later, and marriage determined full maturity.

Today child development texts and pediatric departments consider adolescence a subset of childhood, but medieval people tended to treat it as a subset of adulthood, not signaling full maturity, but nevertheless sharply distinguished from childhood. Barbara Hanawalt argues that society

in the later Middle Ages extended social childhood for males well into
biological puberty.[29] Yet, as she points out, at fourteen males could enter
into service and many other kinds of contracts, enter universities or legal
training, and marry, although they could not inherit property or become
knights until later. Medieval people did not view the boy in his mid-teens
as a child as people do today, contrary to the view of Philippe Ariès that
adolescence was conflated with childhood and youth with adulthood.[30]

Though parents, employers, and society in general accorded the
young man in his mid-teens many adult responsibilities, they still considered him "wild and wanton" as opposed to "sad and wise" adults.[31] The
juvenis, still in early manhood but beyond the beginning of it, was not as
subject to passions and sin as the *adolescens*, in whom virtues and vices,
particularly sexual and gustatory vices, strove for mastery.[32] In artistic
representations—for example, a Munich manuscript of the five ages of
man from the mid-fourteenth century—the adolescent is shown with a
woman but the "youth" as a knight with military gear.[33] According to
Froissart, who assigned each age of life to one of the planets, Venus, who
controls the age from fourteen to twenty-four, teaches the man the plea-
sures of the table and the bed; from twenty-four to thirty-four, the Sun
spurs the man to seek honor; and from thirty-four to forty-six Mars, who
loves wars, combats, and fights, governs him.[34] A poem from an English
manuscript of about 1430, which its editor called "The Mirror of the Periods of Man's Life, or Bids of the Virtues and Vices for the Soul of Man,"
depicts Reason and Lust speaking to a twenty-year-old: Reason says, "Go
to Oxford, or learn law," while Lust suggests music, pikestaff and buckler
play, making cheer with women at a tavern, and drawing wild fellows together.[35] According to one didactic poem on the seven ages, the vice of
womanizing prevails among youth: the character of Youth says, "With
women me lyst both play and rage."[36] The Scots poem *Ratis Raving*
makes the fourth age, from fifteen to thirty, "joly, proud, and gay," an age
of wasting money on women, but also of learning to discern vice and
virtue.[37] These depictions indicate that young men were not considered
yet fully grown up, and were expected to be rowdy and sexually active.
These expectations, as we shall see, worked out differently under different
social circumstances.

Other kinds of texts besides these theoretical or didactic ones also
give an idea of the way medieval people perceived the process of growing
up. James Schultz argues that Middle High German texts saw childhood
(including what people today would classify as adolescence) mainly as a

deficiency, modeled on adulthood but unable to attain it. Didier Lett finds that in hagiography of the twelfth and thirteenth centuries, the terms *adolescens* and *juvenis* in Latin (or *bachelier* and *valet* in French) began to compete with *puer* (boy or child) from about the age of fourteen.[38] At the entrance into "adolescence," or around thirteen or fourteen, children in hagiographical sources begin to show more independence, deciding for themselves, for example, whether to seek assistance from a saint. At this age, too, representations of children become differentiated by sender. Hagiographic texts depict boys as moody, undisciplined, sensual, pleasure-seeking, and disrespectful to God, girls as virginal, sedentary, and silent.[39] Scholars have done less work, however, on how literary or hagiographical texts treat the age of young manhood than on childhood.

This book focuses on young manhood. People certainly recognized it as a stage of life by the later Middle Ages, whenever they may have begun to do so.[40] However, neither in medieval culture nor in this work does it have a strictly defined beginning and end. Mary Dove equates it with "mature adulthood," arguing that in Middle English texts *youthe* (translating the Latin *juventus*) is synonymous with *middel age, manhod, mannes age*, and *ful age*. She does not use the term "mature," however, as we today might understand it. It is "middle" in that it is between adolescence and old age, but it is not middle aged in the modern sense. It is "perfect" or "full" in that bodily growth has been perfected, and it sometimes begins at legal majority.[41] Medieval texts use the terms with a certain looseness, however. The age group discussed in this work ranges anywhere from the teenage years to the thirties, but often for individual men we have no idea of their age; we only know that various medieval institutions put them in a category of those who have not yet achieved full maturity. Medieval society did distinguish, although not always sharply, between younger and older grown (mature) men.

Many scholars have identified a distinct youth culture in the Middle Ages—not a culture of childhood, as today with the huge toy industry marketing to children as consumers, but one consisting mainly of men in their late teens and twenties. (Most of the study of "youth culture" has focused on men, some of it unthinkingly, some of it informed by feminist concerns but nevertheless recognizing that age operated in different ways for women and men.) Youths participated in this culture not as a vestige of childhood or out of lack of readiness for adult responsibilities; rather youth culture attempted gradually to integrate them into adulthood.[42]

Youth culture in late medieval and early modern Europe often included formal or quasi-formal organizations. They served to help prepare young men for their masculine roles, and did not aim to subvert or upset the social order. Tensions persisted, however, among different definitions of masculinity within medieval society. The family might try to teach boys one set of behaviors, the church another, and the youth fraternity still another set, involving drinking, nonmarital sex, and violence. These latter behaviors composed part of an adult masculine identity, but not a universally accepted one, and led to what Michael Mitterauer calls "a tension which is characteristic of the social integration of young men, a tension which is already present in childhood when boys are rewarded for being naughty."[43] Mitterauer speaks here of a somewhat later period, but his words are relevant to later medieval Europe. We shall see later in this book some of the tensions in youthful masculinity created by different demands on men.

According to the didactic literature the transition out of this youthful stage, in the mid-twenties to thirties, accompanies marriage. Once married, the man heads his household; his roaming days—whether as knight-errant, traveling journeyman, or wandering scholar—are in theory over. This relatively late age of marriage for men agrees with what the demographic evidence suggests. Age at marriage for women varied greatly across later medieval Europe, but age at marriage for men, as far as we can tell, tended to be late in most regions and in most social groups (except the aristocracy, and there only eldest sons married young).[44]

Men today may think of "getting married and settling down" as confining oneself to one sexual partner rather than dating a wide range, and drinking less with the "boys." Marriage in the Middle Ages may have had some of the same results—to the extent that a man had a licit sexual outlet he would not need to search elsewhere—but married men encountered few sanctions for extramarital sex with an unmarried partner.[45] The more important result of marriage for a man in the Middle Ages was his fathering of legitimate children. Until a man did so, he had not claimed his place in the genealogical chain. Genealogy held more importance in some social settings than in others, but even without property or title to pass on, fatherhood formed a central component of the medieval ideology of manhood.

A man did not actually have to become a father in order for people to recognize him as an adult, but he had to have the potential to become one, which meant marriage. Susan Mosher Stuard notes how, from the twelfth century on, marriage in Italy became more than just a passage in a man's life. Marriage defined his identity. Wealth devolved to him at marriage; the family might allocate him a share in the estate even during his father's lifetime, and he also gained control over his wife's often sizeable dowry. He joined the decision-making body of those who controlled the family patrimony, but he also had obligations and restrictions on the use of dowry wealth.[46]

Vowed celibates—priests, monks, canons, and friars—had not even the potential ever to have legitimate children. One could indeed make a case that such men were never fully adult or fully masculine. Ordained priests took the title "Father," and as representatives of God they had as much or more authority as a head of household. Within the monastic context, however, monks remained in the position of a child, subordinate to the abbot-father.[47] In some ways, as discussed in the final chapter, monks never achieved mature masculinity, yet perhaps it is better to think of them as embodying a different masculinity rather than a defective one.

Three Kinds of Manhood

Other points of transition besides marriage, none of which necessarily depended on chronological age, led young men into full manhood. This book will examine the operation of these points of transition, what constituted the jump to manhood and how medieval society marked it. I will examine these questions through three case studies, particular social contexts within the later Middle Ages that shaped adult masculine identities. These contexts are the court, the university, and the craft workshop.

I begin to examine these institutions in the fourteenth century. This may seem a bit unusual, since scholars often take the heyday of knighthood as the twelfth century, and that of the universities the thirteenth. I choose this strategy deliberately. Discussions about chivalry in the twelfth century and the universities in the thirteenth tend to focus on the question of origins. I propose a somewhat different emphasis. Where the institutions, or the models of masculinity embodied in them, came from is an important and interesting question but beyond the scope of this work. Rather, I look at the institutions at a point where they have become institutionalized, not to say fossilized. We do not need to concern ourselves with whether dubbing to knighthood originally came from pre-Christian customs or has its roots in Christian ritual; rather, we will attend to what it meant to fourteenth- and fifteenth-century knights who underwent it and to their compatriots who witnessed it.

Particularly in the final chapter, I will consider masculinity in other institutions and among other groups in the later Middle Ages, and expand the range of possibilities for masculine identity formation. The main focus on these three contexts, however, allows us to probe deeply enough to identify similarities and differences and witness all the complications of such a concept as "medieval masculinity."

The later Middle Ages witnessed a number of changes that affected these three institutions. The demographic crisis following the Black Death, for example, affected the status of craft workers in significant ways. The changing political configurations of northwestern Europe, particularly the Hundred Years War, affected the way courts and courtiers thought about knighthood. The Great Schism, the threat of heresy, and other politico-theological developments had an impact on both the structure of the universities and the content of their teaching. The ways in which these institutions shaped masculine identity changed over time. But the fourteenth and fifteenth centuries still form a relatively coherent time period that can conveniently be treated as a whole.

The study of medieval masculinities is especially important because modernist scholars so often leave the Middle Ages out of cultural history. For historians who believe that capitalism and its attendant social changes caused fundamental reconfigurations of all social categories—and many historians of gender and sexuality fall into this group, due in part to the influence of Michel Foucault—the Middle Ages constitute a static and not very interesting period. For historians of the United States, history often seems to begin with European expansion. In his excellent (although not mainly historical) book on masculinity, Tim Connell argues that the modern gender order emerged between 1450 and 1650, caused among other things by the Reformation's disruption of the monastic ideal and positive revaluation of marriage; the emergence of the individual; the emergence of compulsory heterosexuality; the creation of overseas empires; the growth of cities, with their culture based on rational economic calculation and their sexual subcultures; and large-scale European civil war.[48] Not one of these causes, however, erupted full blown in the early modern period; the Middle Ages form part of their history.

It should go without saying—but perhaps does not—that a feminist scholar's writing a book on men and masculinity does not represent a recantation of feminist views. I do not believe that there is no more to be said about medieval women, nor do I think women have received too much emphasis in recent years at the expense of men. Rather, this project grows out of the recognition that we cannot understand women's lives without understanding men as men (as opposed to men as the normative humans, the traditional focus of historical study). Scholars have made great progress in working out the complexities of femininity in the Middle Ages but have barely begun the parallel work on masculinity. Dismissing men as wielders of patriarchal oppression and unworthy of feminist examination is as reductive as dismissing women as unimportant historical actors.

Men's relations (or lack thereof) with women form an important part of their masculine identities, but so do their relations with other men. Sometimes women's very oppression occurs because men value them mainly as objects or commodities in the struggles among individual men or groups of men. Violence against women, for example, affects women deeply; but the men who commit it may intend it against the male relatives of those women, not even considering the women themselves. Regarding women as insignificant or irrelevant is misogynist in a different way than overt antifeminism. Relations among men are worth studying for what they reveal about women as well as for themselves.

Understanding how boys learn to be men in a variety of historical contexts lets us understand the gender and class dynamics of the societies in question. In medieval Europe, boys learned to compete physically, intellectually, and economically with each other to achieve mature masculine identity. In so doing they defined what a man should be and what a woman could never be.

2

Mail Bonding: Knights, Ladies, and the Proving of Manhood

KNIGHTS ARE WHAT MEMBERS of the general public think of when they think of the Middle Ages. Camelot still exerts a powerful hold on the imagination. The knight epitomizes a modern idea of masculinity, although perhaps not the dominant one: the "knight in shining armor" who rescues the maiden from all her troubles. The idea of performing great feats for no reward but honor and renown strikes many as especially appealing. The junk mail that offers us wall plaques with the Karras coat of arms (although the name in that form goes back no further than Ellis Island) attempts to cash in on this fascination.

The knight exercised a similarly powerful hold on the medieval imagination. People from all literate segments of late medieval society, including monks and nuns, read chivalric literature. ("Chivalric" can mean many things, but I use it here in its original sense—"having to do with knights.") Not only aristocrats attempted to emulate the activities of Arthur and his Round Table; the theme also became an important part of town pageants as well. The church often used knighthood as a metaphor: crusaders and members of the military orders were "knights of Christ" in the most literal sense, but anyone who fought against the forces of the devil could be discussed in the language of knighthood. (We shall see in Chapter 3 how this language was used in the universities as well, to describe intellectual combat.) Although the social organization and military practice of knighthood varied across Europe, an international chivalric culture of shared values gave the aristocracy a set of common ideological features.

Knighthood epitomized one set of medieval ideals about masculinity. The purpose of this chapter is to delineate just what those ideals were—how medieval culture constructed a particular, socially situated model of masculinity different from those found in other segments of society. The knight competed with other men through physical aggression. Physical prowess and military success were always an important part of what medieval people admired in their leaders, and it was in feats of arms that young boys received their first knightly training, although medieval authors suggested that they should learn battle strategy and tactics as well. Violence was the fundamental measure of a man because it was a way of exerting dominance over men of one's own social stratum as well as over women and other social inferiors. Both medieval and modern people tend to see "chivalry" as a civilizing ethos, controlling the violence that otherwise would have reigned unchecked. As Richard Kaeuper and other scholars have pointed out, however, chivalric honor ultimately could be defended only by violence, and the people whose chivalric deeds were most admired were those who were the most successful at violence.[1] The degree of control that kings or other military leaders exerted over knightly violence, however, led to conflicts over the masculine ideal.

Violence as a central feature of masculinity is, of course, by no means limited to the medieval aristocracy. Pierre Bourdieu is hardly alone when he generalizes that "manliness must be validated by other men, in its reality as actual or potential violence, and certified by recognition of membership of the group of 'real men.' "[2] It is much more prominent, however, in some historical contexts than others. In the late Middle Ages, violence was the mode of masculine expression within knighthood, while in the university men fought with verbal weapons and in the craft workshop with economic ones.

In discussing knighthood this chapter focuses on the ideological aspects, the role of chivalry in medieval mentalities. Men with the social and legal status of knight played an important role in the governance of many late medieval polities, on both the local and the national level. This role was more significant for political history than the one they played on the battlefield. Yet it was not political but military activity that defined social identity and the masculine ideal for young men of the aristocracy, from scions of great noble families to younger sons of petty landholders. Even a man whose life was spent on property management, litigation, and parliamentary service, like John Paston II of the famous Norfolk letter-writing family, participated in tournaments, in part as a way of getting the patronage he needed from his social superiors.[3] The number of those who were knights by occupation as opposed to status was limited, but even those who did not participate themselves in wars or tournaments were deeply affected by the chivalric ethos.

This ethos was to a large extent created by chivalric literature. The literature varied in different parts of Europe as well as across time, and the discussion here, which focuses on northwestern Europe, notes some of that variation, but the similarities were at least as important as the differences. The same stories were told in various literatures; young men from different regions encountered each other at tournaments or when they became each others' prisoners, and had an opportunity to develop a shared outlook. Chivalric culture was to a great extent international, despite regional variation. The eclectic selection of examples here reflects that international character. This literature does not and cannot tell us how knights actually behaved, any more than cop shows tell us how police officers actually behave. It can, however, show us what the expectations of its audience were, and something about how that audience understood the world.

The Significance of Chivalry

A discussion of knightly masculinity requires us first to sketch out the social context of knighthood in the later Middle Ages. The relation between chivalric ideals and social practice was always problematic. Certainly many men who held the title or exercised the military function of a knight led lives that bore little relation to the ideals expressed in either didactic or narrative literature. Just as literature did not reflect the chivalric life of the later Middle Ages, neither did life directly reflect art. But art surely influenced life, and the ideology of chivalry exercised a powerful influence on late medieval mentalities, which in turn influenced how people behaved. Understanding the ways people thought about knights, and the ways knights thought about themselves, goes a long way toward helping us understand medieval society and culture.

So much of what has been written about medieval knighthood deals with the twelfth century and the origins of the institution that it is important to remember that in the era discussed here, the fourteenth and fifteenth centuries, we are hardly even dealing with the same thing. Originally the German *Ritter* and French *chevalier* just meant a mounted warrior.[4] The English *knight* originally had connotations of service, and the Latin *miles* meant a soldier or a foot soldier in particular, but they too came to refer to mounted warriors. Over the course of the twelfth and thirteenth centuries—spurred by influential works of literature like those of Chrétien de Troyes—the term "knight" (or its equivalents) came to have an ethical meaning: it was someone who lived by a code of chivalry.[5] At the same time, it also came to have a concrete social or economic meaning: a knight was someone who held enough land to finance the purchase of a war horse and armor, neither an inconsiderable expense. In England, for example, from the eleventh century, a specific amount of land came to be called a "knight's fee" and anyone who held that much land owed the service of one knight to the lord's muster. Mounted and armored troops, however, played a smaller role in battle by the later Middle Ages than they did earlier. Knighthood remained important socially and culturally but less so militarily.

By the later Middle Ages, the status of knight was much more clearly defined, and the hereditary aspects of knighthood had become much more important than earlier. In Germany, for example, one could not compete in a tournament unless one could prove knightly descent for four generations on both sides. Knighthood meant being part of a fixed social group as well as accepting a particular way of life. Elsewhere in Europe, too, knights were normally expected to come from a knightly class and male members of that class were expected to become knights, unless they went into the church. But holding the socio-legal status of knight did not mean fighting as one. As a social class, knights or those eligible to become knights were roughly equivalent to the male half of the aristocracy (including much of the petty aristocracy). The knights whom this chapter discusses, however, are those who actually fought in tournament or in battle, or imagined themselves doing so. They might be described as the military arm of the aristocracy.

Both in the later Middle Ages and earlier, those who were knights by occupation as well as by status tended to be young men. They were typically knighted around the age of twenty-one (although this was not a hard and fast rule), and married somewhat later. The factor that determined when they married was often the acquisition of land, so a married knight was a landowner and householder, although he might still attend tournaments or accompany his lord on a campaign. It was the younger knights, the *juvenes* or knights bachelor, and the young men who had not yet been knighted who were able to devote themselves full time to the practice of arms and the social world that went with it, and it is these knights and knights-to-be we focus on here as they learned how to be men.

The fourteenth and fifteenth centuries witnessed something of a blossoming of interest in chivalry all over Europe but especially in the northwestern regions on which this study focuses.[6] This was the era of the Hundred Years War between England and France, which lasted, on and off, from 1337 to 1453 (followed in England by the Wars of the Roses from 1455 to 1485). The war made knighthood a matter of actual combat, not just tournaments, and raised the level of public interest. Although knighthood at this time had a concrete military meaning, however, its administrative meaning remained important as well. In England, for example, being a knight meant that one was a member of the county gentry. This status could not be separated from the knights' military role; a significant portion of the county gentry had fought in the royal armies in France or in border campaigns, and used the profits they made from booty and ransom, as well as the networks of patronage and clientship they developed, to improve their local standing.[7]

Knighthood, then, was a matter of social status as well as—or even more than—military function. Court display and the ideology of chivalry that emphasized the honor and importance of the knight gave the lower aristocracy something by which to distinguish themselves from bourgeois merchants, who were beginning to wield substantial economic, and in some places political, power. Chivalry allowed one social group to see itself not only as an elite who followed a higher code, but also as the real men whose activity was indispensable to society. It was not an outmoded game but an integral part of how the ruling elite defined itself.[8] Indeed, the ideal of knighthood could be part of the aristocracy's defense against royal power.[9] As the aristocracy's struggle with the monarchy played itself out in many regions, chivalric literature emphasized how crucial they were to the king's military success and brought out the fundamental tensions between loyalty and personal renown, between individual bravery and prowess and collective military success. As infantry and artillery threatened to make knights obsolete, the chivalric ethos measured a man's worth by how bravely and strongly he fought as an individual rather than how he contributed to the winning of a battle.

Some scholars suggest that in the later Middle Ages there were distinct models of knighthood, one embodying the virtues of skill in arms, bravery, and loyalty, one piety, chastity, and humility, and one love and courtly accomplishment.[10] Although not all knights described in literature or biography exemplify exactly the same values and not all treatises on knighthood have exactly the same emphases, the sets of virtues in fact overlap, and not all literary (or historical) figures can be easily classified in one of these three groups. All the seemingly contradictory aspects occur in varying proportions across a wide range of texts, and together compose the type of manhood to which potential knights were taught to aspire. When Gawain in Malory's *Morte Darthur*, who embodies the less "courtly" model of prowess and loyalty, is criticized for his lack of courtesy, Malory tells his readers that true knightly perfection requires a combination of these values.[11]

Military prowess—expertise in the use of violence—was far from the only important feature of knightly masculinity. In the later Middle Ages it was in constant tension with another ideal, that of gentility and courtliness. The successful man in the chivalric world was one who not only could fight but also knew how to behave appropriately at court, and this included behavior toward women. The knight in shining armor had to have his damsel. Unlike the university scholar's masculinity (Chapter 3), defined in a context where women were absent, the knight's was defined in large part by his relation to women. The achievement of manhood depended on mastering the sometimes conflicting, sometimes complementary ideals of prowess (successful violence) and love (successful commodification of women).

Success in love was an important part of knighthood. This did not mean that the knight's goal was to impress women. Rather, he used women, or his attractiveness to women, to impress other men. Much of chivalric culture was built around a myth of women's power over men through love. This system denied what real political and economic power women had and gave them an empty authority. Women, as signs and as stand-ins, mediated relations between men.[12] Scholars have debated the relation of "courtly love" to the position of women in the Middle Ages— was the woman in this system a subject or merely an object? Did it express real respect for women and reflect their social and economic power, or did it only put them on a pedestal in order to deny them power in other areas of life? Was the whole system merely a literary conceit or did it affect people's lives?—but the understanding of love also affected the position of men. For every woman represented as a powerful decision-maker, granting or withholding her love, a man is represented as a supplicant. Part of the knightly model of masculinity involved ritualized submission to women, even if it masked a more fundamental relation of dominance.[13]

During the later Middle Ages those who were knights by social status appropriated the Arthurian chivalric ethos and wrote new versions of it. Malory's *Morte Darthur* is the most famous late medieval English

example (based on thirteenth-century texts, which Malory adapted substantially), and was very popular among Malory's peers.[14] Knights and
their protégés wrote or translated handbooks of chivalry: Geoffroi de
Charny's handbook was written in the mid-fourteenth century, and in the
fifteenth century Ramón Llull's thirteenth-century book was translated
into various vernaculars. Vegetius's Roman military manual was heavily
used as well, as translated into French by Christine de Pisan and in an English verse paraphrase. There were notable differences among these and
other texts, including a greater emphasis in later works on the importance
of lineage, but their fundamental similarities about knightly ideals allow
them to be treated as a group.[15]

The literature of chivalry was widely read. The typical knightly household owned several books that quite often included chivalric literature.
(The influence of this literature into the early modern period, indeed, is
what Cervantes satirized in *Don Quixote*.) Numerous passing references
indicate that people did know this material. Kings and dukes had romances read to them, and authors like Philippe de Novare, Philippe de
Beaumanoir, Ramón Llull, and Geoffroy de Charny show familiarity with
Arthurian romance in their nonfiction works.[16] Orders of knighthood
founded in the fourteenth century, like the Garter in England, the Star in
France, and the Golden Fleece in Burgundy, drew explicitly on romance
models (although the Golden Fleece also had classical echoes); indeed,
before establishing the Order of the Garter, Edward III had previously attempted to revive the Arthurian Round Table.[17] Tournaments and jousts
picked up literary themes; some were called "Round Tables," others were
fought in Arthurian costume.[18] Literary tournaments also copied from
real ones in giving detailed descriptions, for example, of the coats of arms
of Arthur's knights, something not found in twelfth-century versions.[19]
Even more influenced by Arthurian literature were the *pas d'armes* in
which a knight would defend a spot against all comers for a period of
time. These defended spots often included legendary and magical elements: a fountain, a lady dressed all in white, a chained giant led by a
dwarf.[20]

Literature provided entertainment, but it also affected the ideals,
interests, mentalities, and aspirations, if not the actual behavior, of the
knightly class in the late Middle Ages. It worked to reconcile several sets
of competing ideals: romantic love, gentility, knightly prowess, and piety.
Those who read it, and took it seriously, in the later Middle Ages internalized the aristocratic ethic, the ludic aspects, and the Christian tinge as

parts of the definition of the ideal man. Young men also learned appropriate chivalric behavior through listening to conversation and personal recollections as well as literary and historical narratives. A household book of Edward IV of England noted that it was the custom of squires at court, in the evenings, to "keep honest company . . . in talking of chronicles of kings and other policies."[21] They would have learned about appropriate court behavior as well as the chivalric values like loyalty and courage.

Johan Huizinga used the Burgundian court—the one most renowned in the fifteenth century for its chivalric pageantry, much of it based on literary models—as his primary example to demonstrate that the fifteenth century was a period of decadence.[22] To him, all this pageantry was an empty sham, a "deliberate and insincere renascence of ideas drained of any real value," "a literary and sportive fashion of the nobility and nothing more."[23] Chivalry had outlived any real military or social usefulness and was now an aristocratic game. The same has been said about chivalric literature and practice in other regions of Europe. Arthur Ferguson suggests that in England, at a time when knighthood in the military sense had little to do with political or administrative life, and when military defeats were leading to threatening social changes, "[t]he chivalric tradition was thus the last refuge in secular thought for a bewildered and bedeviled aristocracy."[24] The new military orders—the Garter in England and the Golden Fleece in Burgundy—have been dismissed as cynical manipulations of chivalric notions of a knightly elite, in the service of a monarch's political goals.

Recent scholarship, however, has shown that chivalry remained active as an ideal in northwestern Europe in the later Middle Ages.[25] If it was a game, it was a very serious one: people took up the attitudes associated with chivalry not just as part of a charade, but as part of their whole outlook on life. The new orders may be seen as an indication of how seriously people did take chivalric values: they would not have worked as a means of royal patronage if the symbolism had not been meaningful.[26] Attitudes drawn from literature about military activity, about gender, about class, were internalized as people modeled their lives on chivalric ideals. Indeed, knighthood in the late Middle Ages was not so much a decaying version of an older institution as an institution created by aristocrats who wanted to glorify their own public service in the face of competition from other elites. They looked back to a golden age of chivalry that may or may not have existed in the twelfth and thirteenth centuries. This does not mean that knights were really running the society—in fact it is in part the weakening of the power of the nobility in relation to the monarchy, at least in England, that led to the emphasis on chivalry. Men of low birth who rose through merit might acquire money and political power, but they could never acquire chivalric honor.[27] Nor could women. The Low Countries in the later Middle Ages, for example, saw a large number of female rulers and regents, but the actual political power these women wielded did not affect the chivalrous ideal of masculinity in the Burgundian Netherlands.[28]

Nor do all scholars agree with Huizinga's statement that the mounted, armored knight was largely irrelevant to warfare by the fifteenth century.[29] It is true that foot soldiers did occasionally defeat knights, as at the battle of Sempach in 1386, which spurred the use of hired infantry.[30] With the increasing use of gunpowder and artillery weapons, warfare took on a new character. This revolution was in progress but far from complete by the end of the fifteenth century, and the knight had not yet become an anachronism. Malcolm Vale suggests that knights continued to be useful in warfare because of their great psychological importance.[31]

The tournament and the joust by no means reflected actual battle-field conditions—in fact, in war conditions knights would participate in *chevauchées* or cavalry raids more often than in pitched battles—but they did allow the knight to exercise skills that he would be likely actually to use in battle against other knights. The mêlée, where the knights of a lord's retinue gained valuable experience fighting together, lost favor to the joust in the late thirteenth and fourteenth century, but even later some jousts were fought *à l'outrance*, that is, with battle weapons instead of blunt ones.[32] War, to an individual knight if not to a prince, had much in common with a tournament in that both were opportunities to demonstrate skill in arms (although battle, involving foot soldiers as well as knights and much more complicated tactics, was far more demanding and dangerous).

Young Knights in Training

Unlike the models of masculinity discussed in Chapters 3 and 4, in which young men's aggressiveness came into conflict with the institutional norms of manhood for their social group and created conflict, the norms for a young man of the chivalric class welcomed aggressiveness. Whether he was to fight in tournament or battle—or neither—he was to train his body in martial skills from an early age.

Learning military skills was not the only purpose of the tournament, let alone the only purpose of the training of a young potential knight. A future knight (for one did not actually have to be knighted to joust) was to learn aristocratic masculine behavior through attendance at and participation in jousts, but he also learned how to behave to other knights in situations other than battle, as well as how to behave with women. A fifteenth-century version of Ramón Llull's didactic work on chivalry explained what it is that a young man needed to learn:

It behooves that the son of a knight, during the time that he is a squire, can take care of a horse. And it behooves him to serve, and that he be subordinated before he is a lord. Otherwise, he should not know the nobility of lordship when he is a knight. Therefore, it behooves every man who wishes to achieve knighthood to learn in his youth to carve at the table, to serve, to arm and dub a knight, for in the same way as a man who wishes to learn to sew to be a tailor or a carpenter needs to have a master who can sew or hew, in the same way a noble man that loves the order of chivalry and wants to be a knight needs first to have a master who is a knight.[33]

The young knight must emulate his mentor, both in military pursuits and in other aspects of demeanor (carving at table and manners at feasts, for example). Llull did not mention the love of women, but the imitation worked in the same way. One who had achieved knighthood could serve as a model for others.

The education of a young man of the knightly class took place in a world in which women were not absent, but peripheral (in England, for example, aristocratic households were heavily male).[34] In the fourteenth and fifteenth centuries young men might be educated in knightly skills and behavior within their fathers' households, but more likely in the household of another: an uncle or other relative, a patron of the father's. All great households included a number of such boys. Here they would have heard the romances they were to emulate, practiced the military skills they would need, and learned courtly pastimes.[35] The hero of *Petit Jehan de Saintré* became a page to the King of France, and this text shows us what a late medieval audience might learn from literature about the education of a future knight: "Furthermore, for a thirteen-year-old, he was a very skillful and hardy youth, whether for riding a very rough horse, for singing or dancing, for playing tennis, for running, for leaping, and for all the other contests and amusements which he saw the men do."[36] Royal or other especially large households had teachers in various subjects for the boys.[37] Manuals of behavior and morality include material on table manners for boys in such households. The boys were also expected to learn music and chess, and to play with weapons and hunt. In noble households they were given special training sessions with arms, and special tournaments were organized for them; by their mid-teens they were expected to play an actual role in fighting.[38] Although they might not be knighted yet, they could hope to serve as pages to noble men or women. This put them in a servile position, but only temporarily, as part of a life stage.

Although a boy or young man at a royal or noble court would have been highly aware of his family background, he did not live the formative years of adolescence among his kin, but in a military atmosphere, highly charged with knightly values. Women were by no means absent from this life, but they were present in an eroticized rather than a familial setting, and the daily companionship was with other men, with whom a knight competed for the favor of a higher-status man. The young knight-to-be thus learned that women were objects to be won, while men were comrades and rivals in the winning of honor. Young knights had a greater or lesser opportunity to be exposed to, and to internalize, these ideas depending where they fell on the social scale. Not all families would have been able to place their sons in a noble household, which required connections. But even for relatively obscure or impoverished members of the county gentry or petty nobility, service in a noble household or retinue remained an important goal and knightly military activity an important path to social advancement.

The lives of late medieval knights, as written by biographers and chroniclers, show a strong resemblance to the lives of knights in literature—in part, no doubt, because their biographers were steeped in that literature, in part because, in behavior at court, people imitated models they knew from literature. At any rate, these biographies can show what was expected of a young man if he was to develop into the ideal knight. A look at several of these accounts shows how the chivalric ideals were interpreted in the lives of specific individuals.

The Burgundian knight Jacques de Lalaing died young, and his entire biography is an account of the training and development of an ideal young knight. Jacques came from a family of Burgundian petty nobility affiliated with the duke of Cleves, who took Jacques with him to the court of Burgundy "at the end of his childhood."[39] According to his biographer Georges Chastellain, he showed a great precocity in chivalric combat, as well as in hunting and chess. This attracted many women to him. After he maintained his *pas d'armes* for a year, says Olivier de la Marche, "you may believe that the ladies of the land made gracious mottoes in his praise, and called him a good knight."[40] In one joust he wore the tokens of two duchesses. But, although he always spoke with ladies in a courtly and genteel manner, and became involved in some mild intrigues with great married ladies, he did not marry. Jacques decided that his goal was to defeat thirty worthy opponents before he was thirty years old.[41] He traveled around Europe, challenging knights in France, Spain, Scotland, and England to jousts; he then returned to Burgundy to hold a *pas d'armes*, the Fountain of Tears.[42] It took place at a pavilion with an image of the Virgin Mary on it, inhabited by a damsel in a robe covered with tears and a unicorn bearing three shields, also covered with tears. Challengers touched one of the three shields to indicate their choice of weapon. Jacques maintained this *pas* for a year against twenty-two challengers.[43] This was only one of many such *pas d'armes* in the Burgundian realm in the middle of the fifteenth century. The fairy-tale trappings gave a game-like quality to the fighting, turning it from sheer force and violence into part of a courtly story.

For Jacques de Lalaing, however, fighting was not just a game. He fought on behalf of the Duke of Burgundy in Luxembourg and against the rebellious citizens of Ghent. Confirming the views of historians who argue that mounted shock troops were obsolete by this time, Jacques died in a rather un-knightly way: he was struck down by a cannonball outside the walls of the town of Pouques at the age of thirty-two.[44]

The story of Jacques de Lalaing, renowned as the greatest knight of Europe, tells us something about what masculine qualities late medieval people admired. They looked for military prowess in a knight, but at least for a young man as opposed to an experienced general single combat much more than the actual campaigns in the field brought him his renown at the European courts. The latter may have been more practical, but the former was a more important part of the mental world of the knight. His biography also stresses his courtly manner, his treatment of those around him, including women, and his elaborate dress and accouterments, part of an aristocratic ethos of masculine display.

The description of Galeas of Mantua written by Thomas of Saluzzo in 1394–95 contains similar chivalric elements. Among other adventures, Thomas recounts how Galeas jousted for the sake of his lady with a German knight who had taken a vow to fight whatever man would take up his challenge. He fought on the French side in the Hundred Years War and was knighted there; he also fought in the service of the kings of Cyprus and Hungary. Thomas compared Galeas at thirty years of age with Sir Tristram of Lyonesse or Sir Palamedes.[45] Whether or not love really motivated him to undertake his adventures, this author put him into that romantic mold; his life as written combined prowess and courtesy, and the author was very aware of the literary context in which contemporary knights operated.

Don Pero Niño, a Castilian knight of the late fourteenth to early fifteenth century, was taken into a great household at an early age like Jacques de Lalaing. His biographer describes his exploits as more military than sporting: he was involved in battles, especially at sea, more than tournaments. However, to fit the chivalric ideal, he had also to succeed at jousting and other sports.[46] He did his greatest deeds after coming to the age of "his manhood" (*virilidad*), that is, after his twenty-fifth year.[47] He married well, the sister-in-law of his patron Ruy Lopez, and the biographer claims that it was because the two were often together and fell in love. The widowed Doña Costanza "had heard many gallant things told of this knight, young, fair, generous, bold, courageous, gentle" and had chosen him. The political advantages of this union are not mentioned. The author also describes a planned second marriage, to a French widow of noble family, and a second marriage that actually took place clandestinely, to Beatriz, daughter of the Infante Don Juan, as love matches.[48] In all three biographies, then, the authors stress heterosexual love as an important shaping force in the young man's quest for prowess, central to what it means to grow up as a man. The lesson was not lost on other young men.

In these accounts, and in Arthurian and other romance literature as well, the knight's youth is a time in which he travels around in order to prove himself, demonstrating his prowess to, and in competition with, other men. Not all young men in practice imitated this literary convention; some attached themselves quite early to a particular lord and served him for an entire career, as Pero Niño did. Jacques de Lalaing also served one lord, but received permission to travel about in order to challenge other knights and prove his prowess. Galeas, on the other hand, traveled in search of both adventure and pay; he went where his services were in demand. The careers of all three illustrate the notion of a period of youth during which one proved oneself before taking up one's position as a full member of society, as a landholder or petty noble. It is during this period that the knight had to demonstrate his achievement of the chivalric masculine ideal. Biographies like these, together with more fictional chivalric literature, provided models for potential knights to emulate. Their focus remained firmly on the need to prove themselves in physical combat against other men.

Birth, Prowess, and Conduct

The ideal of knighthood that young men were to emulate required, as a prerequisite, knightly birth. By the later Middle Ages many texts both fictional and ostensibly nonfictional treated this as a sine qua non, strictly limiting knightly masculinity to the elite. In a sense the young knight, by being born into the right family, had already proven himself against most other men. The challenge issued by Jacques de Lalaing, for example, specified that only those who could prove their knightly ancestry "in four lines" (that is, all their grandparents must be of aristocratic birth) were to take it up, and he himself put up banners with his family tree to indicate his noble descent on both sides.[49] Although occasional exceptions in practice show that the boundaries of the knightly class were in fact somewhat permeable—men could be knighted on the battlefield or as a reward for other kinds of service—the ideology was generally that they were not.[50]

When men were ennobled or knighted (which in many places amounted to the same thing) for deeds of arms, they were often men of substantial wealth, but wealth alone did not do it: military achievement was also necessary. Without some degree of wealth, however, promotion to knighthood and nobility would be meaningless, because the new knight would not be able to maintain his state.[51] Some knights were self-made, coming from petty aristocratic, albeit relatively impoverished, families, and earning the wherewithal to support a knightly state through their achievements in battle. For a young man from a non-knightly family in the later Middle Ages to achieve his way into this class, however, was quite unusual. When men were knighted on the battlefield, as in the Battle of

Aljubarrota in 1385 when Juan I of Castile created sixty knights, those men already had horses and armor or the title of squire, and probably came from knightly families.[52]

The boundaries of the knightly class could be especially permeable in societies where, as in Spain, the threat of conflict and the need for manpower were constant; even there, the knightly class became more exclusive by the later Middle Ages.[53] They were also permeable where large royal bureaucracies developed and knighthood might be a reward for service, as at the Burgundian court. Philip the Good knighted several hundred men before battles in his war against Ghent in 1452–53; among these were members of his ducal court, some of them noble, but others perhaps not. Normative Burgundian texts emphasized the necessity for noble birth, but practice diverged.[54] Elsewhere a non-knight who married into a knightly family might be knighted. The Dutch jurist Philip of Leiden discussed whether someone dubbed a knight automatically became noble— an indication that someone who was not already noble could indeed be knighted.[55] Underlying these rules and practices was the question of whether true knightliness was a given for certain people or whether it had to be earned by demonstrating one's manly abilities. Young men would have learned from chivalric literature that knighthood required both birth and achievement.

Literature reveals a great concern with paternal ancestry, not always requiring legitimate birth. One need only think of the story of Arthur in its many versions: in a land of anarchy, the only one who can seize power and bring peace, despite his youth, is the son of Uther Pendragon, the remaining descendant of the ruling dynasty. The Burgundian chronicler Olivier de la Marche invoked Arthur's illegitimacy (as well as that of many other historical figures) by way of proving that a man born out of wedlock could be king of Portugal.[56] In practice, illegitimacy did not have to be an obstacle to knighthood, especially if the father were of sufficient importance. One of the great jousters of the fifteenth century, who conducted a *pas d'armes* at his half-brother Charles the Bold's 1468 wedding to Margaret of York, sister of Edward IV, was Antoine "Bastard of Burgundy." In Malory's fictional world too, illegitimacy is not a stain if it means royal as opposed to common birth. Sir Tor is honored to find out that his father is a king, rather than his mother's indigent husband.[57]

While legitimacy of birth may not be that important, however, late medieval Arthurian texts do stress nobility of ancestry. In order to pull an enchanted sword from a sheath, a man must be a "pure knight without villainy, and of gentle strain on father's side and on mother's side."[58] Malory's Lancelot refuses to knight Gareth until he knows "of what kin you are born."[59] It is still possible in Malory for someone of lower birth to become a knight, however: a poor man's son becomes a knight through his own prowess and hardiness, and receives lands from a duke in recompense for his deeds.[60]

The fact that sons were depicted as inheriting their fathers' knightly abilities as well as status indicates the importance of the male line in the understanding of aristocratic manhood. Female lineage was not insignificant; men inherited noble blood, lands, and titles from their mothers. But late medieval people saw knightly prowess as coming from the male line, and the development of heraldry indicates this gendered transmission. Coats of arms originally had begun as simple devices worn on the shield so that knights in armor could distinguish their friends from their enemies. By the later Middle Ages, however, heraldry had developed as a discipline with very strict rules.[61] Coats of arms were registered and no one was allowed to use the arms of another. Major disputes over entitlements to specific coats of arms erupted during the later Middle Ages: for example, the Scrope-Grosvenor controversy in England in which, over a five-year period, numerous knights and churchmen testified as to which family had the most ancient claim to *azure a bend or*.[62] An illegitimate son had to place a mark, usually a bendlet or baton sinister, on his coat of arms. The female line was of subsidiary importance. A knight or nobleman who had a female ancestry that he particularly wanted to publicize might quarter his mother's family's arms with his father's: the inclusion of the fleur de lis in the coat of arms of the English royal house in 1337 is one example, expressing a claim to the French throne through the female line. Normally, however, like property and names, coats of arms were inherited through the male line.

The young man seeking to become a knight would situate himself in a long line of his male ancestors, and would hope to pass on his prowess along with his property to a son. Control over women, discussed on pp. 60–61, became an important currency in which masculine status was measured in part because it implied control over reproductive resources. In seeking a wife a young man might be seeking a trophy, but he was also seeking a mother for his sons. Marriage was a goal because it meant continuing the patrilineal chain.

Ancestry mattered because medieval aristocrats found it hard to imagine someone having the requisite knightly qualities who was not born to them. The story of Perceval as told by Chrétien de Troyes reveals as early as the twelfth century this importance of ancestry in terms of what we today might be tempted to call a genetic predisposition. Perceval is the son of a knight, raised in isolation in a forest by his mother. She does not want him to become a knight and leave her as his brothers have, so the education she gives him includes nothing about knighthood and chivalry. One day, however, he comes upon some knights in the forest, and they impress him so much that he thinks of nothing but how he can become like them.[63] Perceval has knighthood in his blood; as his father's son he will never be content to spend his life without it. This popular tale, retold in many versions, shows how medieval people envisioned the importance of blood.

Geoffroi de Charny, in his mid-fourteenth-century handbook of chivalry, seems to have in mind much the same concept of an inborn inclination to knighthood:

[The highest standard in deeds of arms] is embodied in those who, from their own nature and instinct, as soon as they begin to reach the age of understanding, and with their understanding they like to hear and listen to men of prowess talk of military deeds, and to see men-at-arms with their weapons and armor and enjoy looking at fine mounts and chargers; and as they increase in years, so they increase in prowess and skill in the art of arms in peace and in war; and as they reach adulthood, the desire of their hearts grows ever greater to ride horses and to bear arms.[64]

The aptitude for knighthood was inborn, although practice and training were necessary to bring it to fruition.

The inborn aptitude for knightly manhood could not be assumed in all men of aristocratic birth. The process of becoming a successful knight was the process of proving to others—and to oneself—that the aptitude was there. Manuals of chivalry make a clear distinction between nobility of ancestry and nobility of character. Caxton's printed version of Ramón Llull's *Book of the Order of Knighthood* traced the origin of knighthood to the selection of one man out of every thousand: the "most loyal, strongest, and of most noble courage and better educated and mannered than the others." Nobility was to be found in virtue, not in aristocratic speech, or a fine horse and elegant garments.[65] Guttiere Díaz de Games, the biographer of Don Pero Niño, defined nobility as having "the heart adorned with virtues," but nevertheless emphasized Pero's noble birth.[66] Humanist writers at the Burgundian court in the fifteenth century also stressed virtue as the basis for nobility.[67]

The manuals do not go so far as to suggest that nobility of character is enough: noble birth was not sufficient but it was necessary, and in any case how could a peasant be expected to acquire nobility of character, which came through education and training as well as noble birth? High birth definitely gave one a head start in the competition with other men. The texts make quite clear, however, that nobility of birth alone is definitely not enough if unaccompanied by nobility of character. In practice, ancestry and possession of the appropriate horse and armor might qualify one to participate in a tournament, but the ideal knight could not rely on his birth alone. A young man had to prove not only the nobility or gentility of his ancestry, but also that he himself lived up to it. The performance of acts of prowess demonstrated one's good character.

The physical prowess by which a young man of gentle birth was expected to show his manliness and his worthiness for knighthood included both skill and strength. Handbooks for knights comment on the importance of training in the skills necessary in battle.[68] A great deal of simple brute strength was also necessary, to be able to give and withstand the kinds of force created when two knights with couched lances rode against each other. The fifteenth-century English translation of Vegetius's treatise on the art of war describes the ideal man at arms thus: "young adolescents, of grim visage and vigilant looks, straight-necked, broad-chested, strong-boned, brawny, big arms, long fingers, deep knees, small belly, and valiant legs to run and leap."[69] Along with skill and strength, a certain aggressive attitude contributed to knightly masculinity. Malory draws the connection between gender and violence in his telling of the Tristan story. When Tristan's mother dies in childbirth, she comments that this reflects well on his masculinity: "And therefore I suppose that you, who are a murderer so young, are very likely to be a manly man when you come of age."[70]

Malory emphasizes repeatedly that physical promise appears at a young age. Sir Lamorak and Sir Gawain say of Breunor le Noir: "it would be well done to make him a knight, because it seems from his person and face that he shall prove a good knight and a mighty one. For, sir, if you remember, even such a one was Sir Lancelot when he first came to this court."[71] Early promise becomes a motif of chivalric biography. Pero Niño, when he fought at Gijon at the age of fifteen, "performed so many great feats in arms, that all spoke well of him and said that he had begun well and showed that he had a great desire to gain honor in arms and knighthood."[72] The repeated use of this theme put pressure on young men to succeed early in their path to knighthood.

Prowess and aggression were not only important because of their usefulness in warfare; they were also means by which one young man could measure himself against another. The skills that led to winning jousts might not be useful in battle or in any other area of life, just as the skills today that lead to winning in football are not necessarily transferable to other areas of life. The fact of winning and of dominating other men, however, is and was very transferable. Prowess did not have to entail the direct use of violence to dominate others. Rather, the successful use of violence gained one honor, prestige, and status in relation to other men.

The criterion of physical strength and skill in knightly masculinity, however, while it remains primary, is not the sole focus of the historical or imaginative narrative sources. The "virtual identification of chivalry with knightly prowess" in chivalric literature[73] cited by Richard Kaeuper is clearly central to medieval understandings of knighthood, especially those texts written by knights (like Charny). Some late medieval texts, however, let knightly prowess emerge through assertion, adjectives, and lists of defeated opponents rather than through detailed blow-by-blow descriptions of battle. Malory's battle scenes sometimes take the form of long lists of "A smote B," rather than giving details of the action, and Froissart is similar, although some chroniclers describe jousts and battles in more detail.[74] Strength and skill are a sine qua non for a young aristocrat but are not the entire focus of the story.

The rules that hedge around knightly battle in literary sources also suggest to the audience that strength and skill are not all that matter. The idea is not just to defeat an opponent, but to defeat him fairly, according to set procedures of battle that include allowing an unarmed man time to arm, lending weapons to an opponent, accepting challenges to fight at a certain time and place, and so forth. This is what distinguishes knightly violence from simple aggression. As Malory's Palomedes says to Tristram, "you know full well I may not fight with you for shame, for you are naked here and I am armed, and if I slay you the dishonor shall be mine."[75] Arthur gives the rules as: "never to do outrage or murder, and always to flee treason, and to give mercy to him that asks mercy . . . and always to succor ladies, damsels, and gentlewomen and widows, and never to rape them, upon pain of death. Also, that no man do battle in a wrongful quarrel, neither for love nor for any worldly goods."[76] Some knights took their cue from literature and did live up to what they understood as the chivalric code, or tried to, at least with respect to other knights. The custom of ransoming rather than killing prisoners had crass enough financial reasons, but it also became a point of honor: knights were expected to treat their prisoners well, and prisoners were expected not to try to escape.

Adherence to these ideals bolstered masculine honor, but only so far as they applied to others of the same social class. Rules or conventions governed fights against other knights, just as rules or conventions about love governed relationships with women of the knightly class, and men do seem to have taken these conventions seriously. Even when followed, however, the rules of chivalry did not make warfare more humane for the infantry or for civilian noncombatants. Knights had no problem, for example, burning and pillaging.[77] When the French Marshal Boucicaut founded a chivalric order for the defense of women, his biography recounts, it was not women in general but "ladies and demoiselles of noble lineage" that he sought to protect.[78]

The fact that chivalric ideology was not universally applied does not mean that there was a disjunction between ideal and reality, but rather that the ideal did not include people outside the knightly class. The mass slaughter of unarmed peasants or burghers was not something that much disturbed aristocrats, although handbooks of chivalry might warn against the mistreatment of non-knights, and the "free companies" of the fourteenth century were criticized by their contemporaries in terms of chivalric ideals.[79] Many men with a past of pillaging became leaders in the French army in the mid-fifteenth century after Charles VII made an effort to recruit at least those *routiers* of good birth.

A hypermasculinity that combined aggressiveness with pride in birth did not always sit well with the political structures of medieval Europe. The young knight was learning the behavior expected of him by his peers and that expected of him by his lord and the civil authorities, and the two were not always the same. The difference between a model imposed by those who wanted to control the behavior of knights and one adopted implicitly by knights themselves comes through in an examination of attitudes toward courage. Physical bravery, a component of masculinity in many societies, is obviously very important in a military setting, and is universally celebrated in accounts of knights or prescriptive discussions of knighthood. As Andrew Taylor points out, literary and historical works stressed that fear had no place in war—an emphasis that had a clear didactic purpose, even though it may later have caused young men anguish when their own emotions did not measure up to the ideal.[80]

Yet the prescriptive literature is very careful to stress the difference between courage and foolhardiness. The *Boke of Noblesse*, published in 1475 and written by a client of Sir John Fastolfe to encourage Edward IV to invade France, made the distinction:

> I have heard my authority Fastolfe say, when he was entertaining young knights and nobles, that there are two kinds of manly men, and one is a manly man proper, and the other a bold man. He said the manly man is more to be commended than the bold man. The bold man spontaneously, without consultation, advances in the field, to be called courageous, and escapes after great adventure and leaves the field alone, but he leaves his company in distress. And the manly man's policy is that before he advances himself and his company into a skirmish or sudden encounter, he does it so discreetly that he will plan to have the upper hand over his adversary, and save himself and his company.[81]

In its emphasis that taking up every challenge, no matter how unreasonable, is not courage but foolhardiness, and is unmanly, the *Boke of Noblesse* is reacting to the tendency of knights to understand masculinity as bravery in the face of huge odds. Texts like this consider the knight in a military context; they talk more about actual battle than about tournaments. They express concern that the individual's search for glory will get in the way of the interests of the prince or general. From the point of view of a military leader this is obviously something to be avoided.[82] Texts in a variety of genres made the same point. When Sir William Felton fought in Spain for the Black Prince, according to the Chandos Herald, he "very boldly and bravely charged among the enemy like a man devoid of sense and discretion"; he fought "like a lion-hearted man," but was killed.[83] The author admired his bravery but did not endorse his action wholeheartedly; it did not advance his general's cause. In the *Alliterative Morte Arthure*, Sir Cador describes a battle to Arthur, who responds: "Sir Cador, your courage will ruin us all! / Basely you are bringing down my best knights; / To put men in peril is prized as no virtue." Cador angrily replies that he has done his duty, and that Arthur should reinforce his knights better. Arthur, although angry, praises Cador's prowess.[84] This text presents a conflict between knight and general in which the knight's position is that he is obliged to fight bravely and hard, but not necessarily to go along with the general's strategy or tactics; the knight's ideal of masculine prowess does not include being a good soldier. The prescriptive literature shows us that this problem did not arise only in fiction.

From the point of view of the individual, personal glory might well seem more important than victory for one's army, and the values of knights themselves might come into conflict with a chivalric ethos propounded by and for princes. Literary representations of knighthood show knights rushing to take up any challenge, even when it entails great risk. Sir Lancelot, in various Arthurian texts, is particularly known for his fights against overwhelming odds. These stories would have sent the young knight a very different message than that of the prescriptive texts. Froissart describes the Black Prince's freeing of his French captive, Bertrand du Guesclin, as putting his personal reputation for bravery ahead of the interests of his army. Du Guesclin had implied that he was kept prisoner only because the prince feared him, and the prince released him to save his own reputation.[85] This was clearly undesirable from a policy point of view but necessary, in Froissart's view, to maintain the prince's manly image.

The experiences of tournament and joust, with their focus on individual glory, taught the young knight a very different lesson from the discipline needed for an actual campaign, and in practice, except for certain periods of the Hundred Years War, it was tournaments rather than wars that tended to bring a young knight his reputation. In tournaments the ladies watched and awarded prizes, although the prizes were no longer a major source of wealth for knights in the later Middle Ages (plunder and ransoms in battle were more important). Tournaments, fought with dulled weapons, were also less dangerous. Tournament experience might lead a young knight in actual battle to take on more of a challenge than he could handle. Part of becoming a knight meant learning two sometimes conflicting roles, military service and individual achievement in what was fundamentally a sport (albeit one with military applications). Much as authors could urge knights to use prudence and restraint, and praise wisdom as part of what makes an ideal knight, the demonstration of prowess remained more important than prudence to the knights' own idea of their masculinity.

Christianity and Courtliness

If part of the chivalric code espoused in didactic texts came from the needs of princes, part also came from the church, and here too there was some dissonance between idealized visions of knightly masculinity and the way knights themselves experienced and thought about it. Although the church never made dubbing to knighthood a formal sacrament, its deliberate efforts since the eleventh century had infused knighthood with a good deal of religious symbolism and imagery.[86] Books of chivalry stress the religious symbolism of each part of the knight's garb and each part of the knighting ceremony. The sword used to tap the knight on the soldier, for example, by its shape signified the Cross.[87] White linen clothing represented purity, a red tunic represented the blood the knight was to shed, black hose stood for the remembrance of death, a white belt signified chastity, and a red cloak humility. The spurs given to the new knight, although of gold, were intended for the feet to signify that he should not be covetous.[88]

The whole process of initiation into knighthood, as the church suggested it should be performed, had a distinctly ecclesiastical flavor. The sword and other knightly apparatus were to be blessed. A vigil in which the candidate spent the night in a church in prayer the night before his knighting ceremony, as well as a Mass that the new knight attended directly after the ceremony, became a part of the initiation ritual in theory if not always in practice. The various elements of the ceremony did not in fact have their origins in religious symbolism but took it on later, in an attempt by the church to claim knighthood for itself, to reduce its violence and increase its social utility. It is not origins that concern us here, but rather the way the rituals were understood by those who underwent them, and in this regard the church was successful.

Knights could and did understand knighthood as part of the service of God, in which they could fulfill religious obligations without abandoning the masculine ideal of prowess. Ramón Llull made the defense of the faith the primary duty of a knight, before governing, serving his lord, and maintaining justice, all of which came before military prowess and personal glory. Llull, of course, had his own agenda, but translations into English, French, and Scots as well as Catalan in the fourteenth and fifteenth centuries spread that agenda widely.[89] Even a practical man like the author of the didactic fiction Le jouvencel could write that "if God wishes, we can acquire our salvation in the exercise of arms just as well as we could by giving ourselves over to contemplation and eating nothing but roots."[90]

Arthurian literature also presented knighthood as part of the service of God. Malory has a bishop bless the Round Table at its establishment.[91] The legend of the Grail quest is the most significant place where religion enters the Arthurian world. Late medieval audiences understood the Grail story as Christian, whatever its origins, and it cast doubt on the idea of prowess as the sole measure of a knight. Lancelot, the best knight in the world, cannot be the one to achieve the Grail, because he has committed sins of the flesh (notably adultery and fornication, but the stress on Galahad's virginity in some versions indicates that even marital sex might have led to disqualification).

This emphasis on sexual purity as the standard for achievement of the greatest quest of all sits uneasily with the glorification or at least acceptance of adultery found elsewhere in the Arthurian corpus, as well as with the notion of sexual conquest as a measure of masculinity (discussed in the next section). By saying that the Grail quest is too "high a service" to bring a lady along,[92] Malory implies that the church's goals for knighthood are incompatible with the ideals of chivalric love, perhaps because women represent a distraction or a misuse of virility. This exclusion of heterosexual activity, however, is far from the norm in chivalric literature. Other writers incorporated the teachings of Christianity more successfully with the ideals of love. Whatever conflict existed between the church's idealized view of chivalry and the romances' idealized view, knights themselves may not have been troubled by it. The biographer of Jacques de Lalaing reports the advice of Jacques's father, who demonstrates how the Christian and the courtly love aspects of chivalry can merge together. He gives a long disquisition on the seven deadly sins, but uses this teaching on moral virtue to advise Jacques on how to be a good lover: "You must flee the sin of pride, if you want to come to good and acquire the grace of your desired lady," and so on for the other sins as well.[93]

Since the late eleventh century crusading had provided knights with the opportunity to demonstrate their chivalric prowess while fighting for God. By the fourteenth and fifteenth centuries there were fewer opportunities for knights to go on crusade. Although the Holy Land was no longer an option, however, there were still battles to be fought in Spain and in the Baltic region (Chaucer's Knight was involved in the latter). In 1453 the Duke of Burgundy held a "Feast of the Pheasant" at which his knights swore to take up arms against the Turks. Some swore not to sleep in a bed or to sit down to eat until they had done so. This crusade in fact never happened, but the vows were sincerely meant.[94] Even for knights who did not crusade, there were other opportunities to demonstrate religious devotion, by all the means open to other lay people (pious donations, joining confraternities, and so forth), and also by placing military orders under the patronage of saints. And there was not necessarily any inherent contradiction, in the knights' minds, between this and an active sex life or participation in violence. Religiosity and masculinity did not come into conflict.

If the church had been in effect attempting to tame the organized violence of knighthood, it was not the only institution pointing in that direction. In the same way that some scholars have identified a "Christianizing" of knighthood, others have identified a "feminizing" of knighthood. This supposedly came about as courtly love literature required the knight to venerate a woman and behave in such a way as to make her love him.[95]

Late medieval aristocratic behavior placed great emphasis on manners and decorum for men as well as women. This emphasis appears in literature as well as in books of conduct. The good knight of the late Middle Ages, these texts suggest, can now be distinguished not by his aggressiveness but more by his mannered demeanor—indeed, the Middle English poem *Cleannesse* associates hypermasculine aggressiveness with sodomy and gentle, feminine manners with appropriate aristocratic male behavior.[96] The knight must know how to behave at table and to eat without making a mess and embarrassing himself, how to speak in a genteel manner, and other refined manners, which some cultures might consider effeminate. William Caxton's *Book of Curtesye*, directed at a child or very young man, assumes that he is a member of a noble household, assigned to serve at table as young squires did. Caxton goes in detail into table manners:

> Soil not your cup, but keep it clean
>
> . . . .
>
> Blow not in your drink, nor in your soup,
> Nor stuff your dish too full of bread,
> Bear not your knife toward your face
> For therein is peril and great dread
>
> . . . .
>
> Loosen not your belt sitting at the meal
>
> . . . .
>
> Take care also that no breath resound from you,
> whether up or down.[97]

This advice goes on for twenty-five lines. But the young man must pay attention not only to his own manners but also to the people around him. When serving the food he must give particular attention to waiting on men who will help him get ahead in life: "And especially use your attendance / Wherein you shall yourself best advance."[98]

The importance of genteel table manners to the education of a young knight may be explained by the importance of the feast to the chivalric world. Feasts marked weddings, treaties, and other events, and symbolically displayed friendship, seigneurial largesse, and the solemnity of the occasion. Froissart depicts these feasts as impressing the populace at large as well as the actual participants. He notes of a group of English knights who were living sumptuously in Hainault: "They behaved such that they were praised by the men and women, and even the common people to whom they gave nothing, for the handsome state they kept."[99] Chroniclers described in great detail the elaborate dishes, the guests, and the entertainments at banquets, reflecting their importance in aristocratic social relations. The printed edition of Olivier de la Marche's chronicle takes 41 pages to describe the feast at Lille held by Philip of Burgundy in 1453, with detailed discussion of entertainment and food (which overlapped in elaborate presentations).[100] These banquets, of course, were not just military affairs, but included ladies as well, and it was important that the knight understand how to comport himself properly in them.

Indeed, the didactic literature of the later Middle Ages directed toward young gentlemen emphasizes the social aspect generally—how a knight should behave, both in battle and out—at the expense of the military.[101] Perhaps this is because the military skills had to be taught through experience and not from books. Nevertheless, the detailed instructions as to how a young man should properly serve at table found in a text such as Caxton's *Book of Curtesye* seem somewhat at odds with the ideal of knightly prowess and its attendant aggressiveness. It is no wonder that the emphasis on genteel manners here and in narrative has led some people to describe a process of "feminization." For example:

The romances profess a code of ethical values that betrays a somewhat feminine bias, with its emphasis on polish, elegance, social grace, refinement of manners, and the more gentlemanly aspects of chivalry. Here [in stories of classical heroes like Hector, Alexander, and Caesar] we find a strongly masculine ethos, adapted to *Herrendienst* rather than *Frauendienst*. The key virtues are courage, pride, disregard of material comforts or possession, willingness to endure risks and hardships.[102]

These virtues, however, are not in stark opposition to each other: the difference is one of emphasis. Elegance and refinement in material possessions can coexist with an attitude that those possessions are fundamentally insignificant and can be disregarded when necessary.

The argument about courtliness as a feminization of knighthood has been pursued as well by feminist scholars. E. Jane Burns, for example, argues that when a romance knight is not dressed in armor, his gown is similar to a woman's and he is in effect feminized. He is, in a sense, cross-dressing, and his social status is lowered accordingly.[103] Yet, although a knight like Lancelot, when he removes his armor, may be described in the same kinds of terms as the romance lady, no one would take him for a woman. That there may be a non-gendered or gender-blurred ideal of appearance does not mean that men are actually re-gendered as women when they approach that ideal.

Medieval aristocrats considered the aesthetic virtues characteristic of women, but that does not mean that men who exhibited them were effeminate. Rather, such men were worthy of the society of women, and of heterosexual fulfillment. Taste, breeding, and manners were class-linked and not necessarily gender-marked. In a later age working-class people may have regarded the clothing and manners of upper-class men as effete, but in the later Middle Ages refined dress and manners among the aristocracy were not necessarily regarded as feminine, and to label them as such is to apply the standards of another period. Extravagant dress and courtly manners were condemned in the later Middle Ages as wasteful or dishonest, but the critique was quite different from that in the twelfth century when the effeminacy of the courtier was connected with sodomy.[104] (It was connected also with heterosexual debauchery; medieval people did not see same-sex and opposite-sex lustfulness as mutually exclusive.) Rather, writers complained about the extravagant dress of both men and women, which they condemned on the grounds of vanity and lust, not on the grounds that men made themselves like women. Jean de Venette in the mid-fourteenth century, for example, comments on the indecent dress of the French aristocracy, but does not call it effeminate.[105] To be a courtly man was to be pleasing to women, and to engage in many of the same activities women engaged in; but as long as these activities were coupled with military pursuits, they were not considered effeminate.

Attention to appearance, in particular, did not feminize a man. Men did not demonstrate their class status simply by the clothing of the women associated with them, but through their own as well. Charny suggested that elaborate clothing was more appropriate for women than for men, because "the qualities of men are more quickly known and recognized and in more ways than the qualities and reputation of women can be known." Men demonstrate their rank as well as personal qualities through their deeds, whereas women have only their clothing to signify it. Excessive adornment may make men neglect deeds. Even he, however, allowed that it befits a young man to be "elegantly dressed and in good fashion," as long as it is not done out of pride and does not lead to neglect of deeds.[106] Chroniclers could comply with the moralists' strictures against too-elaborate clothing by describing their subjects as well dressed (with ample detail) but denying that they took pride in their clothing or that it was "curious."[107] And even critiques of extravagance in clothing from some quarters did not stop chroniclers and authors of romances from describing it (as well as horses' trappings) in loving detail.[108]

The courtly behavior a knight had to learn included not just clothing and manners, but culture generally. In England in the later Middle Ages, for example, English had become the native language of the aristocracy, but French was the cultured language that both men and women had to know to be courtly. Malory's Tristan, sent to France as a young man to learn "the language and nurture and deeds of arms,"[109] is one of the figures that reinforce this expectation. He has to be educated in the language of his class as well as the behavior ("nurture," breeding or manners) appropriate to a man, and the physical prowess necessary for a knight.

Women, Love, and Male Competition

Part of the reason for a young male aristocrat to learn good manners, ostensibly at least, was that they appealed to women and could bring him the validation of heterosexual love. A knight who appealed to women through his behavior simultaneously demonstrated to other men that he knew how to behave with women. But the appeal through good looks and manners was not sufficient. The display that knights put on, with their elaborate clothing, armor, and coats of arms was also believed to appeal to women, who in both fictional and biographical narrative marveled at the knights as they went by. In the story of Huon of Bordeaux, the Emperor and Huon ride through the streets, "the windows garnished with ladies and damsels, bourgeoises and maidens, melodiously singing."[110]

Jacques de Lalaing's biographer describes the women leaning out of the windows to watch him go by on the way to the joust.[111]

Women served as a central part of the knights' recreation. The courts put on entertainments, ostensibly for the sake of the ladies, as Froissart claimed of Edward III's court; this provided a convenient excuse for the men to enjoy the ladies' presence as part of the entertainment, spending the evening "in revelry, speaking of arms and love."[112] Charny suggested that the company of women was the only honorable entertainment:

Yet it should be apparent that the finest games and pastimes that people who seek such honor should never tire of engaging in would be in the pastimes of jousting, conversation, dancing, and singing in the company of ladies and damsels as honorably as is possible and fitting, while maintaining in word and deed and in all places their honor and status.[113]

The Black Prince's victorious return to England in 1357 was celebrated by "dancing, hawking, feasting, and jousting, as in the reign of Arthur," with "many a lady, many a damsel, right amorous, sprightly, and fair."[114]

Entertainments like these gave men the opportunity to display themselves before women, but women observed not only manners and accouterments but also ability in battle. Illuminations in René of Anjou's fifteenth-century *Livre des tournois* depicting the ladies watching the tournament (and very few male spectators) graphically illustrate the importance of the female gaze to the way medieval people understood the tournament.[115] Díaz de Games depicts ladies watching a joust with a great deal of technical knowledge about why one knight defeated the other; it was clearly within the realm of possibility that aristocratic women would have this knowledge.[116] In a Middle Dutch lyric, a high-born lady is wooed by a fashionable and well-spoken young man, but she prefers a crippled old man who has "proved his manhood by dint of arms. . . . By his arms you can tell the man, not by his dancing."[117] Audiences learned, then, that not only manners but also prowess won women.

Although the texts describe women as the spectators, the knights used the display of their appearance at least as much to appeal to the male gaze as the female. To men it might express not sexual desirability but wealth, nobility, and prowess. The fact that a knight appealed to women could in itself increase his worth in the eyes of other men. As Louise Fradenburg suggests, the tournament promotes homosocial bonding in that it "brings men together but allows them to constitute themselves as 'men,' who fight for and who are watched by women. The 'lady' thus enters the tournament—as spectator, as prize—in part to signify the masculinity of the knight. . . . The lady dramatizes the masculinity of the warrior by being what he is not and by watching his effort from another place."[118] Aristocratic men reaffirmed their masculinity by performing deeds before the gaze of those who were not masculine, and displaying the rewards of women's admiration before other men.[119]

Revels like dances, which involved ladies, were an integral part of a tournament.[120] Knights fought with favors from their ladies displayed on their helmets, and the lady whose knight did well in a joust or tournament was honored by it. In literature, ladies might be asked to judge who had won a tournament.[121] In practice, a lady would give out the prize at the end of a tournament, and might kiss the victor.[122] The reward was not really the kiss, but the public recognition via the kiss of the knight's prowess and desirability. Christine de Pisan made the point, using the classical example of Paris, that a man who appeals to the ladies is not always the best choice for a military endeavor, but for the most part the two were equated.[123] The desire to win the love or approval of ladies was also represented as the occasion for extreme behavior on the part of young knights, who were posturing as much for each other as for the ladies. Froissart reports on a group of knights bachelor who went about with one eye covered, because they had made a vow to some ladies not to uncover their eyes until they performed deeds of arms in France.[124] Men who made such vows were emulating the behavior of literary knights, but the audience was not really the ladies: they made the vows in competition with each other and in order to impress their peers.

The role of display in the tournament begins earlier than the period in question here. Thirteenth-century poems on the theme of the "Ladies' Tournament," depicting a role reversal in which women fight, emphasize the display aspect of the tournament.[125] One might expect that the poems would present women as ridiculous for attempting to usurp a man's role that they cannot adequately perform. This is not the case, as the poems include little description of actual fighting. They express admiration for the ladies, but that admiration comes not from military ability but from beauty and decorum, features that characterize the male knights as well. By casting women—whose beauty was to be admired by men—in the position of knights, these poems carry the implication that the beauty of male knights was also to be admired by men. Putting the women on display serves to emphasize how much the men were on display to other men, with a definite tinge of the erotic.[126]

To prove one's masculinity it was not enough to create a display that appealed to women. In the later Middle Ages a variety of fictional texts construct knighthood as requiring participation in heterosexual love relationships. Malory's Isolde can question Sir Dinadan's knightliness because he criticizes love: " 'Why,' said La Belle Isolde, 'are you a knight, and are no lover? Truly, it is a great shame to you, for you may not be called a good knight except if you make a quarrel for a lady.' "[127] No matter how much prowess a knight has, he needs a woman to symbolize it. A knight who was not interested in the game of love was mocked as discourteous to women, as was the case with Gawain in *Sir Gawain and the Green Knight*: "As good a knight as Gawain is held to be / With courtesy so pure in him, / Could not have dallied so long with a lady / Without craving a kiss, by his courtesy."[128] Malory's Tristan says that "a knight may never be of prowess, but if he be a lover."[129] In *Petit Jehan de Saintré*, a lady of the court upbraids the boy for saying that he has no lady love: "Oh, feeble gentleman! And you say that you love none? By this I know that you will never be worth anything! And, feeble heart that you are! from where come the great valor, great enterprises and knightly deeds of Lancelot [here she lists other knights] . . . if not to obtain the service of love and keep them in the graces of their most desired ladies."[130] This attitude, repeatedly emphasized, could have led young knights to seek a lady to love, not out of any particular desire for her or any emotional bond, but merely because of the necessity of doing love service.

This love, in which young men participated as part of their life stage, might be characterized by secret letters, by wearing the lady's favor on his helmet, by the man's pining away. It probably was sometimes, but not as a rule, characterized by an actual sexual relationship. Knights certainly would have had many women of lower social status available—prostitutes and serving women—for sexual purposes, but the elaborate intrigue of love could only be carried on with a woman of comparable or higher status. Jacques de Lalaing's father, when he gave him his parting admonitions, told him not to frequent prostitutes, who can cause a man to lose not only his soul but also his physical strength, but rather to seek the love of noble ladies.[131]

The need for a lady to love does not mean that knighthood excluded other types of desire. Late medieval knightly masculinity was defined by sexual object choice, that choice being what we today would call heterosexual, but it did not have to be exclusive. It was not a desire for men that might make a knight less than knightly—that issue did not arise—but simply lack of desire for women. While several twelfth- and thirteenth-century French texts depict one character castigating another for loving boys instead of women, this theme is less prominent in the fourteenth and fifteenth centuries, when those who are not interested in women are implied to be socially lower rather than sexually different. For a man, to have a heterosexual relationship was to gain status in relation to other men by dominating a woman; whatever same-sex relationships he may have formed were not part of this game.

Yet knights often expressed their desire for women so ostentatiously that it amounted to protesting too much. The masculine bonding in which knights engaged led to anxieties that could be resolved by claiming that all that went on among the men was in the service of women and caused by a desire for the latter. Why such anxieties might appear in the later Middle Ages is a complicated question. The aristocracy were very concerned with lineage. However, love as played at the court was not necessarily closely connected to marriage (although it certainly was more so than in the twelfth century). Nor was there a great concern over sodomy, which did not receive as much attention in sermons and didactic literature, or indeed in romance literature, in northern Europe as it had earlier or as it did in Italy.

The importance of heterosexual desire to late medieval knighthood comes less from an attempt to overcome male anxieties about homosexuality or to promote marriage and reproduction, but rather because women were one of the currencies in which a knight's success was measured. Although the knight performed deeds of prowess ostensibly to earn the love of a woman, the subplot was that the knight ostentatiously served a woman so as to advertise more widely his deeds of prowess. Because it was the convention for women to be used in this way, the love of ladies was a necessary part of aristocratic masculinity—a sort of "compulsory heterosexuality." Knights felt compelled to demonstrate to other men not their "sexual orientation," which was not a medieval concept, but their superiority to other men in the competition for women. The adultery triangles that appear in Arthurian literature further indicate that women were tokens in a game of masculine competition. It is women who threaten male community because men fight over them.[132] It is they who bring conflict into the chivalric world, even though it is through men's desires that they activate that conflict.

The idea of love service, in which men did martial deeds in honor of a lady, created a myth of men subordinating themselves to women. Many scholars have addressed this myth in its twelfth-century context, concluding that it did not reflect or support women's power in any practical way.[133] In the fourteenth and fifteenth centuries too, when lyrics dealing with love service were still being composed for female patrons,[134] we must beware of reading such productions as reflections of the high status of women. Love service, to the extent it was practiced, was largely a performance to display to other men the lover's appeal to women. It did not really put women in a position even of symbolic power, because it put them under obligation. Because prowess earns love, the lady who does not grant it where it is deserved does wrong; she has little choice in this understanding of the game.

The idea of knights performing deeds to win the love of women—according women a symbolic importance, even if it bore little relation to the political power women may actually have wielded or the active role women may have perceived themselves playing in love relationships—may not seem especially noteworthy to anyone coming out of a European cultural tradition. We hear from an early age stories of knights or princes striving to win the love of princesses. This particular medieval social arrangement seems unremarkable to us because its legacy is still with us. Yet a look at the social world of the Japanese samurai demonstrates that the medieval European pattern was far from the only possibility for a warrior elite. The samurai achieved honor by winning the love of young boys, whose beauty they celebrated in romantic poetry.[135] The contrast indicates that the European situation requires explanation. Part of it may be the Christian culture's emphasis on heterosexual marriage as a sacrament and not just a means of producing heirs. A large part of the explanation may be that women did in fact wield significant political power, as widows and mothers if not always in their own right. The language and ideology of love were ways of shifting that real power into a realm where it had less impact, and then undermining it by making love a commodity earned by the deserving rather than a matter of women's choice.

The idea that love improves the lover by spurring him on to greatness, which began as a literary topos much earlier, had permeated courtly society by the fourteenth and fifteenth centuries.[136] As Charny suggested, "glances and desire, love, reflection and memory, gaiety of heart and liveliness of body set them off on the right road and provide a beginning for those who would never have known how to perform and achieve the great and honorable deeds through which good men-at-arms can make their name."[137] In a set of questions on hypothetical cases that he probably wrote for the French Order of the Star, he elaborated on the idea that love inspired knights to fight well. Two groups of knights, at war with each other, have lovers in the same town. One set of ladies invite their knights for a day and night of entertainment. The other set sees how much joy the others are having and invite their lovers too. The first group, whose ladies have armed and kissed them and asked them to do their duty for the sake of their love, ride out and encounter the other group on their way to see their ladies. Charny asks, "In which group would you rather be to have the better will to fight well?" The question is whether the experience or the expectation of love is a better inspiration, but it is clear that he and his audience saw both as inspiring.[138]

Valor inspired by women, a staple of romance stories, did not necessarily do the women characters much good. In *The Avowing of Arthur*, Kay and Gawain fight to rescue a damsel from Sir Menealfe, who has kidnapped her and threatened to take her virginity. Although the text repeats that the battle is for her sake, when Menealfe is defeated she drops from the story, and he eventually becomes a knight of the Round Table despite his attempted rape.[139] She is the ostensible occasion for a battle whose function is to incorporate another man into the band of brothers. The focus is on the men and their deeds rather than on the woman who is to be rescued.

Stories of romantic love affected, if not the way aristocrats actually behaved, at least the way they understood and described their behavior. Knights and ladies patterned their speech on romance literature, and used the same language in their letters (and not just love letters!).[140] Chroniclers of historical figures adopted the same themes. When Edward III of England became attracted to the Countess of Salisbury, Froissart cast his desires in courtly love terms rather than as simply another case of a king sleeping with whatever woman he wanted.[141] A sixteenth-century account of the fifteenth-century English knight Sir John Stanley depicts him and an heiress falling in love at first sight; even if more mundane factors like her wealth played a role, the poet who chronicled the Stanley family attributed the love to her beauty and her admiration of what he had heard of his prowess.[142] Whether or not "courtly love" was a reality in the twelfth century, writers in the later Middle Ages constructed their accounts of their contemporaries as though it was a reality for them. These contemporary accounts reflect literary influences, but also an audience that took chivalric romances as historical and attempted to emulate the conventions they found there.[143]

The man's prowess and the woman's love existed in a sort of symbiotic relationship: the man's success in deeds of arms obliged the woman to love him, and her love spurred him to further deeds not only by inspiring him but also by supporting him financially. Froissart tells of Isabel de Juliers who fell in love with Eustace d'Aubrecicourt (whom she later married) because of his gallant deeds of arms. She sent him horses, and love letters, which spurred him on to perform more feats of chivalry.[144]

The romantic and the practical merged in the choice of woman to love. A wealthy woman could be of great material assistance to her chosen knight, and literature recognized this. When Jehan de Saintré names a ten-year-old girl as his love, a lady of the court says "You, sir, should choose a lady of high and noble blood, wise, and who has the wherewithal to help you and supply your needs."[145] When Sir John Stanley chose his lady love, it was because he "made such search not only of her degree / But as well of conversation and beauty / And heard by fame to be honest and fair / Her father old and she his undoubted heir."[146]

The idea that Isabel fell in love with Eustace or Lord Latham's daughter with Sir John Stanley because of his deeds of arms follows a pattern common both in literature and in chronicle: ladies are described as falling in love because of men's achievements in tournaments.[147] This type of love was not primarily an emotional relation between two people, but rather a prize awarded for a man's achievement. Women no doubt experienced it differently, but from the masculine point of view love was a commodity that they could earn. According to the biographer of Marshal Boucicaut, he impressed his beloved at the coronation of Charles VI with his good looks and rich clothing, horse and retainers. Inspired by the sweet glances she gave him, he won his jousts. At this time, aged fourteen, he was not yet a knight, but was knighted in 1382 at the unusually young age of sixteen during an expedition against Flanders. Even though, his biographer tells us, he now deserved the prize of his lady's love, he chose to wait until he had done even greater deeds.[148] The implication is that she grants her love because he deserves it, not because his deeds cause loving feelings to well up within her.

The idea that military success was what made one erotically desirable ties together these two important aspects of masculinity. This is no more implausible than the spectacle of women today offering themselves to sports heroes. When the French knight Jean Bonne-Lance, "a gracious and amorous knight," as described by Froissart, took an English knight prisoner in order to humor a lady's wish, the audience would have understood that he was enhancing his own sexual desirability by his military feats.[149] Texts that refer to women's desire for displays of knightly prowess also serve to displace onto women men's desire for violence.[150]

Women also served to eroticize heroic violence in the entertainment of the *pas d'armes*. The knight's vow to maintain a *pas* for a fixed period of time was often made in front of women, ostensibly to impress them. The *pas* often involved defending a woman—that is, a woman (or mannequin) might stand in the pavilion as the symbolic property of one man that others wished to take.[151] When Giovanni de Bonifacio and Jacques de Lalaing jousted, they did so before a pavilion decorated with the image of a woman and the phrase "Qui a belle dame, garde la bien"—"Whoever has a beautiful lady, let him guard her well." Lalaing's challenge to other knights at the Burgundian court required him, if he lost, to go submit himself to a lady of the winner's choosing. Later, when he defended the *pas d'armes* at the Fontaine des Pleurs for one year, he had a lady he was "defending." At the banquet after the year had passed she appeared and spoke, but when she accompanied him during the year she kept silent.[152] The woman was only an object over which the battles of the men were fought, even when she was placed in a position of ostensible superiority.

Similarly, *emprises,* devices that a knight wore to indicate his desire to be challenged, were also ostensibly taken on for the sake of women, but served as an occasion for male bonding. The Italian knight Giovanni di Bonifacio came to the court of Burgundy in 1445 wearing a mock slave-iron hanging from a golden chain, and offering to fight anyone in defense of the honor of his lady. Jacques de Lalaing took up this challenge, and later undertook a similar *emprise* himself, wearing a golden bracelet with a lady's kerchief on it and travelling as far as Spain. This idea of wearing a bracelet as a challenge was taken over into literature, and women apparently found it there: a group of ladies at the English court fastened a golden ring to the leg of Lord Scales, the brother of Edward IV's queen Elizabeth Woodville, and demanded that he not remove it until he had done battle. He challenged the Bastard of Burgundy, and they fought a duel at Smithfield in 1467. Eventually King Edward had to stop the fight.

The two then refused to fight each other at other tournaments for the rest of their lives.[153] The reaction of the ladies to the tournament and the men's bond is not described; it had become a masculine event, and they were merely part of the background.

This elaborate love game, played by one man against another with women as the counters, did not determine choice of marriage partner; marriage among the aristocracy was still a matter of sociopolitical alliances. Tournaments might be fought on the occasion of weddings, but they were primarily celebrating the marriage as an alliance rather than as the culmination of a romance. Yet medieval authors spoke of even arranged noble marriages in courtly love terms.[154] Whereas part of the twelfth-century conception of love expressed by Andreas Capellanus was that it took place outside of marriage, in the later Middle Ages marriage could be seen as its culmination.[155] The young knight might well enter the game of love hoping to acquire a wealthy wife.

Although marriages might be described in the terminology of romantic love, however, and many tales do involve love between single people who eventually marry, much of the love described in literature, chronicle, or didactic text does not see marriage as a goal or focus on it. Jacques de Lalaing, for example, was not seeking a wife, and when the marital status of the ladies to whom he appealed is mentioned, they were already married. His biographer notes on several occasions that women wished their husbands were like him or would like him to change places with their husbands.[156] When Boucicaut's biographer speaks of love making knights do great deeds, he cites the examples of Lancelot and Tristan, implying that it was appropriate to choose a married woman of rank as one's love object.[157] Knights described as married are relatively few in the Arthurian corpus. The knights are presented as young men. Lords who control castles, older and more established, tend to be married, but even here it is often only by their children that we know this; their wives do not always make an appearance. When a more historical figure, the Black Prince, marries, his poetic biographer calls his wife "beauteous, charming and discreet," but does not name her, calling her only "a lady of great renown."[158] Marriage was peripheral to the stories of chivalry.

Although marriage qua marriage was not central to the acquisition of knightly masculinity, however, it was important as an eventual goal. Marriage was the venue for the engendering of legitimate children, especially sons. The discussion of ancestry (pp. 34–36) showed the importance of the patrilineal link. Having a father whose honor you could live up to or a son whose deeds you could be proud of is an important theme in chivalric literature. The young knight would have looked forward to taking his place in the chain. The appeal to women, and success in the love game, was a way of improving one's status vis-à-vis other men by proving one's future potential for fatherhood. One did not demonstrate manhood by marrying, but the demonstration of manhood could put one in a position to marry and thus reproduce one's manhood.

The most famous examples of love in chivalric literature deal with adultery: Lancelot and Guinevere, Tristan and Iseut. These texts create an ethos of adulterous love between a subordinate man and a superior woman. Scholars have related the earlier versions of these stories to the social structure of aristocratic families in the twelfth century, where often only the oldest son married. The other sons were knights attached to the court of some other lord. Whether their romantic sights were then set on their lord's wife as one of the few women around, whether their lyrics in her praise were really meant to flatter the lord himself, or whether the whole thing was simply a convention since adultery was roundly condemned in practice, are matters of dispute. Christiane Marchello-Nizia suggests that the love of the knight for the lord's wife is a displacement of homoerotic desire. "To love that which the lord has chosen or loves, isn't that desiring oneself to be this object of love or choice, desiring to be in the place of the lady?"[159] Of course, the lord most likely chose his wife for reasons other than desire. Nevertheless the love of the lady had to do not only with the lady herself but also, if not with the lady's husband, then with proving oneself better than the other knights who might love inferior ladies.

Malory's fifteenth-century version of the Lancelot story downplays the adulterous element. Although sexual love is implied in Lancelot's love for Guinevere, Malory never explicitly discusses it. He deliberately deviates from his sources in order to present Lancelot as loyal to his lord, without the conflict between love and loyalty that he (like Tristan) encounters in other versions. Lancelot's love for Guinevere, of such a nature that he can love her without betraying Arthur, becomes inextricably linked to his love for Arthur himself. The love of a woman and the love of the lord are one and the same, and the expressions of romantic love in arranged marriages may also be taken as expressions of feeling about the alliance rather than the women.

Wealth and Honor

Not every young knight, of course, could afford to put on a golden bracelet and travel with an entourage across Europe as did Jacques de Lalaing. The code of chivalry veers away from the actual practice of knightly behavior in the attitudes of knights toward money. The manuals of knighthood stress that the knight fights for honor—his own or his lord's—and not for enrichment. In practice, even the wealthiest aristocrats were not averse to accumulating more riches through the spoils of battle—the practice of ransom was one method—and the average knight was desperately in need of such accumulation. While accumulation of wealth was not part of the masculine ideal, it was necessary to other parts of the ideal. Knightly equipment was not cheap. The higher one rose in the social hierarchy, the more elaborate household or group of followers one had to provide for.

Even many nobles could not afford to equip themselves or their sons as knights. A war horse in France in the middle of the fifteenth century cost anywhere from six months' to over two years' wages. This meant that these petty aristocrats, who relied on knightly service for their social identity, had to acquire an income in the service of the prince, whether from plunder, from gifts, or from a direct salary.[160] Tournaments no longer paid as in the twelfth century when a William Marshal could make his fortune from them; rather, they could be entered only by those with very costly equipment, and with the joust replacing the mêlée they offered few opportunities to collect ransom money. Only the wealthy or the well patronized could afford to compete and thus the opportunity to prove manhood might be closed to others.

A young man, of course, had the option of being a mercenary, fighting on behalf of whichever lord or general paid him. This was not uncommon, nor did "mercenary" at the time have the full range of pejorative connotations it does today. Christine de Pisan, among others, discussed the ethics of using mercenaries and came to the conclusion that a knight might ask for payment for his deeds, as long as he performed them in a just war. Geoffroi de Charny also held it acceptable to fight for money, as long as the knight did not give up fighting when he had acquired enough money.[161] It was generally more socially acceptable for a young man to join a particular lord's entourage because of the latter's reputation and the former's hope of glory, and later to be rewarded by the lord, than it was to make the arrangement contractual from the beginning. To the people who were being plundered, it did not matter much whether the knight was a mercenary or a "true knight" fighting for glory who just happened to become rich in the process. The notion of the knight errant—the young knight who goes out into the world to seek adventure and glory—could mask a search for wealth, and such a knight did not look very different from a mercenary to the inhabitants of the region his band was ravaging.[162]

Knights were to avoid the appearance of concern with money not only in their military activity but also in recreation. Geoffroi de Charny considered gambling dishonorable, not apparently for the element of risk but for the associations with greed and crass materialism:

they should not concern themselves too much with nor devote too much attention to any game where greed might overcome them, such as the game of dice, for it is no longer a game when it is engaged in through greed for gain. . . . There is also a game called real tennis at which many people lose and have lost some of their chattels and their inheritance. . . . One should leave playing dice for money to rakes, bawds, and tavern rogues.[163]

Despite critiques of greed, money did, of course, pervade the chivalric world from the kings all the way down to the poorest knights. Froissart reports the Prince of Wales's fury when the king of Spain refused to pay him what he had promised for helping him regain his throne.[164] But chivalric ideology still called for such things to be done out of loyalty. Thus the fifteenth-century Jean de Bueil, author of *Le jouvencel*, a book of advice to young men in the form of a novel, is able to suggest the wealth that may be acquired through service as a knight, without making it sound like the knight is getting paid for his labor: "But the poor men-at-arms, who have abundant labor and suffering, are always ready to use their bodies to acquire honor and renown . . . and fortune finally favors their efforts, and enhances them, and exalts them to a perfect glory in this world; and this should encourage poor gentlemen."[165] To gain money by one's chivalry was not shameful, as long as one could claim as the main motive the honor that was central to heroic masculinity. The disdain for money as a motive that young men learned from chivalric literature, however, could create conflicts with the real day-to-day concerns of mature members of the knightly class, who had to manage property, outfit a household, find dowries for daughters, and equip themselves and their sons for war.

Because largesse was so important as an aristocratic virtue—the medieval aristocratic version of the man as provider—we might assume that knights were supposed to participate in it, and indeed this was the case. For a young man starting out in life, however, this might prove difficult, and many books of advice reminded the knight to keep largesse appropriate to his station. Gilbert de Lannoy urged his reader to avoid prodigality (*folle largesse*). Jacques de Lalaing's father counseled him that ladies love better those who do well in tournaments than those who spend freely.[166] Although presented as moral advice, this counsel clearly was also an accommodation to economic reality.

In learning how to fight bravely and skillfully, how to acquire the love of ladies, and how to gain wealth in acceptable ways, the young knight was learning to behave honorably. "Honor" in the Middle Ages was a heavily gendered concept. It could have a fairly simple, class-based meaning: the quality of being a member of the aristocracy—a membership that might be proven by the possession of knightly accouterments—or, if used by a member of the bourgeoisie, a member of that respectable group. In its aspect as a personal rather than a group quality, when applied to women, it referred almost exclusively to sexual behavior. An honorable woman was one who maintained her chastity, either as virgin or as faithful wife.

Honor for men was much more multivalent, and deeply tied to gender identity. To be dishonorable or dishonored was to be unmanly. It could mean "reputation": a man had more honor if people thought more highly of him. It included both prowess and trustworthiness, but also gentle behavior. It was not constituted only through violence, but the successful use of violence was a sine qua non, and violence was the ultimate means of maintaining it. Prowess included courage and actual military success; trustworthiness included keeping one's word, and loyalty to one's lord. The proportion of each of these elements, however, varied, depending on the context. Honor in late medieval European courts was not a zero-sum game. A man could acquire honor without taking it from someone else. He could gain honor by defeating an opponent in battle or joust, but if the defeated man fought bravely and well he did not necessarily lose honor. It was not, then, equivalent to dominance.

One primary way of acquiring honor, however, was a zero-sum game: the acquisition of women. A man could gain honor by acquiring the love of a woman. Other men lost honor when one man gained it in this way; she too might lose honor if she surrendered to him sexually. A woman was only won if she was totally possessed, and therefore she could only be won at some other man's expense, either by preventing him from winning her or by taking her from him. Honor could be acquired through the making of a good marriage; a high-ranking man's willingness to give his daughter to a particular knight accorded him honor. It could be acquired through winning a tournament and the reward of a kiss. It could be acquired in literary texts by rescuing a damsel in distress. In all these cases, the knight, by acquiring a woman, proved that he was not a woman.[167]

Learning to be a knight involved learning to keep one's word, another important aspect of honor. It was obviously in the interests of lords to cultivate loyalty as a knightly virtue; Richard II of England, for one, used the Order of the Garter to do just this.[168] Handbooks of chivalry reflect these interests. Christine de Pisan, for example, compared the man-at-arms to a dog:

the dog naturally has many characteristics which the good man-at-arms ought to have. The dog loves his master marvelously and is very loyal to him. And the man-at-arms should be also. He is tough and exposes himself to death for his master. . . . He will not bite the friends of his master but naturally sniffs at them. . . . He is very tough and fights with great skill. He has a good understanding, knowledge, and is very amiable to those who do him kindness.[169]

Though it promoted the interests of lords, this ideal seems to have been internalized by the chivalrous class generally. It was certainly part of the ideology of lordship that existed in the later Middle Ages.[170]

Loyalty was not only to one's lord but also to one's kin, notably brothers, and friends. Knighthood created close bonds among men. These bonds might arise because they were knighted at the same time, because one had knighted the other, or because they were involved in the same military enterprise and had gone through the same harrowing battle experiences together. The orders of knighthood sponsored by the various kings were supposed to create these sorts of bonds of brotherhood, but they were instituted for political purposes, intended to place the knights more directly under royal control.[171] Still, these orders attempted to exploit the sense of belonging and companionship that knights shared. The knights of the Golden Fleece, for example, were called brothers, although this was a formal designation and it is not clear how personally it was taken.[172]

Tourneying fraternities also grew up in the regions of Germany where tournaments were popular in the fifteenth century. Similar groups were found in France, although less specifically focused on tourneying. These confraternities pledged mutual military assistance, friendship, arbitration of disputes, and aid in raising ransom money. Some tried to emulate the orders founded by princes, taking on special insigna and rituals.[173] They served to give unaffiliated lesser knights a sense of belonging and of knightly formality. They also sponsored feasts and, in parts of Germany, tournaments, which these knights could hardly hope to be able to do on their own.[174]

More important must have been the bonds that grew up spontaneously among knights. Because women were excluded from the military activity that was the knights' raison d'être, the shared experiences of hardship and of violence created homosocial bonds—links among men in which women could never participate. Such homosocial bonds are evident everywhere in Arthurian literature. That between Malory's Lancelot and Gareth is one example: "For there was no knight that Sir Gareth loved so well as he did Sir Lancelot; and always for the most part he wanted ever to be in Sir Lancelot's company."[175]

The bonds are also apparent in the historical narrative sources: knights rejoice in each others' victories, declare their love for each other, even celebrate together after fighting against each other.[176] Even one's opponent, held for ransom, might be more closely bonded to one than members of one's family who were not men at arms. Knights who were fighting on opposite sides even in bitterly fought wars like those between the English and the French might socialize together during a period of truce, as Boucicaut did with the English who admired his arms and feats of chivalry.[177] Boucicaut's biographer chooses to present his subject as admired rather than feared by his enemies; they have a great deal in common simply because of their knighthood. Indeed, he also reports that Boucicaut went to avenge the death of the Scottish knight William Douglas, whom he had never met; he admired his knightly qualities and saw it as his obligation to take action on his behalf.[178] The 120 knights and squires of Hainault who, Froissart tells us, set out one day to do great deeds "through love of one another" were expressing this bonding; what might otherwise have been done for the love of ladies was here expressly done for their companions.[179] Jean de Bueil's *Le jouvencel* speaks of the joys of war predominantly in such terms of male bonding: "You love each other so much in war. . . . A sweetness of loyalty and pity comes into your heart, to see your friend, who so valiantly exposes his body to accomplish the commandment of our Creator. And then, you get ready to go die or live with him, and out of love, not to abandon him. From this comes a delectation such that no man who has not tried it can say how good it is."[180] The emphasis on this theme in such a wide variety of texts would have taught young men that this bonding was a central part of knighthood.

Sometimes this bonding was in pairs rather than in a group, and could be formalized. "Brothers-in-arms" might write up a contract sharing their plunder, a written recognition of a relation that probably grew up on the battlefield. Whether or not the relationship between Edward II of England and Piers Gaveston fell primarily into that category, as Pierre Chaplais has suggested (and whether, if it did, that meant it was not sexual), is not as important as the fact that this sort of bond did exist. Sexual or not, it was close and passionate, and it might also confer legal rights.[181] The tomb slab of two English knights who died near Constantinople in 1391, which shows them bearing the same shields, is a record of this kind of relationship: according to the inscription they had been constant companions for thirteen years, and one refused food and died a few days after the other. The coats of arms of both families are impaled on both shields (each coat of arms takes up half the shield); this was usually done with the arms of a husband and wife, or a bishop's personal arms and those of his see, but is very unusual with two men. Maurice Keen calls them "companions in a very special sense."[182] Whether or not they were lovers, their military companionship and their personal bond reinforced each other. Indeed, with such brothers in arms, the fact of martial prowess may have made it possible for them to enter into such a bond without concern for their masculinity. It is possible that participation in such a homosocial world left men open to accusations of sodomy, but it is more likely that the military context of such a bond served to justify relationships that might otherwise have been called sodomitic.

Such bonding with another knight might help a young man negotiate his way in the world into which he had been initiated. It was not the ritual of knighting, but the participation in tournament and battle that made him part of the knightly community. The ritual, however, developed its own symbolism and eventually became a clear marker of who did and who did not belong. Those who had not been knighted could still be part of the knightly world; as squires, or even as fighters who were not officially knights, they could participate in battles. Honor in many tournaments, however, was restricted to those who were officially knights.

The initiation into knighthood was supposed to take place at the entrance into manhood. It was a rite of passage comparable to marriage for a woman; indeed, in many places a lord had the right to a special "aid" or payment from his vassals on two occasions: the wedding of his eldest daughter and the knighting of his eldest son. The knighting of a king's or duke's son could also be the occasion for extended celebrations and spectacles.[183] Knighting usually took place about the age of twenty-one, but the age could vary. Biographies of knights often stress the unusually early age at which they were knighted, as evidence of their prowess; Boucicaut, for example, who began to bear arms already at the age of twelve, was knighted at sixteen and was Marshal of France by the time he was twenty-five, a very unusual elevation but one justified by his biographer with reference to Roman examples.[184]

For the greatest lords, the knighting ceremony of a son was a splendid occasion, often accompanied by days of tournaments and feasting.[185] For others it might be a much less elaborate affair, and there were also battlefield knightings.[186] The actual ritual of the knighting itself, by the later Middle Ages, called for a bath to purify the candidate, then a prayer vigil followed by a ceremony in which the knight was struck on the shoulder with a hand or sword (the actual dubbing, a late development) and given arms, usually a set of spurs.[187] The didactic literature explained this ritual with heavy religious symbolism, as discussed above. The prayer vigil certainly can best be explained this way. The other elements, however, call for other explanations. The giving of arms represented the bond between lord and man, and the loyalty that would be expected from the new knight, one of the major characteristics of aristocratic masculinity.

Especially in the later Middle Ages, it became important who did the dubbing. Knights took great pride in receiving their knighthood at the hands of someone whom they greatly admired for his prowess. Keen calls this an "apostolic succession" of knighthood: members of the aristocracy were very aware not only of their own genealogies, but of the deeds of those whom they considered their role models, and sought to create a bond with them by being knighted by them.[188] Others were knighted in mass ceremonies on special occasions, and a bond was created too among all those knighted on such an occasion.

The bath may have had other purposes as well, besides that of symbolizing moral purity.[189] Physical cleanliness, of course, was a class-linked quality; peasants were considered dirty, whereas aristocrats wore clean clothing and smelled nice. These stereotypes may not have been borne out in practice, as even aristocrats did not bathe frequently, though they did wash their hands at mealtimes. The bath may also have functioned to display the male body. A prospective knight bathed in the company of other knights, giving them an opportunity to verify a lack of deformity and disease and to see displayed before them a physical masculinity. Being "whole of limb" was one of the criteria for knighthood, at least in theory, and the bath allowed that to be verified.[190]

After being knighted a new knight had to demonstrate his prowess. He joined the mass of young knights attached to the household of a great lord, known as knights bachelor. It would be years before they were able to marry; they would have to acquire land first. Elder sons might await the death of a parent, and younger sons awaited their own opportunities to accumulate wealth. A lord might give them land and wealth in return for meritorious service, but in the meantime they lived in an aristocratic household with other men, had intrigues with women, practiced jousting, went to tournaments, fought in the lord's battles, and participated in the male military culture.

These knights performed for the sake of other men. Their battles were with and before men. Although women formed part of the audience, and the knights claimed to be jousting to win their love, it was ultimately the renown they earned among other men that spurred them on. Women were a distraction from the real world of violence: a necessary one, because they were one of the means by which a man measured his manhood, but not the end. The display that was such a big part of knighthood was for other men, and it was other men who ultimately evaluated the young knight and ruled him a full man. Display was important not only for the individual knight wishing to demonstrate his aristocratic masculinity to others, but also for the knightly caste generally. The tournaments, ritual entries of towns, banquets, dances, and *tableaux vivants* of fourteenth- and fifteenth-century Europe were all ways of making visible power relations in the society: between ruler and ruled, between the knightly classes and others, and also between masculine and feminine.

The display of emotion was no exception to the visibility of both fighting and love. Public emotion on the part of knights and great lords was not frowned upon, but indeed admired. Even tears were not unmanly; it was manly to have deeply held feelings, and important to display them.[191] Some texts contest the masculine nature of extreme grief. In the *Alliterative Morte Arthure*, when Arthur embraces and kisses the dead Gawain, spattering himself with blood and fainting away, his companions suggest that his grief is womanly—"to weep as a woman is not appropriate"—and that he must "be knightly of countenance as a king should." Arthur's extended answer indicates that he disagrees strongly.[192] Even if Arthur's grief is seen as excessive, however, it is not so unusual, and it in no way disqualifies him as a king or leader; the audience is not necessarily meant to agree that he has behaved effeminately.

The knightly model of masculinity came into conflict with other roles and responsibilities of the late medieval aristocracy. Many people who had the social status of knight, or who came from knightly families, were in a position where they could choose other careers that would bring them wealth and prestige. In England, for example, many knights were also educated in the law. The *Boke of Noblesse* complained that manliness could only be demonstrated in the field and not in the law courts: "But now of late days, the greater pity is that many who are descended from noble blood and born to arms . . . set themselves to singular practice . . . as to learn the practice of law of custom of the land, or civil matter, and so waste greatly their time in such needless business."[193]

To take up other careers was not necessarily incompatible with bearing the title of knight, or with participating in knightly activity on occasion. True adherence to the knightly model of masculinity, however, required living up to literary models by devoting one's life to the attempt. The successful deployment of violence remained the main measure of success. Perhaps the whole emphasis on the manliness of the knight was an effort to maintain the popularity of a fading institution that was criticized by townspeople and clerics as useless to society and contrary to religion. And yet, although there were other avenues to pursue, knighthood remained real to many men in the later Middle Ages, and an important ideal to even more.

3

Separating the Men from the Beasts: Medieval Universities and Masculine Formation

IF THE ACQUISITION OF MASCULINITY in the European later Middle Ages was primarily a matter of proving oneself against others, nowhere was this more true than in the single-sex environment of the university. The absence of women was taken for granted rather than contested. University thinkers—despite the common and accurate image of the influential Aristotle as arch-misogynist—did not spend a great deal of time or effort justifying women's exclusion or demonstrating male superiority. It was still important for a young man to learn to reject the feminine within himself, but this was by no means the primary goal of his education. Rather, that education was to give him the skills to compete verbally against other educated men, and to prove his superiority over the uneducated. Simply by belonging to the university he had already proved himself not a woman; his task was now to use intellect to dominate other men. He proved his manhood by his rationality, which distinguished him not only from women but also from beasts.

The number of men actually involved in the medieval universities was relatively small—at the largest universities probably four to five hundred students admitted annually, barely fifty at the smallest. Unlike the knightly model, the university model of masculinity was not admired, let alone personally emulated by the population as a whole. However, the process of training young men at universities had an influence on medieval society disproportionate to its numbers. Universities were the training ground for a substantial portion of the clergy and nearly monopolized the formation of the intellectual elite. The university systems established in the Middle Ages provided a model of gender-differentiated education that persisted into the twentieth century. Within monasticism men and women were separated for the most part, but education and intellectual life had been open to both, separately if not quite equally. The university, however, was the province of men only. This does not mean that women could not be educated; recent scholarship has shown that lay literacy, including that of women, was more widespread than previously assumed. But they were educated in a quite different context. The fact that women were excluded from the universities had profound implications for the history of learning, especially science.[1]

It is precisely because they were the province of men only that the medieval universities have received limited attention from feminist scholarship. That women were excluded, however, does not mean that the institution is therefore not relevant to the study of women, and it is certainly relevant to the study of gender. The universities developed their own model of masculinity, distinct from the aristocratic knightly model although related to it, that was closely connected with late medieval misogynist traditions. The norms established within the universities by both masters and students show how young men were expected to take up their masculine position in the world.

Although the origins of the medieval university as an institution lie in the schools of the twelfth century, the intellectual achievements that gave scholasticism its renown came during the thirteenth and first half of the fourteenth centuries. Thomas Aquinas, the great synthesizer of Aristotelian philosophy and Christian theology, is probably the best known of the great thinkers working at that time. Aristotelianism was not the universal rule, but Aristotle's methods predominated in a way his views did not. University teaching and writing came to be governed by the strict rules of Aristotelian logic, especially in the universities of northwestern Europe with their emphasis on undergraduate education in the arts. This study focuses on the period after the origins and heyday of medieval universities—the fourteenth and fifteenth centuries—when universities were exercising stricter control over their undergraduates and taking seriously their responsibility to shape not just the mind but the entire man.

Student Backgrounds and University Structure

As with knighthood, it is necessary first to know something about the social setting of the university student in order to understand the process by which he learned masculine norms. By the later Middle Ages, logic was the main subject that undergraduates studied at medieval universities in northern France, England, and Germany, although natural philosophy (what we today would call science) was increasingly important. The first degree, Bachelor of Arts, was supposed to cover the seven Liberal Arts: the *trivium* of grammar, dialectic, and rhetoric, and the *quadrivium* of music, arithmetic, geometry, and astronomy. Logic emerged as the most important subject, however, at least north of the Alps. The seven-part schema was supplemented by the study of the "three philosophies," natural, moral, and metaphysical, which were part of the curriculum for the Master of Arts degree.[2]

Not all students remained at the universities long enough to receive the baccalaureate degree (half to eighty percent left before getting a degree). Those who not only took the degree but chose to remain for further study in the arts could receive the title of Master of Arts, which carried with it the license to teach. Many of these masters did not intend to make a career of the university; they were required to remain as regent masters, teaching for a few years, and then moved on to other careers in the church or royal administration.[3] Those who did remain might continue to study for a higher degree in law, medicine, or theology. The universities of England and France tended early on to focus more on theology, while those of Italy, southern France, and Spain specialized in law and medicine, which did not necessarily require a previous degree in arts. By the later Middle Ages law had become important all over Europe. Not all universities had all these faculties; students might spend their whole university career at one institution or they might move around.

The social background of university students varied greatly. In the earliest days, universities were merely schools that drew together the studious, mainly clergy, from over a wide area. The mendicant and other orders developed their own schools or *studia* affiliated with the universities; they were not allowed by their orders to study in the arts faculty, and some could not study law, so they were concentrated in theology.[4] As universities became more institutionalized and regularized, matriculating students were younger (except for members of monastic or fraternal orders, or beneficed parish clergy licensed to attend the university to improve their preaching and teaching).[5]

Data on the ages at which students came to the universities are unclear. The arts faculty at Paris by 1350 apparently allowed fourteen-year-olds to determine as bachelors if they had attended lectures for two years; the age in 1282 had been twenty.[6] On the other hand, just because students could attend at that age does not mean that most did. References to young boys at universities could refer to pupils at grammar schools affiliated with the universities, rather than matriculated students. In both Germany and England in the sixteenth century, the median age of students on entrance was seventeen, with the majority of entrants between sixteen and eighteen.[7] We cannot assume, however, that in the fifteenth century, from which less data survive, the situation was the same. In late medieval Oxford it seems to have been the mid- to late teens; at New College, where the records are best, statutes required entrants to be between fifteen and twenty, and the actual average in the fifteenth century was seventeen and a half.[8] Yet at the University of Rostock in the fifteenth century, minors (under fourteen) constituted a third of admitted students in some years, and R. C. Schwinges suggests that the majority, throughout Europe, were fourteen to sixteen.[9] At the institutions focusing on law and medicine, students were on average older. At Bologna, the average age of scholars (not necessarily on entrance) was between twenty-three and thirty; the statutes of the Spanish College there provided that while "boys" could be present at business meetings of members of the college, they could not vote until age eighteen.[10] Given the ages at which young men were considered able to do other things—fight, marry, take monastic vows—when they came to the universities they were for the most part considered men rather than boys, much more ready for adult responsibility than fourteen-year-olds today. Still, they were young men, at an age to be shaped and influenced by the people and the institution around them.

University study was not cheap. There were university fees to pay, room and board to provide, books and parchment to obtain, and a lifestyle to live up to. Jean Dunbabin calculates that a family below the level of the lower aristocracy (a poor knight) would not be able to support a son at a university.[11] Even to prepare himself with the education in Latin necessary to attend a university, a boy needed to come from a family that could afford basic schooling, or else to have been identified quite early as a promising student and given scholarship assistance. Model letters home from university students indicate that they expected their families to support them.[12]

For the dedicated youth, there were other options besides family support. Some colleges set aside positions for poor scholars. Some bishops funded poor boys from their diocese to attend universities—sometimes by granting them benefices. Indeed, it may be in part a "crisis of patronage"—a falling-off in the availability of this financial support—that led to the increasing importance of endowed colleges in the late fourteenth and fifteenth centuries, at least in England.[13] Poor students might also take the "work-study" option, sometimes even working as servants for their richer peers, their college or hall, or their master. Such students tended to take longer to attain degrees.[14]

If university students were unlikely to come from the poorest segments of society, they certainly did not all come from the wealthiest or highest status. Before the fifteenth century, sons of the nobility had generally only attended universities if they were preparing for a life in the church.[15] There were a few exceptions: in the early fourteenth century a number of sons of the aristocracy who were not seeking clerical careers attended the University of Paris, at least briefly.[16] By the end of the Middle Ages, however, particularly in northern, central, and eastern Europe, universities proliferated and more young men began to attend them not for specific career preparation as much as for social cachet and a general level of education. Here students from noble families were given special privileges within the university. By the early modern period the university was well on its way to becoming a finishing school for the sons of the nobility, a normal part of the aristocratic life cycle.

The majority of university students for whom we have data on origins were sons of lower aristocracy and to some extent merchants and professional men. Matriculation records from the university of Heidelberg from 1386 to 1450 reveal that 57.4 percent of the students fell into the category of *divites*—students who were well enough off to pay their entrance fee, but not identified as noble or clerical. 6.5 percent were members of the high nobility (of whom there may have been more at Heidelberg than elsewhere); 13.7 to 16 percent (depending on how one counts) were members of the clergy, either secular or regular. The number of *pauperes* who could not pay their entrance fee grew over the period.[17] At Cologne between 1395 and 1495 there were 2.3 percent nobles, 10.5 percent beneficed clergy, 63.8 percent from the middling group, and 15 percent "pauperes," again more in the later fifteenth century than earlier.[18] Knights and gentry, called by historians "middling" because they were neither nobles nor peasants, were still among the most privileged in society; their participation does not indicate extensive social mobility.[19] In Spain, too, scholars have concluded that most of the students were neither poor nor nobles.[20] At Oxford the majority seem to have been neither gentry nor bourgeoisie but the sons of yeomen and husbandmen farmers—at New College, at least, from 1380 to 1500, 61.4 percent of students were sons of "rural smallholders" (anything below gentry status, including possibly wealthy yeomen). 12.5 percent were gentry, 17.6 percent urban bourgeois or sons of artisans.[21] Even those students classified as *pauperes* were hardly destitute: to be admitted to a special college of *pauperes* a student could have a personal income of up to 20 florins per year, equivalent to the income of an urban craftsman. There may, however, have been a large social difference between those classified as *divites* and *pauperes*.[22]

Matriculation records also reveal the geographical origins of students, which varied a great deal from university to university. Paris and Bologna drew from a pan-European clientele at higher levels of study, though even in Paris the majority of students came from northern France.[23] As the Middle Ages wore on, however, universities proliferated so that most students remained in their native country, even native province, for their undergraduate education, going elsewhere if they pursued a higher degree.

The move toward localism or regionalism in universities reflected a broadening of their clientele and the fact that this clientele was no longer limited to the church. By the fifteenth century the student bodies of the universities had become laicized: fewer clergy and students preparing for the clergy, more lay men who were not training for an ecclesiastical career.[24] Many students went to the university to acquire connections and status, not just to pursue learning for its own sake or for spiritual reasons.

Even in the early thirteenth century, where the universities had been much more restricted to the intellectual elite, many (even of those ordained) had gone into royal administration, and of those who remained within the church many were administrators rather than spiritual leaders.[25] The jurist universities of the south had always been geared to producing practicing lawyers for secular as well as canon law courts, although a background in law was also often a stepping-stone to high church position. Later on, an arts degree seems to have been an advantage in obtaining a position as parish priest, but by no means a sine qua non. Indeed, at some points a university graduate may have been overqualified to be a parish priest.[26]

Graduates sometimes sought patronage from bishops and others, and sometimes became landholders, manorial officials, or royal administrators.[27] In part such graduates were valued employees because of the skills that they learned: not knowledge of Aristotelian science or scholastic theology, but rather logical thinking and disputation. It may also have been the case that bishops or other university men tended to patronize their fellow graduates, or even those who spent a few years at the university without obtaining a degree.[28] University education, however brief, gave one a cachet as a certain kind of man.

The way students lived while at the university in the later Middle Ages reflected the laicization of the universities, although this depended a great deal on which university they attended. Students were more heavily regulated in the fourteenth and especially fifteenth centuries than they had been. The university undergraduate was now seen as a young man growing up and being molded personally as well as intellectually, rather than primarily as a scholar seeking learning. The regulation of students was one way of controlling disorder within the towns, particularly impor tant in the later Middle Ages as the civic authorities played a greater role in the founding and management of the newly proliferating universities. Surviving regulations also reveal the ideals of behavior that the young men were meant to follow as they grew up.

At the southern law-dominated universities, it was largely individual townspeople—independent of the universities, although licensed by them— who rented rooms to students. Sometimes one enterprising student would rent a house and then rent rooms to his colleagues. North of the Alps, as at Oxford and Paris, students had to live in authorized halls, *bursae* or pedagogies, often run by a master.[29]

By the end of the fifteenth century the English universities, Oxford and Cambridge, were moving toward a collegiate system, in which university teaching and administration were decentralized. At its inception, however, this system did not include most of the undergraduate students. The colleges were founded by charitable bequests for the support of advanced students (who might also be teaching as masters in arts). King's Hall, Cambridge, endowed in 1337, and New College, Oxford, founded by William of Wykeham, Bishop of Winchester, in 1379, were innovators in focusing on undergraduate arts education. There may have been some undergraduates connected with other colleges, but undergraduate education was far from the primary function of most colleges.[30] Most undergraduate students, well into the sixteenth century, lived in "halls," something like an American dormitory but run by private individuals who were nevertheless responsible to the university. Oxford in 1410 tried to require all students to live either in colleges or halls and not lodge with townspeople.[31]

Paris had a similar mix of residential arrangements; by the end of the Middle Ages more and more colleges were being founded and student life was more closely controlled. Some colleges were founded by and for the benefit of particular groups. In addition to secular colleges, religious orders with a large number of members studying at a given university would have their own colleges. For the most part, where colleges did provide places for and fund undergraduates, it would have been the more serious and not the average student who benefited from them. Some students in Italian universities were organized into colleges in the fourteenth and fifteenth centuries, although teaching was not connected with them as in Oxford or Paris. The officials were students, elected by other students, and there was also outside supervision.[32]

The increasing control over students' lives in the northern universities in the fifteenth century can been seen in the proliferation of college and university statutes about their behavior. The statutes from Erfurt from 1447, for example, required that the rectors of *bursae* promise to police the students' morals, make them speak Latin, close the gates at the required hour, and evict incorrigible vagabonds and misbehavers. The University of Cologne strictly regulated the student halls.[33] Effective control was not always possible, and groups of students got together and made their own housing arrangements, along the lines of a college fraternity in the modern United States.

The more or less centralized living arrangements for students in various regions also reflected more or less centralized institutional arrangements. There were two basic models of university administration. In Italy, the universities were run by the students, who were chiefly studying for graduate degrees. They made decisions, appointed masters, and determined regulations. In Paris and other universities that followed its model, the body of masters governed the university, collectively by faculty (arts, theology, medicine), and within the faculty of arts by nation. In the German universities founded later on in the Middle Ages, the masters often had less autonomy as the local secular authorities played a greater role.

Each faculty of the university made its own regulations governing instruction and teaching. At Paris and the English universities, some of the teaching (especially tutorials and disputations, although not always lectures) was carried out through the colleges, at least for the 15 percent or so of students who belonged to them. There were also lectures and tutorials in the English halls, in addition to the general public lectures of the universities.[34] At some German universities, the masters who ran *bursae* organized their teaching through them.[35] Within the faculty of arts at Paris, teaching, disputing, and examining were organized by nation. Paris had four nations: the French (also including students from Italy and Spain), the Norman, the Picard, and the English or German nation. Students chose a master to study with and became affiliated with the nation to which he belonged. At Bologna, the transalpine and cisalpine students formed nations, with smaller subgroups. The nations provided not only a form of organization of instruction in some universities, but also a social network. There were periodic outbreaks of violence among the nations, which indeed led to the abolition of the northern and southern nations as Oxford in 1274 as administrative units (although it did not stop violence between students from different regions).

Paris and Oxford in the thirteenth and fourteenth centuries have often been considered to constitute the pinnacle of medieval intellectual achievement. The reality of the university for most of the students, however, was much more workaday. Most were in the arts faculty and would not have come into contact with the great theologians, although they might indeed have attended their lectures or disputations for their entertainment value. They attended the university mainly for the credential and career advantage it would give them, whether this came because of what they learned, whom they met, or what type of behavior and style of life they adopted. This did not mean that they were unaffected by the intellectual life of the university; this chapter will suggest some ways in which they were profoundly affected by it. But here we focus not on how their university experience changed their views about theological issues, but rather on how it shaped their sense of themselves as men. Placed in this all-male environment at a formative time in their lives, they learned a particular type of manhood.

Women, Gender, and Sexuality in the University

The most salient feature of the universities with regard to masculine identity was, of course, the absence of women.[36] Men may understand themselves as men quite differently in an all-male environment than in a mixed-gender environment. A university man's appeal to women did not have the same implications for his competition with other men nor for his future prospects for marriage and fatherhood as it did for young knights. Heterosexual aggression, however, could represent a challenge by young men to the idea that they were supposed to focus on the mind and not the body. Their own ideas about masculinity did not always accord with their institutional position.

Women had a small presence in the university environment, but not as the peers of university students and scholars. Men holding administrative positions in their colleges or universities might have to deal with women who were their social superiors: aristocratic women who were donors or potential donors. They would also have to deal with towns-women over rent. Indeed, there were even a few married students and masters in the late Middle Ages.[37] Even the typical undergraduate student would come into contact with women, although perhaps not on a daily basis. The universities, after all, were located in major European cities and towns; they were not isolated as monasteries were. But the universities and colleges did their best to discourage such contact, largely on the grounds of the sexual temptation it offered.

Anyone of the social classes who would be likely to attend the university was used to having servants to wait on him. Wealthy students might bring their own personal servants; for others, there were hall or college servants, including some students using this means to finance their education. These servants were mainly men. Many colleges required that all the servants be men, although the Sorbonne had a female porter (*janitrix*).[38] Washing, including the washing of hair as well as clothing, was one job traditionally done by women. Some colleges recognized this, specifically providing that a man should be appointed for this task if one could be found, that the laundry should be taken out of the college to a laundress, or that if a woman were hired to come into the college she should be old.[39] Authorities may have been particularly concerned with laundresses because, of all the tasks to be performed in the college, this was the most likely to be women's work; it could also be because of the traditional connection of laundresses with prostitutes or at least women of dubious sexual morals, and because of the personal contact.[40] Even old women as laundresses might be suspect as go-betweens or because they might bribe secrets out of servants.[41] Old women, though, were less of a threat than the nubile. The Dominican college of Notre Dame de la Pitié at Montpellier, according to its 1491–94 statutes, allowed the novices to have "one old and respectable maid who is called their mother," a reflection on their lack of adult status. At the Spanish College at Bologna, although members were not allowed to have any woman, even mother or sister, in the college overnight, with the permission of the rector "old women, or such of whom no evil could realistically be suspected," were allowed to look after sick students.[42]

Even had it been possible to keep students from coming into contact with women within their colleges, it was not possible to keep them from doing so within the towns. Students who took lodgings in the town might have landladies to deal with. They would have had to deal with tradeswomen every day in the purchase of their victuals, their parchment and books, and their clothing. They even sometimes had to deal on an official basis with women: for example, when the beadle of the English/German nation at Paris had died, the nation had to enter into negotiations with his widow to obtain the return of his regalia.[43]

More threatening to the university, and to the potential clerical calling of the students, than contacts with servants or tradeswomen were encounters with women who were the students' social equals. In some places this was less of a threat than others. At Paris, where the university was both large and self-contained, town (at least the respectable segment) and gown did not mingle as much as elsewhere. The university had its own churches, so students would not likely have run into members of the public there. In Oxford, there were confraternities which included both town and gown, but the women included were wives of male members; these groups would perhaps not have involved young students nor the daughters of townspeople.[44]

In both of these university towns, as well as others, a main way in which students interacted with women of the town was through violence. Universities throughout Europe—and the towns in which they were situated—repeated admonitions for students, especially when inebriated, to avoid harassing the wives and daughters of townsmen. In Paris in 1269 the local official excommunicated students who "wound, kill, abduct women, rape virgins, break into houses, and commit theft and other enormities."[45] At Orléans in 1307 the university stated that it would not defend students accused of nightwalking, rape, brawling, or housebreaking; at Copenhagen ambushing the townspeople, breaking into their houses, or raping women were grounds for loss of university privileges.[46] As Marjorie Woods has pointed out, many of the standard texts used in grammar schools to teach Latin include stories of rape.[47] When boys were taught in this environment, which naturalized sexual violence, they would have learned that it was if not acceptable, at least not unusual to demonstrate or fulfill their heterosexual desire by force.

In the German universities of the later Middle Ages, which were smaller and drew on a more local student body, there was more integration of students into the town. The *Manuale scholarium*, a book of Latin dialogues for the use of students, indicates what some of the relations may have been.[48] The *Manuale scholarium* was probably first published in Heidelberg, sometime in the 1480s; there were seven editions in various cities before the end of the fifteenth century. It consists of eighteen dialogues between two students, Bartoldus and Camillus, about various aspects of student life. Because the titles of many of the chapters begin with "How students talk about . . . ," commentators have taken the *Manuale* as a guide to the kind of everyday Latin a student would need to know. Some aspects of it can be substantiated from other sources: the giving of (prohibited) gifts to examiners, the disputations, the regulations about clothing. It is still not entirely clear, however, whether it was meant, or can be taken, as a direct reflection of practice, or whether it is in part tongue-in-cheek, depicting stereotypes that have some truth to them but are nevertheless stylized or exaggerated.

The authorship of the *Manuale* as we have it is not known. Most of the work, however, also appears in a book by Paul Schneevogel (Paulus Niavis) of Leipzig. Scholars at first suggested that Schneevogel had simply copied the text, claiming it as his own; more recent work, however, gives priority to Schneevogel and considers the *Manuale* a revised version of his book.[49] Schneevogel's work was entitled "Conversational Latin for New Students," and if the work was in fact originally written for this purpose, it probably bears the same relation to social practice as a tourist phrasebook does today—close enough to make it useful, but not a reliable description. It seems most likely that the book was originally written at Leipzig, then reworked for a Heidelberg audience. As it stands it probably refers to practices that would have been recognizable to students at most German universities, even if they did not correspond in precise detail to the practices at any one.

In one section of the *Manuale*, entitled "How They Speak About Women when they are Inflamed with Love," Bartoldus tells Camillus about a young woman whom he has seen in church. He thinks he is in love. His companion replies that she is menstruating and therefore poisonous.[50] The idea that a menstruating woman can poison men, kill at a glance, and wither fields goes back to ancient times.[51] The dialogue, of course, lacks verisimilitude, for how would one student know when this particular woman was menstruating? The purpose, clearly, is didactic. Yet the passage does reveal that it would be plausible for a student to meet, or at least see, a respectable young woman in church.

The impression of regular contact between students and towns-women is confirmed by another passage, where Camillus has received a ring from the daughter of a local judge. His companion warns him that she is already pregnant by another man who has abandoned her, and is only looking for a husband in order to obtain a father for her child.[52] In another conversation Camillus says that he plans to go to a dance, and Bartoldus warns him against it, listing the problems love causes to a scholar and discussing how women will tempt and corrupt him. "What plague is more harmful to the studious than women?"[53] Even though Camillus insists that these are respectable women and that he wants to go to the dance to enjoy their company rather than to gratify his lust, Bartoldus says that attending a disputation would be better. It is precisely repectable women who present a threat.

These misogynist commonplaces are hardly new and their deploy-ment in a university context, where students are presumed to be prepar-ing for a life in the clergy, is not surprising. What is notable is that they are used to warn students away from marriageable women, women of their own social class. Nothing in the *Manuale* talks about prostitutes or dis-courages men from all sexual activity; rather, it is emotional entangle-ments and the burdens of marriage that they are to avoid. Women who can be used instrumentally for sexual gratification are not seen as prob-lematic in this particular text. Similarly, a mock disputation from Heidel-berg from 1500, although entitled "On the faithfulness of prostitutes to their lovers," speaks of women generally, trotting out the commonplaces of distracting men's attention from God, deceiving them, taking financial advantage of them, and so forth.[54] Here again the focus is on the harms of a man's obsession with women, not the sexual act itself.

Prostitutes were extremely common in university towns. Jacques de Vitry's description is well known: prostitutes in Paris attempted to draw passing students into their houses, calling them sodomites if they de-murred, and brothels were located on the lower floors of lecture build-ings.[55] In Paris, the Street of Straw, where the lecture halls were located, had to be closed at night because prostitutes were practicing their trade in the halls, committing their "horrible foulnesses" on the chairs of the mas-ters. If the customers were undergraduates or indeed townspeople, one could easily imagine their glee in using this space for this purpose.[56] Both Oxford and Cambridge made attempts to ban prostitutes, although this was clearly ineffective.[57]

The authorities condemned students' (and masters') relations with prostitutes largely for reasons of order and decorum. The statutes of colleges at many universities prohibited members of the college from having carnal knowledge of any woman within the college, or indeed bringing her into the college at all, but did not speak to what students did elsewhere.[58] Others, it is true, prohibited students from visiting prostitutes, or taverns where they were likely to be found. Still, some were concerned only with preserving the reputation of the college itself. The College of the Blessed Virgin Mary at Leipzig in its 1445 statutes required that any member of the college report it to the authorities if he learns of any other member who visits a woman in or outside the city or brings her into the college "in such a way as to bring notoriety or ill repute to the college." University regulations there provided that members of the university could not publicly keep in their residences a loose woman, nor live with one, but there was no restriction on having sex with them.[59] Some of the Oxford colleges made "a lapse of the flesh" grounds for expulsion; the university provided that any student, in a college or not, who kept a woman in his dwelling could be expelled.[60] The Spanish College of Bologna and the College of St. Ruf at Montpellier went so far as to give reasons why *all* women were forbidden from the college: "because woman is the chief of sin, the weapon of the devil, expulsion from paradise and corruption of the ancient law."[61] These university and college statutes, the *Manuale scholarium*, and other texts indicate that the universities were more concerned to regulate the location of students' relations with women than to impose chastity upon them.

The university authorities did not enforce, much less the students adopt, the teachings of the church about celibacy and chastity as part of their model of masculinity. Rather, they recognized them as sexual beings and called for them to relate to women in that way alone. The potential implications of this for their future lives and careers are apparent. The emphasis on sexual activity was not an emulation of aristocratic models. Courtly ideas of love played little role.[62] Rather, university men used sexually available women—servants or prostitutes—to demonstrate their assimilation into manhood.

This instrumental use of women was in part a reaction to the expectation or norm that most students would become clerics, which persisted into the later Middle Ages even after it had ceased to be universally the case in practice. Displaying an aggressive heterosexuality could help university men avoid the implicit charge of emasculation attendant on a life of chastity in the eyes of the laity. Women served in this context not as transmitters of land or providers of genealogical links, but as advertisements that university men were not feminized.

The emphasis on aggressive heterosexuality does not mean that the homoeroticism one might expect to find in such an all-male context was absent. Even without widespread homosexual behavior, the formation of erotic bonds that may never have been acknowledged or consummated nevertheless could have had a great impact on how the students related to one another. Aggressive heterosexuality need not have been a denial of homoerotic desire. Love or affection for another man was not considered feminizing and did not necessarily conflict with instrumental use of women. As in other same-sex environments, men might interact with women sexually but had little opportunity to develop more complex relationships with them (whether as son, father, helpmeet, mentor, breadwinner, or friend). They could, however, develop complex emotional relations to men while still using women as a sexual outlet.

Of course, homosexual behavior was present too. The transvestite prostitute John Rykener, who lived in Oxford for five weeks in 1394 under the name of Eleanor, confessed that while he was there "three unsuspecting scholars" had "practiced the abominable vice" with him often. This activity took place "in the marsh" in the late summer, so it is possible that the partners did not disrobe and the students in question (who were in orders) did not in fact know he was a man. But it is also entirely likely that they did.[63] Other examples are also ambiguous. In 1431, a student of one of the masters of the college of the Sorbonne was punished for spending the night away from the college without permission: he confessed that he had slept at the stews (bathhouses) "with a foreign man."[64] It may be that the two were visiting female prostitutes together; or it may be that the two men were sexually involved. The punishment—being stripped and beaten in the schools, as an example to others—was worse than for other university members who visited prostitutes.

Somewhat clearer is a case from Merton College, Oxford, in July 1491. Richard Edmund, a fellow of the college, was accused of "the sin against nature." He was accused of having seduced boys to this sin, to the peril of his soul and scandal to the reputation of the college. Found guilty by his fellows, he was expelled but allowed to remain until Christmas "for the honor of the College." By the next February, he had left the college, but not Oxford, because he appears on the list of those who incepted as masters at that time.[65]

The ambiguity or certainty of these records referring to male same-sex activity within the university is in one sense irrelevant. Within this all-male environment involving boys from the age of 14 on up, such activity must surely have gone on, and it does not matter whether a particular case is an example of it. The writings of Jean Gerson further indicate that homosexual activity was a concern within the university; we do not know whether his concern over teachers having sexual relations with their students was based on widespread practice or simply his own anxieties.[66] A more interesting question is how such activity was handled and dealt with within the university setting.

The expelled master of Merton College notwithstanding, the authorities seem generally to have ignored male-male liaisons. Legislation from universities across Europe repeats admonitions to the scholars not to bring women into their residences, or not to frequent taverns where female prostitutes are known to be available, but not to avoid having sex with one's fellows. This does not mean the practice was accepted; what it probably means is that the colleges preferred to keep it hushed up, as did Merton in avoiding the publicity of expelling a fellow in the middle of the term. There is no evidence that such involvements made the active partner in any way unmanly. Indeed, the students who had sex with John/Eleanor Rykener may have been demonstrating their masculinity to other men as much as did men who had sex with biological women.

Although students learned a masculinity that involved sexual activity, that activity was supposed to be rational and controlled in contrast to the irrational and uncontrolled feminine. Even though to be a man was to be sexually active with women, it was the woman to whom lust was attributed. An aggressive masculine sexuality and an attitude that women are the seductresses are not necessarily incompatible, as anyone with a passing acquaintance with late twentieth-century popular culture can attest. The idea of man as sexual aggressor and man as rational and moderate in his passions can coexist even in the same individual and certainly in the same subculture. This understanding of masculinity helped medieval students reconcile the idea of sexual aggressivity with the life of the mind. This rationality and self-control contrasted, as we shall see, not only with femininity but also with the behavior of other men against whom university men might define themselves.

Logic, Disputation, and Masculinity

The ideal of masculine moderation, as opposed to feminine excess, echoes some aspects of Aristotelian teaching. As discussed in the previous section, there was plenty of misogynist rhetoric in the university environment, much of it intended to discourage student contact with women.[67] The reliance of the university curriculum on Aristotle, however, does not explain all that rhetoric. Aristotle exercised a dominating role over logic, theology, and medicine in the later Middle Ages, and the misogyny of his views is well known. He was far from the only authority scholastic writers cited nor did all agree on interpretations of his work, but Aristotelianism had set many of the parameters of the discussion, and Aristotelian ideas remained a presence.[68] Most of Aristotle's influence, however, was in his method and the way he categorized knowledge, rather than the specific content of his thought. Aristotle's misogyny per se may not have had a great effect on the arts curriculum, although the absence of women from Aristotle's works except to dismiss them as inferior no doubt had a more subtle impact on the students. It is worth reviewing Aristotle's views on women and their impact on the higher faculties, because these shaped the environment within which arts students operated. The writings of an Aquinas or an Albertus Magnus, who wrote in the thirteenth century and most of whose works were not read as part of the undergraduate curriculum, still commanded great authority in the universities of the later Middle Ages.

The influence of Aristotelian ideas about gender was perhaps most apparent in the medical faculty. The idea of woman as a deformed man was expressed in terms of reproductive biology, and there were also biological reasons why woman's intellect was thought to be inferior to men's. Joan Cadden notes that the influx of Greek and Arabic learning in the twelfth and thirteenth centuries, although on the surface it "suggest[s] a simple pattern of concepts about sex difference," by no means created a univocal view of women's biological nature.[69] Yet, while in their disagreement over such issues as the reproductive contributions of males and females, the causes of sex determination of the fetus, and the nature and function of sexual pleasure, academics might reject Aristotle's one-seed theory, they nevertheless collectively shared his assumptions about woman's physical and mental weakness.[70] They could not accept entirely the idea of woman as deformed man because woman was specifically created as such by God. Still, in Aquinas's terms, although women as a group were necessary to procreation and deliberately created that way, "with respect to individual nature woman is something deficient and manqué."[71]

The biological differences between women and men were thought to determine character and personality type.[72] They were important not only in the study of medicine, but also in theology, because they determined each gender's relation to the divine. Albertus Magnus, in his works of natural philosophy, set the tone for other scholastic writers: women's small size and weakness were natural, due to their cold and wet nature.[73] The *De secretis mulierum* (On the Secrets of Women), a text attributed to him and incorporating many of his ideas in a less systematic, scientific way than his own writings, was extremely popular. The text, apparently intended for male rather than female readers, contributed to misogyny outside the university as well as within, where it was heavily commented upon.[74]

The biological understanding of man as stronger and woman as weaker had, for Aristotle, clear implications for society, and the scholastics were not slow to amplify. For example, Aristotle justified men's dominance over women by reference to nature, in a similar manner to the way he justified free men's dominance over slaves.[75] Albertus explained that although some woman may be "wiser and stronger than a man," this is against nature, "for it is according to the nature of woman to have mutable ideas, because of moisture; men, however, because of the opposite composition, have constant ideas."[76] Aquinas, too, wrote that women's frailty is "not due to a flaw of nature, but intended by nature"—it was part of the divine plan.[77] His commentary on Aristotle's *Politics* argued that woman "has the power of understanding but this power is weak, because by the softness of her nature, her reason does not firmly adhere to plans, but quickly is removed from them because of some passions, whether desire, or anger, or fear." He added the Biblical admonition about women keeping silent in churches.[78]

According to Aquinas, women were subjected to men not because of feminine or human sin but inherently. "There is another kind of subjection, domestic or civil, according to which the dominant one uses his subjects for their own utility and benefit. And this subjection would have been even before sin. . . . And thus, in such a subjection woman is naturally subject to man, because by nature man has more rational discernment."[79] Nicole Oresme, in his commentary to his French translation of the *Politics*, written in the 1370s, translated Aquinas's statement about women's power of deliberation being weaker because of the softness of their nature. He went on to give a few counterexamples, like Semiramis, but stated that "it does not happen often that a woman has great virtue and constancy."[80]

These particular Aristotelian ideas and medieval thinkers' responses to them are well known,[81] but in fact they are not all that typical of scholastic writing. Misogyny in the curriculum of the medieval university came not only from Aristotelian commonplaces but also from a pervasive assumption of women's insignificance—a far cry from chivalric literature that expressed misogyny by putting women at the center but denying them agency. While in their commentaries upon particular Aristotelian passages they accepted and amplified Aristotle's misogyny, medieval scholastics did not devote their lives to a critique of women and femininity. A study of extant quodlibetal disputations in theology from the University of Paris that deal with issues involving women and gender shows that scholastics tended not to expound gratuitously on feminine weakness but rather as much as possible to ignore the fact that the issue involved women.[82] This was not because they were gender-blind egalitarians, but because women simply were not interesting to them as women: they were not part of their intellectual world. The masculine stood as the norm for all.

A few examples of quodlibetal questions will give a flavor of the sort of misogyny at issue in the universities.[83] Questions that dealt with strictly theological issues were discussed in very abstract terms, and whatever may have been said in the actual discussion the recorded quodlibets are brief and do not use many concrete examples. When they speak of humans they use the neutral "homo" and, while the authors undoubtedly had men in mind, what they said in general about the human intellect and the soul was not gender specific. They excluded women not overtly but more subtly. Other questions, however, did refer to women. Questions about marriage were generally in the province of canon law, but this did not prevent their being asked in quodlibetal disputations, in which various fields of study did overlap. Even so, the theologians who discussed these questions often did not consider women qua women.

Durandus of St. Pourçain in 1312–13, for example, considered the question of whether a woman who was left a legacy on condition of her marriage could receive it if she became a nun. Durandus did not need to explain the superiority of virginity for women; he simply assumed it, and reasoned that someone who chose a better course should be seen as having fulfilled the requirement. The point was not the good of feminine chastity—which one might have expected him to discuss, if the nature of women and their sexuality had been a great concern—but the nature of legal conditions; a vow of continence counted as matrimony for this particular legal purpose.[84] The questioners had posed the issue in terms of women, but that was not what interested the respondent or the master who determined.

Another question, on whether marriage was valid if performed after a vow of chastity, was answered by "Master R. of Arras" with reference to papal power to dispense from vows, without reference at all to the nature of marriage or masculine or feminine chastity.[85] The same master used a question about the marriage debt not to discuss the reasons for this doctrine or the nature of human sexuality, but to assert the superiority of theologians over canon lawyers. If a man contracted marriage but took holy orders before consummation, is he obliged to render the debt to his wife? Yes, although he cannot exact it from her: "for that which concerns the nature of marriage is of Christ's instituting, and is to be considered by theologians; the other issues [about holy orders] are of positive law and pertain to the jurists."[86] Again the relative position of a husband and wife is irrelevant. A question of Guy of Cluny on whether virginity lost in mind can be restored became a discussion of the technical concepts of material and formal; he did not take the opportunity to refer to masculine or feminine tendencies to sin.[87]

Even when quodlibetal questions discussed women's subordinate position, the masters did not often refer to Aristotelian doctrine on women's weaker nature. Gerard d'Abbeville considered whether a Jew who converted to Christianity could remain married to a spouse who did not. One of the possible answers he discussed was that a male convert could stay married, but a female could not, because her Jewish husband might cause her to relapse into error. Gerard did not say, however, whether this is because of women's fickleness, weakness of character, or legal and social subjugation to her husband.[88] In a discussion of whether a wife could make pious donations without her husband's permission, Adenulf of Anagni, nephew of Gregory IX, made clear that the wife was subject to the husband. But he derived this subjection from biblical (1 Cor. 11) rather than from Aristotelian authority, and when he spoke of the husband and wife as the "superior" and "inferior" parties, he seems to have been referring to status rather than to nature.[89] He did not need to condemn women as incompetent or deny their spiritual equality in order to deny their right to any control over the property of the household, even for pious purposes.[90]

For the most part, women were simply nonactors. The irrelevance of women's will is reflected in an anonymous quodlibet where, in answering the question, "is *scandalum* a moral sin," the theologian gave the following example: "if someone plays around (*ludat*) with a woman in the presence of others, and in that he embraces her and kisses her in front of them and throws her on the ground and does such things, even if he does not have the will to commit a sin, to him is imputed whatever happens as a result, since perhaps those who are present, nor the woman, did not have the will to sin before they received the will to sin from his deed, and perhaps they will sin with this woman or with others, or she with these men or with others, which otherwise they would not have done."[91] The man, not the woman, is blamed; he is committing the *scandalum* by what he does to her. She is entirely passive, having no will to sin when the man was "playing around" with her.[92] That does not mean that she was being assaulted. Neither consent nor lack of consent is implied. Consent is simply irrelevant. This lack of importance placed on feminine consent to intercourse is not a peculiarity of this author or of theologians in general; it is pervasive in medieval culture.[93] Yet it is another indication of the insignificance of women as actors to scholastic theologians.

In a remarkable example of how women simply fell out of the picture, Gervaise of Mont St. Eloi addressed the question of whether a woman who had taken a vow of chastity but then married committed a mortal sin in every act of marital intercourse.[94] Gervaise began by using a gender-neutral term (*homo*): "a person [who has taken a simple vow] retains power over his/her own body" (the Latin possessive does not distinguish the gender of the possessor). Then as he turned to the specific case, he slips into the masculine: "[he] did not give the power over his body to his wife until after their first carnal intercourse." Even when the original question had been posed in terms of a woman's moral status, Gervaise preferred to discuss that of a man. The answer would probably not have been different had he considered a woman rather than a man. However, his shifting the question to the masculine side, while it appears a gender-neutral move, is a sign that to him the masculine was the norm and the feminine insignificant.

Even questions about feminine sexuality were turned into questions not about women themselves but about the nature of the divine. When asked whether God could restore lost virginity, Gerard d'Abbeville replied with a discussion of whether God's omnipotence included the power to falsify.[95] While it may be significant for an understanding of medieval gender relations that women's loss of virginity was so permanent that restoring it might be falsification, whereas for example restoring the dead to life was not, Gerard ignored this issue and used this question as a way of discussing God. Another discussion of whether a man or a woman is more meritorious in preserving virginity became a question not of gender comparison but of what constitutes spiritual merit.[96]

It is hardly surprising, in theological disputations, that the participants would attempt to turn the discussion as much as possible to theological issues. They did so, however, by largely excluding women from their mental world. The theologians were doing what they were supposed to do: using the specific questions asked to generalize to larger issues. The women referred to in the questions became in effect tools to think with, or stimuli to the larger discussions. And yet the application of reason and logic to theological questions was not ungendered. In refusing to follow up on the feminine aspects of the questions offered, the masters were saying that they did not matter. The difference between men and women did not matter, not because men and women were equal in all things, but because women fundamentally did not matter.

The exclusion of both real-life women and real-life men from what was theologically important also reflects how this masculine thought worked. Affective piety, a typically (though not exclusively) feminine approach to religion in the Middle Ages, tended to humanize the divine, if only metaphorically, in order better to identify with it. Masculine scholastic thought, on the other hand, dehumanized the human: it was not primarily concerned with pastoral issues but with principles and abstractions. It focused on an intellectualized conception of the world, not a personalized one.

The attitude that women were theologically and philosophically insignificant fit in well with a model of masculinity which recognized men's sexual nature and therefore treated women only or largely as sexual outlets (very different from the other medieval views that treated women as love objects or bearers of children). The theological faculty, where these disputations were held, was for more advanced students, not the younger ones under discussion here; but some arts masters also studied theology and the ideas of theologians had an impact in the arts faculty. The medieval university was a world without women not only in the student body but also in the curriculum.

More than the specific content of the arts or other curricula, however, it was the process of education, in particular the disputation, that shaped the young men's masculinity. The disputational process promoted not the sexual but the rational aspect of manhood. The idea that men are rational and women emotional was not new to the Middle Ages any more than was misogyny. However, whether or not it was caused by the Aristotelian revival, in the later Middle Ages a strand of misogyny that saw women as intellectually inferior began to develop alongside an earlier and concurrent strand that saw women as morally inferior (more lustful, more sinful). The counterpart to women's intellectual inferiority was men's rationality, and university education put a premium on this aspect of masculinity. University students learned that the ideal man was rational not so much from explicit teaching or preaching as from the constant example of scholastic disputation.

The intellectual method of the universities, especially in arts, was based almost entirely on the study of logic, and disputation was the pedagogical technique deemed most suited to its practice. We know the most about disputations in the faculties of theology, where more of them have survived, but they proceeded in similar ways in the arts faculties. Students in their third or fourth year of study in the arts were expected to participate. In ordinary disputations, a master would put forward propositions to be debated by his students; each would take a position as "opponent" of the thesis or "respondent," answering objections. The master (or a bachelor about to complete his course) would then "determine" the disputation by summing up and giving his own view of the question.[97] In addition to private disputations held among a master and his students, there were also public disputations, which might take place weekly at certain times of the university calendar. In the theology and possibly also the arts faculty, there were also disputations *de quodlibet* ("about whatever") in which the audience put forward questions about anything they liked.[98] It is from the records of these disputations that I have taken the examples above of the insignificance of women.

The disputation gave scholasticism its distinctive characteristics; indeed the statutes of medieval universities explicitly stated the importance of the disputation for developing the students' minds.[99] The disputation form had substantial effects on the texts that were used in the universities. Commentaries were written mainly in the form of questions, and although some of them were based on lectures, others grew out of discussions originally conducted orally in the context of a disputation.[100] Peter Lombard's *Sentences*, the main theological textbook, was especially conducive to this way of approaching problems: it presented authoritative texts on both sides of a question and then resolved the issue, just as might happen in a disputation. The *quaestiones disputatae* that survive do not reflect the process as it happened; they comprise the master's *determinatio* or resolution and are much more systematic than the disputation itself presumably was.

The disputational process was inherently competitive—in Walter Ong's term, agonistic. Ong sees the agonistic or adversarial structure of medieval and Renaissance education as deeply determined by the cultural understanding of masculinity. The whole basis of formal education was to take a stand on one side or another of a thesis and defend one's position against attackers, in the first instance one's teachers and later other academic adversaries. This was a sort of ceremonial combat.[101] William Courtenay notes the language used to describe debates: *impugnatio, adumbratio, evasio*—terminology from swordfighting. "There was, at least in the fourteenth century, some of the atmosphere of a tournament about scholastic debate in which, along lines similar to the 'round table' with capped lances, young scholars would enter the lists to prove their skill, their *subtilitas*, against an appointed foe without intending to damage him in any serious way." Courtenay suggests that the tournament analogy is particularly useful in understanding the ethos of scholasticism and its disputations.[102] John of Garland wrote that in disputations you should hide your own ignorance but "barber" your opponent.[103]

Jody Enders argues that the quodlibetal disputation was a dramatic performance of a ritualized combat. Although the written accounts of such disputations do not convey the active, fluid give-and-take that we may presume went on in the lecture hall, Enders reads literary accounts to suggest how the actual *disputatio* might have proceeded.[104] What Enders does not consider is the question of audience. These disputations might be well attended and quite gripping for the audience, but it was a very

specialized audience who might be as excited by the subtlety and bril-
liance of argument as by the performance itself.

Although the quodlibets that survive from the theological faculties
are no doubt redactions rather than transcriptions, they still reveal that
rhetorical technique and elegance of expression were less important than
logical reasoning, specialized language, and use of authorities. Erudition
and insight rather than presentation were most valued. The combatant,
like the knight in a tournament, needed not only talent, but years of
schooling.[105] The application of logic by the fourteenth century not just
to arts but to all areas of knowledge meant that university training was the
equivalent of training in argumentation according to fixed rules. To be
successful academically was to be a skillful debater, but skillful in logic
more than rhetoric.[106] These skills, available to only a few men, marked
the young man as a member of a special elite.

This academic structure of attack and defense provided a forum
for the demonstration of masculinity. In medieval culture, warfare—with
its vocabulary of attack and defense of a position—was considered the
proper task of the aristocracy, and single combat was considered the most
honorable activity for a man. Some academics, from the twelfth century
on (even before the reception of most of Aristotle and the rise of scholasticism proper) certainly considered their own scholarly activity in this
context. As Peter Abelard put it, "I exchanged all other arms for these,
and to the trophies of war I preferred the combat of the disputation."[107]
John of Salisbury analogized the training of Roman and other military
men to the training of a logician who must master the instruments of his
art. Dialectic teaches the contestant to bear his arms, which consist of
words.[108] These twelfth-century attitudes continued throughout the Middle Ages. The university had adopted the notion of masculinity as violent
domination of other men, but the violence was metaphorical, using words
as weapons.

Not everyone found the combative nature of dialectic a positive
development. Stephen of Tournai wrote to the Pope, "There is public disputation, which is against the sacred constitutions, as to the incompre-
hensible deity; about the incarnation of the Word, verbose flesh and
blood irreverently quarrels."[109] Vincent of Beauvais, in the mid-thirteenth
century, commented, "The contentious disputation of mature and modest
men is repugnant and censurable. And today, hardly one out of many thou-
sands can be found who is modest in disputing, but all are contending

and struggling, and disturbing rather than elucidating the truth." The thrust of Vincent's criticism, however, is directed against barriers to finding the truth, not against unseemly behavior like polemical or ad hominem argument; it is not the combative aspect of the *disputatio* that concerns him. He wants to tone down the performance in order to concentrate on the ideas, but he does not question that the ideas can be best elucidated through disputing.[110] Theologians defended disputation as superior to preaching in the support of the faith: it was more difficult, and it told people not just what to believe but also why.[111]

The disputation form was not unique to the universities. Debate poems were a staple of many vernacular literatures as well as Latin.[112] Scholars have made the case that in the *Romance of the Rose* "the pilgrim-student becomes the audience and the target of an archetypal symposium—one having the particular form of a university *disputatio* of the thirteenth century as conducted by the masters of rival lecture halls."[113] Back-and-forth debate as depicted in poems or embodied in texts written in response to another author, however, was not conducted according to the strict format and rules of the academic disputation. It did not take the formal structure of defense of, or objections against, a thesis, although of course something of that nature is implicit in any argument. Helen Solterer has argued that participation in such literary debates, by both actual and fictional women, was a way for women to talk back and speak out. The woman, however, is always positioned as opponent, leaving the man as the initiator. And women's participation was more often represented in literature than performed in practice: although Christine de Pisan participated in the early fifteenth-century pamphlet war of the *querelle de la rose*, defending women against the misogyny of Jean de Meung's poem and then defending herself against attackers, neither she nor other women participated in oral disputation at the university.

It was not being available only to men that made the scholastic mode of thought characteristically masculine. Single combat was a man's way of resolving questions, because fighting took place in the man's world, and disputation was single combat with the tools of reason. Like knightly prowess, disputation was a way for a man to prove himself in relation to other men. Not too many medieval authors paid much attention to particularly feminine ways of resolving questions, because women were not generally thought of as operating in the spheres where there were important issues to be resolved. When they did pay attention to it, medieval authors took speech as characteristic of women: women flung invective, used injurious or unruly language.[114] This might lead one to the conclusion that language was a characteristically feminine tool and therefore that the dispute might be considered a feminine form. However, language was feminine when it was disorderly. The language of the *disputatio* was very ordered. It was not polemical, but rather supremely rational.

The disputational process, and other university pedagogies, served also as a bonding mechanism. University students spoke a private language—indeed, several. One was the technical language of logic that was used in all fields of study. This was an academic jargon in the same way that the technical language of various academic disciplines is today; there was no pretense that it was intended for the general public. The language of the disputation was a highly technical, precise, and detailed Latin; its written form was highly abbreviated. Minute attention was paid to specific words and the exact order of words in order to draw distinctions and clarify categories. What may seem to a modern reader much like hairsplitting was to a medieval writer a precise and thorough investigation of all the aspects of a question.

Learning the arcane skill of disputation was part of the university man's induction into mature manhood. The student began his disputational training by contesting issues with his master. This, indeed, is what Ong primarily meant by the agonistic nature of education: not the combat between peers but the combat between student and master. As Solterer points out, literary debates nearly always cast men in the magisterial position. Women occasionally have some claim to the disciple position, although men usually end up claiming to speak for women.[115] The fact that women's role could displace that of the disciple also works to cast male disciples as not just junior but less manly than the master. In the university, whether the *disputatio* was between equals or unequals, both parties were male. Students in disputing with their masters could move from a more subordinate and deferential position to claim the full masculine privilege of speech.

In effect, one of the functions of the university was to initiate the student into academic discourse, teaching him the vocabulary and ways of speaking and writing appropriate to the form. And to the extent this separate register of language was used only at the universities, it was available to men alone. The *disputatio* or its derivative, the written *quaestio*, was recognized enough as a form to be satirized within the university milieu. Besides the works of literature like the *Romance of the Rose* that drew in some way on features of the form, there were other, less famous works that more directly used the techniques of academic competition to make a point about some more frivolous issue, but in the language of serious scholarship and rational discourse.[116] These pamphlets were, in effect, inside jokes for those who spoke that language.

On an even more basic level, however, the speaking of Latin served as a bonding mechanism. As an elite language, it set those who spoke it apart both from members of lower social groups and from women. Although there were Latinate women in the later Middle Ages, the bulk of women's writing that survives is in the vernacular. Learning Latin was part of the rite of passage for learned men. It was a sign of social position as well as of gender—not only most women, but also most men would not have the necessary degree of fluency in it. Latin was the language not only of written but also of oral scholarly discourse. At a truly international university like Paris it would have been the language of much everyday conversation as well.

Students were required to conduct all conversation at the university in Latin, not just within the classroom.[117] At Paris this might be a necessity in any case, as students came from all over Europe and did not all have a vernacular in common. At more provincial universities, however, most of the undergraduate students would come from the same region.[118] Here the authorities had to be more vigilant to encourage the speaking of Latin and to prevent the relapse into the vernacular. The terms in which they did so made clear the class associations of the Latin tongue. The statutes of the Collège de Foix at the University of Toulouse in 1427 called the vernacular the language of "cowherds, swineherds, and rural dwellers," to be avoided because of its "swineherdishness, crudeness, and vice."[119]

Evidently these statutes were necessary because some students were coming to the universities not as prepared in Latin as they should be. This was particularly the case in the German universities in the fifteenth century, where officials called *lupi* (wolves) eavesdropped on students' conversations to make sure they spoke only Latin.[120] The publication of phrasebooks for students, like that of Paulus Niavis that formed the basis for the *Manuale scholarium*, also indicated the deficiencies in their Latin. Students needed to learn Latin not only because they needed it for their academic work, but also because it was part of what bonded them into an academic community of men.

Students were also bonded into that community by their relationship with their master and the other students of that master. The social and pedagogical structure of the medieval university system fostered same-sex affective relationships. One force promoting such relationships might be called the erotics of discipleship. The power of attraction that an admired mentor and intellectual guide has for a student is recognized today in the claim that student-teacher sexual relationships can never be consensual because of the power dynamic involved. This erotics of discipleship can clearly be seen in medieval culture. The most famous example, perhaps, is a twelfth-century heterosexual one—Abelard and Heloise—but there is a rich tradition that goes back to Alcuin and involves deep emotional relationships between masters and students.[121] But even if master-student relationships are inherently agonistic—and the medieval university was structured so that they were, with disputation as the main pedagogical method—that does not mean that they are not also erotic. As Stephen Jaeger shows, an important model of love—if not the only one in the Middle Ages—was "ennobling love," a love that was not based on random "chemistry" but on admiration of the virtuous qualities of the beloved, and that ennobled the lover. In learning the skills of logic and disputation, the student modeled himself on a particular master. His character was to be improved by a man, rather than by the love of a woman.

Bonding Mechanisms

Speaking Latin and one's relation with one's master, of course, were far from the only mechanisms for bonding. Another was drinking. Wine, ale, or beer, depending on the region, was the lubricant of university social life. The surviving account books of the English-German Nation at the University of Paris reveal this clearly. Each new master, and each newly appointed official of the nation, had to buy drinks for the members, and the nation itself paid for them on other occasions, as well as providing funds to its members to help cover the costs of the feast they had to provide upon attaining the doctorate.[122] The nation adjourned to the tavern after each of its meetings. Sometimes members tried to hurry the process: at the time set aside for petitions, one member petitioned that they all go to the tavern.[123] A large fraction of the nation's funds were spent on drink. Indeed, it is possible to plot a geography of drinking establishments on the left bank of the Seine in the fourteenth century based on the records of the nations.[124] The English nation passed a rule against drinking except on the feast of their patron, St. Edmund, but this was not followed; there were similar rules among the nations at Bologna limiting the number of banquets with drinking.[125]

The University of Paris eventually had to legislate against excessive drinking by members of the nations on the feast days of their patron saints; the French nation in 1451 agreed not to permit feast days with actors, loud instruments, or "dissolute costumes, distracting the souls of the scholars from progress and leading them into lasciviousness."[126] Alcohol was also involved in violence, whether between nations or between town and gown. The St. Scholastica's Day riot of 1355 in Oxford, which lasted three days and left both students and townspeople dead and several academic buildings sacked, began in a tavern brawl between students and the tavernkeeper.[127] In Paris, the Picard nation on its feast day in 1409 attacked the English nation and a riot ensued.[128]

Drinking went on under other auspices besides those of the nations: at the Paris college of the Sorbonne, wine was so much a part of the everyday routine of the masters that the penalty for any infraction of the rules was to stand a round of wine for the assembled masters. Indeed, one student was fined in this way for saying that the masters were drunkards who, when they did not have any way of drinking for free, would fine their students.[129]

This alcohol consumption was not limited to a small group of rowdies who did not take their education seriously; it involved the whole community. Both solemn feasts and everyday college dinners were well lubricated. Sometimes a distinction was made between drinking in the college and drinking in public as in the Collegium Sapientiae at Freiburg (1497), which attacked feasting at the tavern as softness and effeminacy, connected with the sins of impudent words and shameful jokes, while prohibiting eating and drinking in the college only if excessive.[130] Here again excess is represented as feminine as opposed to rationality and moderation.

It was evidently the college and university authorities, rather than the scholars themselves, who imposed the idea of moderation in alcohol. This does not, however, mean that drunkenness in and of itself was part of the ideal of masculinity espoused by university students. Rather, as in many other groups in the Middle Ages, from parishes with their church ales to royal banquets with their toasts, drinking together was an expression of camaraderie and belonging. For the young man who was being initiated into adult male life, the use of alcohol marked him as part of the group. An element of competition may also have been involved: he had to prove himself to other men by his drinking (and paying) capacity.

The bonds of male companionship created by drinking together did not include women, or when they did, the women involved were either barmaids or women who frequented the taverns—considered the equivalent of prostitutes—or prostitutes themselves.[131] Such group visits to prostitutes could, of course, intensify the bonds among men: communal heterosexual experience may be a displacement of homoeroticism or simply a way of affirming masculinity to each other.[132]

Several other activities in which students in groups engaged after drinking also helped forge a group identity. Students gambled in the taverns, and university and college statutes repeatedly prohibited the playing of cards and dice.[133] At Louvain the concern seemed to be with the reputation of the university: students were not to play dice "in taverns or public places."[134] The appeal of gambling, in addition to the possibility of improving one's financial situation, lay perhaps in demonstrating one's masculinity to one's peers by showing a certain aggressiveness and willingness to take risks. This might seem to contradict the ideal of rationality and moderation, but indeed the same sort of daring was involved in disputations. Chess was sometimes exempted from rules against gaming as long as it was not played for money. More physical games, like the *jeu de paume* (an early version of tennis), also forbidden, were apparently connected with drinking too. The French Nation at Paris complained that young men (*juvenes*) were breaking into their lecture rooms on feast days and playing court tennis and committing "many foul things" there.[135]

Wine could be expected to be followed by song. The music studied as part of the quadrivium was not music performance but rather theory, considered as a branch of mathematics, and to the extent that it was related to performance had to do with the liturgy.[136] Performance with instruments was the province of minstrels rather than intellectuals. Loud singing and playing of instruments was one of the things colleges prohibited as a result of drunkenness, in part because of its potential to disturb the townspeople or other scholars.[137] A Vienna statute for arts students in 1413 referred to an "indecent noise" with musical instruments.[138] The Freiburg college statutes prohibited musical instruments on the grounds that they suggest wicked and abominable things to the adolescent mind.[139] An exception was made for the clavichord, possibly because it was not easily portable and therefore did not lend itself to street revelry. The Spanish college at Bologna allowed members to play instruments in their own rooms if it did not disturb others.[140]

Dancing and dramatics were also prohibited. The dancing to which the statutes refer seems to have been dancing in the streets—"dances through courts and gardens"—and did not necessarily include women.[141] The 1398 statutes of Angers stipulated that the feasts of the nations should be conducted "without drinking, dances, and costumes and actors."[142] In Germany, some dancing was licit. An Erfurt statute of 1447 stated that students may not go to the burghers' dances unless invited; if they were invited, apparently, it was acceptable, and indeed, the *Manuale scholarium* treats it as morally dubious but licit. At Bologna, however, balls were forbidden.[143] The University of Louvain statutes seemed most concerned, again, with publicity, fining anyone who danced publicly with laymen in the town square. At Cambridge there was no dancing in the public square, but an exception could be made for a new master on the day of his inception. Students at Oxford were not to dance with garlands in the porches of churches.[144] The rowdiness of singing and dancing in the streets could lead to vandalism or attacks upon the property or persons of the townspeople. Dramatics could also give rise to fighting, as groups satirized one another.[145]

University and college authorities recognized that the activities they prohibited were connected to the students' age: young men or "adolescents" in the medieval sense were prone to such behavior. The 1497 statutes of the Collegium Sapientiae at Freiburg provided "that the inmates of our house avoid the society of youths and adolescents who are lustful, depraved, and lazy and slothful in their studies."[146] The preface to the 1488 statutes of the University of Poitiers pointed out that "from adolescence human sensuality turns aside a man inclined to wickedness."[147] The University of Paris argued in 1446 for the release of seven students imprisoned in the Châtelet, reflecting a boys-will-be-boys attitude in dealing with outsiders: "Scholars are young men and sometimes do youthful things, the less serious ones of which belong to their masters' cognizance."[148] The statutes of the College of Ave Maria at Paris, which took boys at eight or nine years old, allowed them to remain only until sixteen, "at which age they commonly and habitually incline to evil."[149]

Gender and age were not the only factors affecting students' behavior: social class entered as well for some student groups who drank, gambled, and chased women together. Loud, outspoken public display was the prerogative of the aristocracy, the group with which students were attempting to identify, even if it was not the group from which they came. Students were attempting to become not just men but elite men. Whatever their social background, the young men at universities, aiming at career advancement, attempted to emulate the mores of the privileged groups in society.

This attempt to identify with the elite is revealed also in students' clothing. University and college statutes required academic dress, and prohibited indecent and secular clothing. The prohibitions varied from place to place—at the Collège Duplessis in Paris, no green clothing, at the Spanish college in Bologna no pointed shoes, at Oxford no fur except for masters or those of noble birth—but what did not much vary was the ban on extravagant and fancy costume.[150] Whether or not they or their families were in a position to afford it, students attempted to follow the latest in fashion.[151] As discussed in Chapter 2, attention to dress was not considered an effeminate characteristic in the Middle Ages; women were criticized by preachers for their extravagance in clothing, but so were men, and the finery of men's clothing was often discussed and praised in secular literature.

The refusal of students to follow the rules about academic dress may be an attempt to identify with the class that they hoped to emulate if not join. Some students, of course, were already aristocrats. The regulations were directed, however, not at aristocrats who insisted on continuing to behave as such, but at other students who tried to adopt the customs of their noble colleagues. Indeed, the 1463 statutes of the University of Freiburg im Breisgau specifically made the contrast between knights and scholars, listing among students who could not be admitted to a degree, "those who go about in indecent clothing in the manner of *routiers* or squires or otherwise disobediently and not scholastically."[152] The same attempt by students to adopt an aristocratic lifestyle may be behind the English college regulations prohibiting the ownership of dogs and falcons.[153] While these regulations discouraged students' attempts to live like aristocrats, they were not to live like artisans either, since universities prohibited students from exercising a trade.[154] This may have been in part an effort to avoid annoying the townspeople with competition, but it also reflected a sharp distinction between manual labor and intellectual activity that functioned to maintain the prestige of the intellectual.

Students who bore weapons were also trying to emulate the knightly ideal. Weapons were forbidden by college and university regulations (many referring to both offensive and defensive weapons), which were often violated.[155] Court records from college towns reveal that the weapons were not only carried, but also used. In Oxford in 1299, for example, a student stabbed a prostitute to death when she asked for her payment.[156] Sometimes the weapon carried was only a dagger, but sometimes it was a sword. The common use of weapons might be surprising among a group of men presumed to be preparing for a life in the church, but the presumption that they were future clerics may have made them all the more sensitive to challenges to their masculinity and encouraged them to defend themselves by force.

Collective as well as individual outbreaks of violence were repeated. In 1477 the Picard nation at the University of Paris asked that teachers and principals of colleges be prohibited from leading their students to the fields at the Pré-aux-clercs where "fights and insolences" had taken place.[157] The connection of arms with honor is shown by a privilege of Orléans in 1333 decreeing that members of the Picard and Champagne nations could bear arms on the feast day of their patron saints.[158] The dangers of this sort of honor appear in the cases of feast-day violence mentioned above (p. 96).

Along with the aristocratic virtues of display and swordsmanship, students also attempted to demonstrate the aristocratic virtue of largesse. Spending money freely upon oneself and others was a sign of gentility, and even students who could not afford to do so were expected by their peers to participate, thereby demonstrating their suitability for membership in the community. The purpose of such banquets was not only conviviality but also ensuring that students had the proper social graces. Again, these banquets were all male: men were proving themselves to each other. In the classroom young men adhered to the university model in which elite manhood was based on rationality, but to stake their own claims to masculinity they borrowed from other models as well.

Initiation Rituals and the Construction of the Rational Man

Students were compelled to spend money not just by generalized social pressure but also by specific rituals of initiation or hazing. These helped the student enter into the community of the university, and defined him against all nonscholars, including men of other social classes and women. Like a guild entrance fee, the money required of students indicated a commitment to and an acceptance into the group. The language used to describe student initiations indicates a sharp distinction between in-group and out-group. The student confraternity of St. Sebastien at Montpellier provided that no one could be admitted to the name of student "until he presented himself with humility and honor, and with six *grossi*" to pay for entrance into the confraternity. He was to swear an oath, and after the "feast of his purgation" and a year's probation the "shameful name" of *beanus* (a term for first-year students that first appears in France and may derive from *bec-jaune*) would be removed.[159]

A feast was the most common ritual for a new student or *beanus*. A student might also be expected or required to provide a feast for his colleagues, examiners, or the whole nation when he determined as a bachelor (achieved his degree by taking the leading role in a public disputation) or when he incepted as a master (gave his first lecture) or took up an office in the nation.[160] In Pavia in the law faculty the custom was a gift of sweets and wine on the day after examination.[161]

The custom of having new students give a banquet for their colleagues was criticized at Orléans in 1367, for example, because this practice was impoverishing many students, who had only a little money laboriously acquired by their parents and relatives. These students were being bullied into providing a banquet for their fellows, led to the tavern "like sheep to the slaughter."[162] Sometimes the amount the new student had to pay was on a sliding scale based on his wealth. The University of Paris in 1342 provided that he could not be forced to pay the fee, and if he offered it voluntarily only those with whom he lived could accept it.[163] At Angers in 1398 as well as Orléans in 1365, the statutes provided that students' books were not to be seized to pay the *bejaunium* (initiation fee) and (at Angers) that the money be used for pious causes rather than debauchery.[164]

Hazing of *beani* amounted to more than financial exactions. The College of St. Bernard in Paris had to prohibit "burdening, shaking, or other insolences and jokes . . . in the chapter, the dormitory, the schoolroom or the gardens" against new students. At Angers, the university decreed in 1373 that *beani* should be received benignly without tumult or running about the town or any holiday.[165] Regulations of the College of St. Nicholas at Avignon show a set of hazing procedures that may be what these other institutions were trying to prohibit: no one was to call "polluted and most stinking" *beani* "sir" on pain of a fine of a mark of silver, and if one beanus did so to another he would receive two blows. *Beani* had to serve at table and had to appear before an "abbot" with their heads uncovered in order to "separate the pure from the impure" and segregate "the beanus and those contaminated with the taint of the beanus from those who have been promoted." The *beanus* finally had to be purged with water.[166]

Both of these features—hazing of the freshman or *beanus*, and the use of a feast to mark (or to pay for) one's entrance into the community of scholars—are found in the statutes of the German universities. For example, according to a decree of the Heidelberg arts faculty in 1419, a bachelor who had just been examined for his license was not to invite anyone to a bath or a feast after the bath, except the dean and his fellow examiners, because "in such excessive and abundant banquets poor men are greatly harmed."[167] Inviting the examiners, however, seems to have been routine, and the bathhouse as venue might imply that the examinee hired the services of prostitutes as well. (The Montpellier regulations specifically warned any *beanus* against daring to provide prostitutes along with the feast for his new brothers.[168]) There was a similar provision at Vienna, requiring the bachelor to spend not more than thirty pence for bath and feast.[169] In Leipzig a new member of the Grosse Fürstenkolleg had to give a feast within the first month, as well as (if a master) bonuses to the servants.[170] The 1447 statutes from Erfurt required that "from a *beanus* for the removal [*depositio*] of his *beanium* no more than a third of a Rhenish florin shall be exacted, unless permission to spend more has been obtained from the rector of the University and the Secret Council."[171] Presumably such permission could be obtained in the case of a wealthier student.

The use of *beanium* as a noun, representing the status of freshman as a thing that could be removed by a specific act or ceremony, indicates that being a *beanus* was not just a question of newness but a matter of having some taint from which one had to be purified. Besides purging, hazing could also take the form of taunting or other harassment. At Vienna in 1385 students were prohibited from exacting money from or insulting the *beani*; at Leipzig they were told not to harass them during the procession of Corpus Christi. Other university and college regulations provided a penalty for students who threw urine or feces at *beani* or otherwise physically molested them.[172] Clearly the ritual humiliation aspect of initiation was present here.

The most detailed account we have of the initiation of a *beanus* is from the *Manuale scholarium*. The relation of this account to social practice is not straightforward. The section that concerns us here is the description of the *depositio cornuum*, or removal of the initiate's horns. One of the two students comments to the other about a horrible stink in the room: "there's either been a corpse rotting here, or a goat, filthiest of all beasts." They find it to be a horrible monster: "for this beast is horned, has ears like an ox, and his teeth, sticking out in both directions from his jaw, threaten to bite like a wild boar. He has a nose curved like an owl's beak, and red and bleary eyes threatening rage." They then discover that the monster is actually a *beanus*. When they offer him wine and he attempts to drink, they call him venomous and say that he "ought to drink water, muddy water, at the brook with the cattle." They then speak of how his mother would be sad if she knew how he was being treated, and accuse him of weeping when he hears his mother mentioned. They address him: "O *Beanus*, o ass, o stinking goat, o smelly female goat, o toad, o zero, o figure of nothing, o you nothing at all! May the devil shit all over you and piss on your stomach and feet!" They discuss cutting off his horns, pulling out his teeth, cutting his beard and nose hairs; one student goes to get implements, and returns with a salve as well, made from goat excrement. They saw off the horns, pull out the teeth, and shave the beard using water with fragrant herbs picked from the garden by the outlet of the privy. They threaten to hang him by a rope in the privy. They then force him to confess to a variety of crimes, from theft to rape to perjury. As "penance" for these offenses, they order him to buy them a generous dinner with fine wine. They all then wish him luck; he has become a member of the community.[173]

To what extent was this ritual of deposition actually practiced? It is well attested from the sixteenth century on, as a more or less official custom of the German universities.[174] The initiate wore a hat with horns (which were sawn off), had false teeth pulled, had his head shaved, and underwent other indignities. It is not so clear what was actually practiced in the later medieval period. Heidelberg records from 1454 contain a list of students who "put off [*deposuerunt*] their *beanium*."[175] This phrase, however, may not refer specifically to the removal of the horns, because the same phrase is used as in Erfurt in the statute limiting the amount a *beanus* could be made to pay. It could mean simply "removal of freshmanness" rather than "removal of horns." There are two other texts from Erfurt, however, that when read in conjunction with the *Manuale* seem to support the existence of a practice similar to that described there. One is Goswin Kempgyn of Neuss's *Trivita studentium*, written sometime in the mid-fifteenth century. This text is a long poem describing various aspects of student life and study. In the one manuscript that has survived, it is heavily glossed, so even where the poem itself is cryptic, the glosses explain what is happening to the *beanus*. The whole ritual is called the *vexatio beanum* (harassment of the *beanus*). The *beanus* is to be transformed by the use of ragged clothing, basin, and blade, and to be bathed. He is advised to bear the ritual patiently rather than fight it.[176] There is no reference to horns, but the shaving and bathing are similar, and the use of excrement is implicit in references to the buttocks and farting.[177]

The other text is a pamphlet from 1494, the *Monopolium der Schweine-zunft* by Johannes Schram.[178] This parody of a quodlibetal disputation discussed the *beanus* as follows:

Of *beani*, whether they can be received in our society, I decree: they must be cleansed of their *beanium* before they are received. And the way they must be cleansed is clear from the third part of Alexander, distinction 23ff., *on horned animals*, line *beasts*, verse *full of stench; A sea, a wave, a body of water purge forth that which makes a shameful sound, and feminine filth; these likewise are good for a beanus, honey, liquid, water, wine (there's some good Latin), the drinking of which pleases the one being purified and the one helping*. Cups, *gantz volle* [completely full], drinking, *das sie werden tolle* [so they get wild], because the *depositio* alone is not enough, but that there be a feast for his colleagues, of good wine (according to others, good beer), which I prove thus.[179]

Clearly the feast itself is connected with the purging of the *beanus*'s taint and accompanies, rather than consititutes, the *depositio*.

As to what exactly is the taint that must be purged, the *Manuale* is our best clue. There we must look for exactly what sort of transition the *beanus* is in fact making. The *beanus* is in a liminal state between the status of unlearned child and that of university student, but what are the features that distinguish those statuses?

One thing that is happening to the *beanus* is the transition from an animal—an especially bestial one—into a human. This transition represents the process of civilization: the bringing of the rude, unlearned, rough new entrant within the pale of acceptable society. The unlearned man is compared to a human beast. Indeed, such an image of bestiality corresponds well to medieval literary depictions of peasants. The image of the uneducated person as bestial is found in the writings of university men throught the high and late Middle Ages.[180] Jacques Le Goff notes with reference to this particular text:

Thus the future intellectual abandoned his original condition, which strongly resembled the images of the peasant, the country bumpkin found in the satirical literature of the time. From bestiality to humanity, from rusticity to urbanity, these ceremonies, in which, degraded and practially emptied of its original content, the old primitive essence appeared, recall that the intellectual had been extracted from a rural environment, from an agrarian civilization, from a rude, uncivilized life on the land.[181]

But it was not an abstract or essential medieval intellectual who was being cleansed of the taint of bestiality; it was students in fifteenth-century German universities. And, in fact, a comparison with the treatment of peasants in fifteenth-century German literature reveals that the connection of this ritual with rusticity is not nearly as direct as one might expect. The representation of the *beanus* as a horned beast does not resonate with particular texts of fifteenth-century German literature: peasants were depicted as stupid, boorish, violent, and with an affinity for excrement, but not particularly as bestial.[182]

Even though the goat image does not specifically refer to a peasant background, the taint of rusticity still remains a part of the pollution from which the *beanus* must be cleansed. Even if fifteenth-century German peasants are not depicted as goats, they are shown as filthy and hypersexual, characteristics connected with the *beanus* (as well as Jews and women). The *beanus* may have been considered a rustic in a figurative rather than a literal sense, simply because he had not yet entered into the community of the educated. The learning of Latin, as discussed above, was taken in medieval universities to distinguish between rustics and others.

The connection of the *beanus* with rusticity was largely independent of the actual demographics of the medieval university. Only 11 percent of all students at Heidelberg between 1386 and 1450 were from villages. And not all of these, of course, would be peasants in any economic sense; they were the sons of the village elite, although they still might be considered *rustici* simply because of their rural origins.[183] Peasants or rural dwellers were a small enough segment of the university population, and the relation of the goat imagery to depictions of peasants is indirect enough, to suggest that a rejection of rusticity is not all that is going on in the initiation ritual of the *depositio*.

If we focus on the goat, "filthiest of beasts," it becomes apparent that the ritual is connected with sexuality and abjection as well as rusticity. The goat is the animal mentioned most prominently in the text; it is also the one characterized by horns and beard, the features that must be removed. Goat excrement also appears prominently. The general function of excrement in the text (which is not all goat excrement) is to connect the initiate with filth. But goat excrement was also thought to have medicinal properties. According to Albertus Magnus, "the fat of a goat, mixed with the excrement of a goat, rubbed on gout, eases the pain; the excrement of female goats, burned, mixed with vinegar or a mixture of vinegar and honey, rubbed in vigorously, cures baldness."[184] Vincent of Beauvais, in his magisterial compilation *Speculum naturale*, gives more recipes involving goat excrement, which was efficacious for wasp stings, uterine flux, snakebite, scrofula, hemorrhage, baldness, excoriation, burns, gout, arthritis, and abcesses.[185] Both baldness and gout are characteristic of men rather than women; baldness is a sign of maturity and gout of luxurious living, both presumably to be obtained in the future by the prospective student.[186] Yet, in the name of healing, and following commonly accepted healing practice, the initiators were going to smear the initiate with feces. The prohibition from Heidelberg from 1466 (p. 102) indicates that feces were used in hazing *beani*.[187]

The goat was connected in medieval culture not only with physical but also with spiritual filth. Goats appear in the Old Testament, especially in Leviticus, as sin-offerings, in passages that were taken as prefigurations of Christ's sacrifice. Medieval traditions about goats drew more often on another Biblical theme, that of Christ as the shepherd separating the sheep from the goats (Matt. 25:32), than on the goat as a type of Christ. Many commentators made the direct connection between the goats and sinners and between the sheep and saints. The sheep on the right hand and goats on the left became a theme in early Christian art. The sin here connected with the goat was not just any sin, but the sins of the flesh and the impurity of the body.[188]

The connection of the goat with the sins of the flesh also appears in the bestiary tradition. Bestiaries described various animals and gave moral explanations for their characteristics; they were intended not just to convey knowledge about nature but also to edify. Many drew on Isidore of Seville, the sixth/seventh-century encyclopedist, who wrote that "the male goat [*hircus*] is a lascivious animal, and wanton, and always eager for sexual intercourse, whose eyes look sideways because of libidinousness."[189] Some bestiaries depict the lascivious male goat, bearded and with long horns.[190] One text quotes a reference to male goats in the Psalms and interprets: "The he-goats are those who follow the depravities of the devil and clothe themselves in the shaggy hide of vice."[191]

The goat's connection with the libido is also found outside the bestiary tradition. In medieval art, the personification of Luxuria (Lust), one of the seven deadly sins, is often shown riding on a goat.[192] Albertus Magnus thought enough of the sexual power of goats to claim that "whoever eats two goats' testicles and has intercourse, from the surplus of the digestion of this meal will engender a male child, unless there is an impediment in the woman with whom he has intercourse."[193] Nuremberg carnival customs in the fifteenth century included a dance where figures of goats, among other animals, symbolized male fertility.[194]

The goat, especially as a symbol of sin, was also associated with the Jew in the Middle Ages. Jews were sometimes depicted with horns. The direct link was with the Devil rather than the goat, but the diabolical horned Jew was sometimes shown together with a goat whose horns were identical to his. Since the goat was the Devil's chosen animal, Jews were often depicted riding goats or with goat-like beards. The odor attributed to Jews in the late Middle Ages further links them to the *beanus* of the dialogue.[195] It is not likely that the *Manuale*'s intent was to portray the *beanus* as a Jew. However, the association with the Jew would have resonated for medieval readers and identified the *beanus* as filthy, depraved, and nonhuman as the Jew was.

The sexual aspect of the goat, and its odor, are both clearly present in the *Manuale* dialogue. The aroma that Camillus smells brings a goat immediately to his mind, and he calls the *beanus* an *olens capra*, echoing the way classical sources describe the *hircus*, but making the *beanus* into a female rather than a male goat. Part of the *beanus*'s preinitiate status, his not knowing how to behave properly or his lack of civilization, is his libido as well as his smell.

One possible reading of the *Manuale* text is that the *beanus* is being feminized, rather than cleansed of the feminine. The cutting off of the horns, the shaving of the beard, and the transformation of the odor into a sweet smell might point in this direction. Given the status hierarchy of the university, and the lack of actual women, the new students, the youngest members, could be effectively cast in the feminine role. However, while perfumes and unguents might be connected with women or effeminacy, strong odors could also be connected with women, and often were in medieval misogynous discourse. Nor are the horns distinctively masculine—female goats also have horns.[196] The cutting off of the horns cannot be a simple castration symbol. Horns, too, were a sign of cuckoldry; their removal might indicate that the *beanus* was no longer to be a figure of ridicule. The language of the ritual clearly points to a cleansing of the feminine, not a feminizing of the *beanus*. The Erfurt mock quodlibet, which refers to "feminine filth" (*lutum femineum*) as that which must be purged along with the foul odor, makes this connection as well.[197]

Rather than feminizing, the ritual was initiating the student into an alternative form of masculinity. It rejected the bestiality of uncontrolled sexuality. Yet it is not likely that a student-initiated ritual would be attempting to turn the prospective student into an asexual celibate. The authorities at medieval universities might have preferred their students have nothing to do with women, and several of the other dialogues in the *Manuale* suggest that this ought to be the case, but it is clear enough, as discussed above, that this was never accepted by the students themselves. Rather, the ritual would seem to be taking away not the initiate's sexuality, but his uncontrolled and indiscriminate sexual impulses. He is now to be civilized, a gentleman.[198]

For those who did come from an aristocratic background, and were not intended for a life in the church, the *depositio* might also perform the function of making the entrance into the intellectual world acceptable. In making explicit the rejection of the feminine, the ritual in effect denied that study or Latinity was effeminate, that it was incompatible with honor. If the uneducated man is like a female goat, then to enter the university was not to deny one's masculinity but to affirm it.

The civilized student might be sexually active but not lascivious and wanton, which were the characteristics both of women and of animals. Many medieval medical scholars, after all, recommended moderate coitus as productive of good health for men; it was the Aristotelian idea of balance and moderation rather than the Christian idea of chastity that controlled in their work.[199] Rational and controlled sexual desire was associated with humans, as opposed to irrational, lustful animals.[200] Uncontrolled, animal lasciviousness was also associated in many medieval discourses with femininity; the initiate here is becoming not only human, but masculine.[201] The masculinity is one that mediates between the church's demand of celibacy (not often honored) and total sexual abandon. University students might emulate aristocratic practices in taking their pleasure where they could find it, but they were not to be controlled by it.

This initiation ritual sums up much about the model of masculinity that a young man adopted as a university student. He rejected the bestial and feminine and formed a bond with a group of men. He related to women in a sexual and instrumental manner. He emulated the aristocratic model of masculinity in some ways, proving himself to other men through display, violence, and largesse, even though these aspects were frowned on by the authorities. What was not frowned on was the idea of rationality and moderation that distinguished the man both from the woman and from the beast.

4

Masters and Men:
Independence and Urban Craft Workers

AS A MASCULINE SPACE, the craft workshop seems quite different from the university, where women were physically absent and insignificant in the discourse, or the court, where women were important symbolically as commodities exchanged among men. In the workshop men and women worked alongside each other. A woman's work was often essential to a family enterprise, and women as well as men worked as skilled laborers. While in practice women might do some of the same tasks as men, however, official recognition for their skilled labor remained for the most part a male prerogative. The normative artisan was the master; except in a very few crafts, men ran the workshops. They hired men as skilled workers. Female servants or family members might help, or run the retail end of the business, but only as widows were women officially recognized as participants.

Masculinity in the craft workshop was defined, however, as it was elsewhere, not only in opposition to women but also in opposition to other men. The goal of artisanal masculinity was domination of others (including women but mainly men) economically through ownership of an independent workshop. Skill and a sense of belonging to a particular craft as recognized by the formal organization of that craft led in theory to economic independence, the ability to marry, civic participation, and the control of subordinates in a workshop. Masculinity depended not so much on proving oneself not a woman as on proving oneself not a boy. Full manhood required maturity, independence, and financial success. The traditional understanding of masculinity as the opposite of femininity is not irrelevant to the situation in the urban craft workshop any more than it was in the university setting, but it is not the whole story.

There were many more urban craft workers than there were university scholars or even knights in the later Middle Ages, although they still did not form anything like a majority of the total population. Compared to university culture or aristocratic culture, both of which were largely international (although with regional variation), the lives and position of urban craft workers varied much more from region to region and town to town as a result of economic, demographic, and cultural factors. Nevertheless it is possible to locate common features of an artisanal masculinity. Across Europe, only being an independent head of household provided a craftsman with honor, full participation in civic life, and a position from which to master others.

Adulthood was not achieved simply by coming of age; full manhood required the assumption of a particular position in society, and not all craftsmen could achieve it in the towns of later medieval Europe. In a hierarchical society young men had to struggle for social status, which required their moving out of a position of dependence and into one where they could dominate others. Those craft workers who remained in a dependent or subordinate position, unable to be their own masters or the masters of other men, had to seek other means, often labeled rebellions, for proving themselves. In the struggle for dominance they competed mainly with other men.

In the workshop the young man learned his trade, which in theory as he became a man he would be able to practice on his own. Since in practice this often proved not to be the case, the dissonance between expectations and reality that many of the wage workers experienced must have had a formative effect upon their concepts of themselves as men.[1] Because of the financial exigencies of raising a family, and also because in many places workers normally lived in the households of their employers, it might be quite difficult for any worker who was not yet a master to marry. This left young men without a stable base within the town, leading (in the medieval view) to gangs and disorder. It also could lead to resentment of married men, particularly those who married younger women. A class of workers might be mired in permanent dependency, the social equivalent of adolescence, because economic and social forces prevented them from taking up the duties and responsibilities of a man as head of household. Their dependence did not make them feminine, but they could not achieve full adult civic masculinity, so they might turn to other means, including violence, to demonstrate their manhood.

Young men learning their craft were placed in a difficult position, preparing for a station in life that they might well never attain. One way for them to claim masculinity was an assertion of solidarity with the masters. Both masters and workers considered themselves skilled, trained at their craft, as opposed to the much larger body of laborers (and women) who had not learned the "mystery," who had looser ties to masters, less stable employment, and more likelihood of falling into crime.[2] On the other hand, however, skilled workers sometimes made common cause, identifying their own interests against those of the masters or asserting independent status through other means than the craft.

The meaning of "honor" was crucial for artisanal as it was for knightly masculinity. Honor, equated with free birth and a good reputation, was a prerequisite for craft guild membership rather than a result of it.[3] However, when texts refer to townsmen as honorable or respectable (*ehrlich, preudomme,* "good") they almost invariably are speaking of masters, not employees. Master artisans occupied a particular niche in urban society: they could participate in government where unskilled laborers could not, but they usually did not dominate the town as the greater merchants did. They put great value on their independence, financial stability, respectability, and status as head of a household as well as skill as integral parts of what it meant to be a craftsman.

The kinds of documents that tell us about craft workers rarely discuss masculinity explicitly. As with university students, we must infer what people thought made a man from their behavior or from regulations whose purpose was something else entirely. This chapter focuses not so much on concepts of masculinity as discussed in an artisanal environment as on the experiences of young men as craft workers. The relation of these experiences to concepts of masculinity remains implicit rather than explicit in the sources.

Artisans in Medieval Society

As with the other models of masculinity, to understand the workings of gender in a social subgroup we must first place it in social context. Artisans who were masters in their crafts were a middle stratum in late medieval urban society. They owned their own workshops and tools; many sold directly to consumers. Many of these workshops were small, involving only the master and one or two family members, but in some places ateliers were larger and had many employees. Craft workshops were largely household based. Workers tended to live in the household, and the line between domestic servants and craft employees was not always clear.

The sharp distinction between masters and wage workers in the same craft was relatively new in some areas. In the thirteenth century in Languedoc, for example, statutes talk about artisans in various crafts, but do not distinguish between masters and workers, although notarial contracts did make the distinction.[4] Elsewhere, too, the assumption was that most artisans were masters or soon would be. Anyone who worked on his own account and who paid a fee was a master. Only in the fourteenth and fifteenth centuries did the dividing line sharpen as mastership became rigidly defined and formalized. Gervase Rosser has suggested that this sharp dividing line is an artifact of the sources, craft ordinances that "enshrine the prevailing contemporary theory of labor relations" but not its practice.[5] However, while the opposition between masters and workers may not have been so stark in everyday experience, its inscription in the law had very real consequences. Court records show that the distinctions were taken seriously by city authorities. The types of masculinity that developed in this context were closely linked to one's position in the craft, and only masters were treated as full adults.

Although a master craftsman could become wealthy and politically prominent, artisans, even masters, did not always play governing roles in the late medieval towns. The constitutional struggles of the high Middle Ages had involved merchants against the aristocracy, and the merchants eventually won out, establishing oligarchies in many towns. During the later Middle Ages, further conflicts developed, pitting craft organizations against the merchant oligarchies. The merchants might be organized into guilds or similar organizations as well—in London, for example, the grocers and the mercers were prominent merchant companies—but the crucial distinction was that they were primarily involved in trade rather than in manufacturing.

When conflicts of the crafts against the merchants did develop, it was not a question of working class against bourgeoisie. The guildsmen who sought to play a greater role in the governance of the towns were the upper stratum of masters, entrepreneurs, and property owners, not the wage workers.[6] Thus any degree of participation in the political and ritual life of the town, a component of mature artisanal masculinity, came not simply through craft membership, but master status.[7]

The industrial organization of some towns, particularly textile towns in Flanders and Italy, stood somewhere between a modern capitalist and a household workshop model. The clothmaking process, for example, included more than a dozen separate crafts. An entrepreneur (clothier, draper, *lanaiuolo*) hired craftspeople—spinners, weavers, fullers, shearers, and so forth—as subcontractors. The master weavers, fullers, and other craftsmen were not technically employees, and their employees worked for them rather than for the drapers, but masters did not provide their own raw materials or work independently, and were in effect little different from employees. In Florence, for example, the petty entrepreneurs of lesser crafts, or *sottoposti*, did not belong to the guilds, and were excluded from political office.[8] By the beginning of the fourteenth century, many workers who in a previous period would have been independent had become part of a large group of wage laborers, perhaps a third to a half of the Florentine labor force. Some of them worked in their own workshops and owned their own tools, but they still worked for wages, either by time worked or by the piece: they were not independent producers selling their product.[9] Whereas apprentices, workers, and supervisors had previously been differentiated primarily by age or position in the life cycle, now few of them had any hope for becoming independent masters no matter how mature they got.[10]

In most towns, the master maintained his independence at least in theory. But the crafts still did not adhere to the textbook model for achieving mature masculinity in which an apprentice worked for a master for a period of time, became a journeyman, worked for another period of time to perfect his skills, created a masterpiece, and became a master.[11] By the later Middle Ages, there were barriers to entry into the crafts, which in many places became hereditary. Even if the number of openings in a given craft were not limited, it might still not be so easy for a journeyman to become a master; there were fees to be paid or expensive materials to be purchased for the making of the masterpiece. For many workers, then, the status of wage worker or journeyman (in French, *valet* or *compagnon*; in German, *Gesell*) was not destined to be a stage in the life cycle as they moved on to better things, but a permanent status. Yet a number of journeymen without hereditary privileges—more in some places than in others—still managed to become masters, which held out hope for others and perpetuated the ideal.

Craft organizations controlled individual crafts in most towns of the later Middle Ages. Royal or urban authorities issued particular privileges or statutes for each craft, in effect granting a monopoly, but the crafts themselves enforced them: they mediated disputes among the brethren, determined who was qualified to be a member, and set standards. The craft collected fees from anyone who took up the mastership (often equivalent to becoming a full member of the organization), or who took on an apprentice. They set the hours of work, sometimes the wages of the workers, and the specific requirements for the items produced, to discourage price competition among the members who held a monopoly on that particular craft. In England, membership in a craft brought with it freedom of the city (citizenship), which otherwise could be achieved by birth (being the legitimate son of a father who was free of the city) or by purchase. Heather Swanson argues that craft organizations in England appear more prominently in the sources than they really were because, as organizations, they left records.[12] Yet even if they had their genesis as she suggests, as creations of municipal authorities with the purpose of controlling craft workers, they did exercise power over practitioners and provided an important focus for their sense of craft community.

The masters were the full members of the craft, and municipalities recognized their authority. Wage workers too could be members—in some cases they were required to join—but usually constituted a second rank with distinctly limited privileges. In London, for example, the confraternities that coincided with some of the crafts had "liveried" and "yeoman" members. Only liveried members could serve as officers, and they had more privileges; there were certain feasts that only they could attend. They carefully supervised the operation of the "yeoman" section of the craft. The lesser masters and wage workers, as "yeoman" guild members, could attend some of the solemn feasts and celebrations, and received the social provisions of the guild—for example, burial expenses. By the late fifteenth or sixteenth century in some crafts the livery company was a small elite, which might include nonpractitioners of the craft, like nobles, admitted for prestige reasons.[13] Yet the distinctions between those who were liveried and those who were not, and those who were masters and those who were not, remained clear.

Most crafts did not permit women other than widows of masters to join. While their husbands were alive, however, wives worked alongside them, as did female servants, participating in the work but not always receiving the credit or privileges. In a few crafts—notably silk-working and other luxury textile crafts—a few towns allowed women to be masters. In other crafts where women were the majority of workers the masters were still men.[14] Though women's work was by no means insignificant, in most places only men (or widows as a stand-in for men) were eligible to be the independent heads of households envisioned by the traditional artisanal model. In particular, full membership in the organizations that held monopolies on particular crafts and regulated their exercise was largely a masculine preserve.

The term "guild" in medieval sources can be misleading to modern readers. In fact, what we think of, and what I occasionally refer to, as "craft guilds" were usually called simply crafts, *métiers*, *arti*, or *Zünfte*, although sometimes also "corporations" or "mysteries." The term "guild" in general referred to a religious and social organization that could also be termed a confraternity. Some of these were parish based, but in others, membership was determined or restricted by craft. These guilds, dedicated to the honor of a particular saint, provided occasions for socialization and the making of connections across trades as well as opportunities for worship.

By the later Middle Ages, the religious guild or confraternity connected with a craft often overlapped with the organization of a craft itself: members of the craft might be required also to join the confraternity, so that a spiritual bond linked masters and wage workers. Sometimes the workers were full members of the confraternity, but its officers or leaders were usually masters, and sometimes the confraternity came with different levels of membership or a structure that replicated the social hierarchy. The confraternity could thus combine vertical and horizontal relationships, reinforcing patriarchal and paternalistic lines of authority while at the same time emphasizing brotherhood.[15] In Salisbury, for example, the ordinances of the tailors and their related confraternity established separate fellowships for masters and journeymen; each group had its own stewards. At the main fraternity celebration, at mid-summer, the members all worshipped together, but the two groups feasted separately.[16] In confraternities that crossed craft lines, artisans (masters and workers) had the opportunity to join together with others of their own social group.[17] For people who were new to the towns, fraternities allowed them to meet people of different crafts, sexes, or social status.

Arrangements in which journeymen were second-tier members of the same craft guilds or confraternities as their masters indicate that the two groups understood themselves as sharing common interests, goals, and aspirations. Such arrangements made sense in a world in which the journeymen saw the possibility ahead of them of promotion to master status, where the manhood that required full independence and civic participation was something they could reasonably expect to achieve. Indeed, as Barbara Hanawalt suggests, even for apprentices, seeing the masters in their livery gave them something to strive for.[18] By the later Middle Ages, however, this expectation was no longer reasonable in many regions, and other arrangements became common, which indicate that masters and journeymen saw their interests as mutually antagonistic.

In parts of Germany in the fifteenth century, wage workers in a number of different crafts had their own organizations. These served largely social functions rather than regulating industry, but the fact that they were separate rather than a branch of the masters' guilds may indicate that the journeymen could no longer expect to look forward to eventually achieving master status. Their links with their coworkers might be permanent, although some wage workers did advance to become masters. Repeated strikes and other conflicts in southwestern Germany between the masters and journeymen as collective groups, discussed below (pp. 139–40), indicate that they had come to see each other as antagonists. These uprisings differed from labor unrest in other areas, like the revolt of the Ciompi in Florence in 1378, which was not a conflict of wage workers in one craft against their own employers, but rather a complex event which included, among other conflicts, masters and workers of the same crafts allied against merchants.

Apprenticeship: From Boyhood to Manhood

A man's life as a craft worker usually began with his apprenticeship.[19] He remained in a subordinate position that emphasized his youth and his ignorance, while at the same time attempting to prove himself worthy of eventual master status. Crafts strongly encouraged the use of the apprenticeship system and discouraged masters from taking on young workers on a less formal basis. For example, the goldsmiths of London prohibited their members from taking a child into service (as distinct from apprenticeship) to be instructed in the craft.[20]

There was great variation in the age at which apprenticeship began, and so few documents give precise ages that it is not possible to arrive at any sort of reliable average; as a generalization with numerous exceptions, one might say it began at around twelve to fifteen years old. Those documents from across Europe that do give exact ages show as wide a range within a single craft as from six to twenty-two years for entering apprenticeship.[21] Steven Epstein has identified two distinct types of apprentices, one whose work began between the ages of ten and fourteen, the other between fourteen and twenty-one. The former group mainly provided cheap labor, at least for the first few years of service; the latter received job training and might get paid.[22] The latter were the ones more likely to later become masters in a skilled craft and achieve the mature masculinity of independence.

Length of apprenticeship varied very widely. Six or seven years was a typical period, but the length could be anywhere from a year to ten years depending on the town and the craft. Most crafts set minima for their apprentices, but the actual period was contractual, and sometimes the contracts stipulated less than the legal minimum.[23] Some of the variation depended on the age of the new apprentice.[24] More highly skilled crafts did not necessarily require longer apprenticeships. Philippe Didier, who has studied apprenticeship contracts from Burgundy, suggests that in fact the apprenticeship period was the shortest precisely in the most skilled crafts.[25] This pattern—or lack of pattern—appears in other regions as well.[26] Apprenticeship as a period of learning does not explain this discrepancy, which must have to do also with employers' need for labor. Didier suggests that in highly skilled crafts with short apprenticeship periods, apprenticeship served to educate the young worker. In other crafts with longer periods of apprenticeship, however, it provided a form of inexpensive labor. Parents might not pay as high a fee to place their son in a craft with a longer apprenticeship period.[27] Even within the same craft, there could be a trade-off between length of contract and amount of fee. The apprentice was not only there to learn; if he served as a source of labor for longer, he paid less. While in general apprentices, who were expected to grow up and become masters, composed a social elite compared to mere servants, for some the distinction between unskilled labor and apprenticeship as training was blurred.

The payments that the apprentice or his family made to the master took a variety of guises. Sometimes they notionally covered the room, board, and clothing that the master would supply over the course of the apprentice's term. Sometimes the apprentice paid a fee per year until he could earn (for the master) a specified amount. Towns paid masters to take on orphans as apprentices, and these fees provided important working capital.[28] In London it was common for the apprentice's family to lend the master a sum to be paid back at the end of the apprentice's term; the master had the use of the income and the apprentice could eventually use the sum to get started in business. In several cases when the master allegedly refused to give the money back, the apprentices' parents implied that the payment was not part of the apprenticeship contract but something extra "to the purpose that their said son shall be had more in favor."[29] The families were clearly concerned with their sons' future position in life, preparing them for a life of independence as masters.

Though the apprentice's family usually paid a fee, payments went the other way as well.[30] In Florence apprentices received wages like other workers. Contracts often specified that apprentices would receive a set of tools of the trade at the end of their contract, which could be worth a substantial amount but also symbolized independence.[31] In several places there were two groups of apprentices, younger ones who got no wages and older ones who did; the older ones may have been unemployed workers willing to sign on for an apprentice's lower wage.[32] In London the idea of wages for apprentices appalled the tailors. William Assheby complained that his apprentice John Hebelthwayte refused to obey him; Hebelthwayte responded that Assheby refused to honor a private agreement between them to pay Hebelthwayt thirty-two shillings in quarterly installments over the length of the apprenticeship contract. Witnesses agreed that there was such an agreement, and the master of the company exclaimed that it was "very heinous and against all the good rules of this city." He feared "the great infamy that likely might have grown in time to come to the whole body of the fellowship by reason of the foolish dealing and seditious demeanor of the said Assheby if this matter should be published and come to light." To avoid such a precedent the master and wardens of the company declared the contract invalid.[33] They clearly felt the principle of apprentices' unremunerated labor worth defending, perhaps on the principle of keeping the relationship one of personal dependence rather than economics.

Even when the apprentice received nothing but his room and board, masters might attempt to get their money's worth by requiring of their inexperienced apprentices other tasks besides those related to the craft, duties that required less training. Some crafts stipulated that masters could ask apprentices to perform household tasks only in the first few years of apprenticeship.[34] Contracts could limit this type of work: in Tournai, for example, Jacques de Grandglise agreed in his contract of apprenticeship to a strapmaker to do everything "but scrub and wash."[35] A number of London cases complain of abuses by masters in terms of the work they asked apprentices to do. The London goldsmith Richard atte Well had to swear in court to teach his apprentice the trade rather than sending him into the country to thresh grain or do other field work, presumably as a result of a complaint about his earlier behavior; Nicholas

Salman complained that his master had made him into a domestic servant instead of teaching him the trade of a draper, and the jury awarded damages to the apprentice as well as cancelling the indenture. Edmund Pellet's master refused to teach him fishmongery but instead had him learn shepstry (dressmaking); when he complained the master put a needle through his thumb and his mistress beat him. He eventually left to become a priest. John Malmayn's master did not teach him haberdashery but made him a babysitter: "he has no other work from his master but to carry a small child in the streets each day." John Ravlyn's pouchmaker master had him dig ditches and cut wood; Thomas March's master had him brew beer instead of learning cutlery.[36] All these abuses resulted in complaints because these tasks were inappropriate either to the apprentice's gender or to his social position, conflicting with his self-image as a prospective skilled craftsman.

The apprenticeship contract, especially when it involved underage boys—or even teenagers—was not simply a transaction between employer and employee for the purchase of labor, but an agreement between families. The procurement of labor on the one hand, and the provision for vocational training on the other, played a role, but for the family of the apprentice it was also important to find someone else who would do a good job of rearing their child.[37] Apprentices usually retained ties with their families (except when, as was the case in some towns, many apprentices were orphans).[38] Some contracts, for example, provide for their temporary return to help with the harvest.[39] The fact that it was often families that brought cases about the mistreatment of apprentices indicates that ties could remain close, especially when they lived in the same city.[40] But the apprentice was gradually forging a new set of bonds with his fellow craftsmen.

Though apprenticeship could be a means to social mobility, more often it served to perpetuate the social hierarchy. In English towns, the crafts put more emphasis than elsewhere on the apprentice's background. In 1406, a statute made it illegal to take apprentices from families with less than 20 shillings' annual income. The mayor and aldermen of London interpreted the statute to apply only to those apprenticed by their families, not those who apprenticed themselves. Even so, however, unfree birth disqualified a candidate for apprenticeship (even though unfree status no longer meant very much legally or economically, this could exclude many rural dwellers).[41] The cutlers required not only free birth but also that the apprentices be "handsome in stature, having straight and proper limbs,"[42] like the requirement of free birth more a matter of honor than of practicality. In 1411, John Mabban, a London goldsmith, wished to make his brothers apprentices, but was not permitted to do so, because one had been a beggar and another a miller and a cobbler.[43] Some apprentices clearly came from quite well-off families.[44] A young man from a wealthy family still needed to go through apprenticeship in order to achieve the skill and recognition he needed for mastership.

Occupational and geographical mobility was hardly absent. In London, many of the tailors' apprentices came from the north of England, a pattern repeated among the other leading crafts. Lesser crafts tended to recruit more from the area around London. Most of the tailors' apprentices were from rural areas. Of those whose fathers' occupations were given at their enrollment, only 10.2 percent were sons of tailors, and 25.4 percent other artisans. Sons of yeomen (farmers who owned their own land) and husbandmen (who did not) made up 50.9 percent, although some of these gave town addresses and may not have derived all their income from the land. Proportions in the skinners' company were similar.[45]

Elsewhere in Europe, too, there was a tendency for apprentices to come from the same social stratum as their employers, although it was not a statutory requirement. In many Continental towns not only could masters take on their children as apprentices without regard to limits on numbers, they could also take on the children of other members with master or apprentice paying a reduced fee (or no fee) to the guild. In some crafts the sons (and occasionally daughters) of masters were allowed to become guild members without going through a formal apprenticeship. If, however, the father was not a master craftsman, or the son wished to pursue a different craft, the full fee had to be paid. In England, by contrast, family members received no legal advantage.

Contracts from Tournai show that apprentices, mostly from within the town, came mainly from prosperous artisanal or commercial backgrounds.[46] In Aix-en-Provence, 96 percent of apprenticeship contracts in the building trades involved boys from the same social stratum as the trade they wished to enter; apprenticeship might be a step toward occupational mobility but not social mobility.[47] Apprenticeship was not just a source of cheap labor but was a period of training in a skill and initiation into a group. Young men who were socially appropriate to the group were more likely to be chosen. In towns where apprentices were older and received wages, they were more likely to be of poorer backgrounds, but also less likely to have the opportunity to become masters.

Apprenticeship created a quasi-familial relationship. The master stood in for the apprentice's father and was responsible for the young man's welfare in many ways, either written into the apprenticeship contract or assumed by custom.[48] The master was supposed to train his apprentices in morals and social behavior, especially with orphans placed as apprentices by town authorities.[49] Usually neither guild regulations nor contracts specified masters' exact responsibilities for either the apprentices' moral or academic education. Contracts state that the master is not to make the apprentice do anything immoral, but do not go into further detail.[50] To describe how the master shall teach, they use terms like "loiaument comme preudom" (meaning roughly "as an honorable man"), "as best he knows," or "according to the customs."[51] These provisions emphasize the master's role as not merely an employer but a head of household. A young apprentice would learn that mature masculinity meant exerting patriarchal control over all aspects of his employees' lives, playing the role of a father to all his dependents.

If an apprentice was to become a master some day and manage his own workshop, as opposed to remaining a laborer, he would need to be literate at least in the vernacular. Usually boys picked up the academic knowledge necessary for the craft along with the technical skill. The goldsmiths' company of London required that boys be literate in order to be taken on as apprentices.[52] A number of Burgundian apprenticeship contracts specifically require that the master teach the apprentice to read and write.[53] Some masters sent their apprentices to school. London haberdasher Robert Chirche promised in an apprenticeship indenture that two of the twelve years would be spent at school, a year and a half on grammar and half a year on writing. John Holand, apprenticed to Thomas Hert, barber of London, complained in 1415 that his master was so poor he could not feed or clothe him or keep him in school as he had agreed in his indenture to do. The mayor and aldermen transferred him to another master. Thomas Batter sent his apprentice William Elmeshall to study with a priest, who, however, "put him in his kitchen to wash pots, pans and dishes."[54]

Although contracts required the master to treat the apprentice as "his own child," whether he actually became part of the family in an affective sense is doubtful.[55] Apprentices did form part of the *familia* or household in the economic sense, the unit that carried out craft production. A statute of the beltmakers of Paris provided that if an apprentice married, he no longer had to eat at the master's table but received a cash sum instead for his board.[56] This provision indicates that under normal circumstances the apprentice did live as part of the family (as opposed to eating separately or with servants). The apprentice was in an even more dependent relationship with the master than most employees; regardless of his level of skill he was still a boy rather than a man. His master, regardless of his level of skill, was a man through his control of the household.

Marriage not only ruptured the quasi-familial relation between master and apprentice; it also laid claim to an independence that the crafts were unwilling to accord to apprentices. The shearers of Ghent in 1362 discouraged apprentices from marrying by providing that a master's son born during his father's apprenticeship did not enjoy the privileges of automatic guild admission as did other sons of masters.[57] In England apprenticeship indentures commonly forbade the apprentice to marry, and indeed to become engaged to marry, without the permission of the employer.[58] The pervasive misogynist idea that women desire money, jewels, and fancy clothes may have played a role in the prohibition on apprentices' marriages, making employers fear that married apprentices would steal.[59]

Contracts that stipulated that masters should treat apprentices as members of the family were not necessarily inconsistent with beating or otherwise abusing them, since fathers could treat their own children in such ways. The master as patriarch could dominate apprentices as he did his family. In 1364, John Everard got into financial disputes with his uncle, the London mercer Alan Everard, to whom he was apprenticed. A group of arbitrators settled the financial issues but added that as a sign of obedience and respect to his master, John should hold his master's stirrup when he mounted.[60] Such deference was appropriate in medieval society both from servant to master and from son to father.

Like a family bond, the bond between apprentice and master was very difficult to rupture. The apprentice's flight did not necessarily break it: some crafts prohibited the master from replacing apprentices who fled, possibly to prevent a master from goading a disliked apprentice into flight. Masters went to great lengths to recover apprentices who fled.[61]

A master usually could not transfer his apprentice's contract to someone else without the permission of the craft authorities, but this provision was not infrequently broken.[62] The Parisian guild of strapmakers limited the circumstances under which a master could sell his apprentice's contract to another: only if he went overseas or became ill. An apprentice could buy out his term only in case of his master's illness. These regulations were necessary "because of the lads who become puffed up with pride once they have completed half or a quarter of their term, and especially so that the craftsmen do not entice the apprentice of another" and "so that the apprentices don't annoy their masters so much that their masters allow them to buy out their service."[63] In Venice, masters could be fined for sending apprentices away "without reason," and apprentices could also be fined heavily for leaving and prohibited from working for other members of the craft.[64] In England, apprentices were allowed to buy themselves out of a term, but only if the master agreed.[65] From both France and England there are examples of apprenticeships being canceled by mutual agreement when the apprentice was unsuited to the craft.[66] It is not possible to know whether mutual agreements to break the contract were really as amicable as they seemed, but it is plausible that other such partings of the ways never found their way into court.

These provisions from various towns about apprentices leaving their masters indicate a primary concern with the loss of valuable labor, but the relationship was never a strictly economic one. The way local authorities intervened to void a contract indicates that especially in England the crafts were deemed to have a collective responsibility for the formation of their apprentices. In London, when a master had failed to enroll his apprentice in the craft before he completed a year of service, or failed to provide him with proper instruction and support (often through having left the jurisdiction or taken sanctuary because of debt), the court dissolved the apprenticeship contract, sometimes transferring it to another master in the same craft.[67] Apprentices who took matters into their own hands and left the service of masters who did not support or train them properly, however, could find themselves under arrest.[68]

In one London case, the master actually claimed that the apprentice was his property, and the court disagreed with him. John Bakton's master Henry Perle, mercer, was going abroad on business and did not plan to keep a shop in London, so he would be unable to train Bakton. He wished to transfer the rest of his term of apprenticeship to Roger de Causton, claiming "that his apprentice is his chattel and he can do with him as he wishes, give or sell him." The court granted Bakton's release from his apprenticeship because he did not have to serve another master against his will. At Bakton's request they assigned him to another mercer, John Fyfhyde.[69] This case underscores the distinction between personal and economic dependence. The apprentice was not, like a slave, merely a tool of his master; the relation was understood as personal. This did not necessarily translate into good treatment, but it did mean that the type of domination the master exercised over the apprentice was not solely economic. The apprentice was less than fully a man because he worked for another, but also because he was in the position of a child.

Court records reveal that apprentices did have some recourse in cases of ill treatment. Masters in Paris had the right to beat their apprentices, as long they did not do so to excess. Yet the courts took note of abuses. Lorin Alueil was made to fulfill his contract to his master Jehan Prevost, a cabinetmaker, but the latter was required to treat him "as the son of a respectable man [*preudomme*] should be." Jehan was specifically admonished not to allow his wife to beat Lorin, although it was all right for Jehan himself to beat him.[70] The courts protected even someone in the dependent position of an apprentice from the emasculation of being beaten by a woman, both in the latter example and in a London case where the wife of an imprisoned master fed his two apprentices inadequately and beat them, causing one to lose the sight in his left eye.[71]

In these cases city courts were asked to intervene, but the crafts settled many such cases themselves. In the late fifteenth century the tailors of London released Thomas Wytney from the service of Richard Buthom because Buthom "gravely insulted him and showed him the evil finger," and Thomas Godfrey from Robert Archer for "unreasonable and undue chastising and unclean keeping" on Godfrey's third complaint. John Bowman's apprentice complained to the Merchant Taylors' court of "unlawful and unreasonable chastising, as well with defensive weapons as with lack of meat, drink, victuals and apparel," and Bowman stormed out of court "in a great agony and ire, saying he would be master over his own apprentice." One of the wardens took the apprentice home with him to keep him safe.[72] These cases indicate the paternalism of the crafts. Apprentices were not just notionally members of their masters' family. They were also in a sense dependents of the craft as a whole; the craft was concerned with ensuring that the masters lived up to their patriarchal responsibilities.

The importance the crafts placed on collective responsibility for proper instruction and training of apprentices appears in the provisions for apprentices whose masters die. In some crafts the apprentice was assigned to another master to finish out the remaining portion of his term.[73] In some guilds widows could carry on the craft unless they remarried; in others, only if they remarried a man in the craft.[74] They most often could not take on new apprentices, but sometimes they could keep apprentices already in service with their late husbands.[75] In 1399, the court of the Châtelet in Paris dealt with the case of Guillemette, the widow of Regnaut Olivier, chandler. She was not supposed to continue in his craft after his death, because she was not "expert and sufficient in the craft." Because she was already keeping the workshop and needed to support her children, however, the court let her continue, with the stipulations that she not take any apprentices besides the one she already had and that if she married someone outside the craft she could not teach it to him or any children he already had.[76]

In London, when a master died and the widow did not carry on the business, the court might release the apprentices, but only because she failed to instruct them; if she remarried, the instruction might be considered her husband's business.[77] The husband's responsibility is shown in the case of John Agmondesham, apprenticed as a goldsmith to his widowed mother (who presumably inherited the apprentice from the boy's stepfather). He made agreements with several men that if any of them should marry his mother, he would be released from the rest of his apprenticeship.[78] The limitations on widows' craft activity may reflect generalized misogyny and a more specific worry about the sexual voracity of widows and the possibility of preying on young boys. In their pronouncements, however, craft and municipal authorities were concerned mainly with the proper provision of education for the apprentices and the maintenance of their monopoly.

Court records, although they can tell us a great deal about normal expectations in medieval life, reveal only the cases in which problems developed. Conflict between masters and apprentices may not have been the norm. In many instances masters and apprentices did form close personal relations, although these do not show up in litigation. In London, of 3,330 men whose wills Barbara Hanawalt has studied, 3 percent left bequests to their apprentices: in 28 percent of the cases money, 33 percent of the cases goods, 7 percent of the cases a shop. Here some sort of quasi-familial bond had been formed. Similar bequests are found in York.[79] Some masters on their deathbeds released their apprentices from part of a term, although the executors did not always let it stand.[80]

Masters did not have to wait until their deathbeds to help apprentices financially. Although apprentices did not participate fully in the social life of the craft, upon finishing their term they were sometimes expected to give a feast. As with the courts and the universities, feasting was an important social ritual marking rites of passage. For the apprentice, whose completion of his term signified not only his artisanal skill but also his attainment of manhood, both in chronological terms and in terms of independence from the master, the feast marked his first membership in the craft or guild community. At the same time, however, paying for the feast presented him with a financial problem. Some apprentices did get paid a nominal salary, especially toward the end of their terms, and some masters gave them the opportunity to take on commissions on their own. Still, the costs of having one's completion of apprenticeship certified put another obstacle in the way of the attainment of mastership. Masters could help their employees overcome these obstacles. Some former apprentices, too, set themselves up in business through loans of money or equipment from the masters with whom they had trained.[81] Such gifts or loans, however, depended upon a personal relationship between master and apprentice rather than any institutional arrangements.

Masters helped their apprentices not just by educating them and providing material assistance, but also by introducing them to social networks. Of those apprentices in the London tailors' guild between 1425–45 and 1453–58 who eventually became free of the city, three-quarters had originally worked for liverymen. That is, those boys who were apprenticed to the leading members of the trade had the best chance of making it in the craft, whether because these tended to be boys from well-connected families or because their masters had the resources to set them up in trade. Former apprentices of liverymen also had an advantage over other apprentices in eventually achieving livery status.[82] The social divisions within the craft gave the apprentices of the most successful men the best shot at replicating that success and achieving full economic and civic independence.

All apprentices, whether attached to prominent or less successful masters, began their training intending to learn a craft and with the strong hope, if not the concrete expectation, of ultimately becoming masters and setting up their own workshops. These aspirations, however, were often frustrated. In the Tournai painters' guild from 1440 to 1480, of 70 apprentices, only 30 ever became masters. In York, of 375 weavers' apprentices in the second half of the fifteenth century, only 45 later became free of the city. Of 40 taken as apprentices in the 1470s, only 5 eventually achieved the freedom, and even then not until the late 1480s. Of 89 apprentice coverlet weavers in Ghent from 1370 to 1396, only 3 became masters.[83]

Some apprentices found a shortcut to eventual success through the instrumentality of women. Marrying a master's daughter or widow could mean skipping the laborious process of accumulating capital.[84] If an artisan had no son to whom to pass on his business, but had one or more daughters, he might well use apprenticeship as a way to audition young men as prospective sons-in-law and heirs. Particularly for young men coming from outside the town, with few contacts, marriage to the daughter of a master provided not only an entrée into a craft but also inclusion in a social network.[85]

An apprentice or journeyman would find marrying into a mastership an attractive goal. It was common enough that some towns had specific regulations about it: for example, the shoemakers of Flensborg, Denmark, specified a fee to the guild if a journeyman or apprentice wanted to marry the daughter or widow of a shoemaker, or a female shoemaker, and join the guild. The locksmiths, blacksmiths, and coppersmiths of Florence, on the other hand, provided for the husbands of guild members' daughters to take up the craft without paying, as guild members' sons could.[86] The Florentine butchers established in 1346 that a woman could bring membership in the craft as her dowry only once: if she were widowed, her second husband would not be eligible for membership.[87] In Cologne, the shoemakers, needlemakers, and tailors all provided that anyone marrying the widow of a member could join the guild for half the usual fee.[88] These mechanisms allowed women to be the bearers of masculine independence.

Since in some crafts a widow who remarried might lose her right to practice the craft unless she married someone who was trained in it, she had an incentive to choose a new husband from among her workers. An apprentice whom she knew well might be a good prospect, even if he were much younger than she, which need not always have been the case. An apprentice near the end of his term could easily be more than twenty years old, and a widow could be in her twenties also (especially in Italy where the age at marriage for women was much younger than that for men). In London, in one example, the tailor William Griffith on his deathbed released his apprentice (and possible fellow Welshman) Harry ap Richard from his term of apprenticeship. Harry then had "certain communication . . . concerning unto matrimony" with the widow, who, however, ended up marrying a goldsmith.[89] The majority of apprentices did not gain a mastership by marrying into it, but it happened often enough to feed the possibility in young men's minds and strengthen the notion that marriage and mastership were entwined.

Apprentices were firmly rooted within the families of masters, whether as child-substitutes or potential sons-in-law or second husbands, but they had social networks outside the workshop as well. An urban environment brought young men, apprentices and others, together and presented them with a variety of temptations. Apprentices who lived as quasi-members of their employers' families might well begin to rebel, especially if the master's wife, often much younger than the master and not much older than the apprentices themselves, gave them orders or disciplined them. The 1445 case in which a goldsmith's apprentice tried to strangle his mistress may have been such an occasion.[90] Within the household these young men had little opportunity to socialize with women not in a position of authority over them, and therefore little opportunity to dominate women. When they could, they sought the company of other apprentices or of unmarried journeymen and constructed their masculinity through solidarities with them. These solidarities might include such aggressive activities as gang rape.[91]

Most of the examples of depredations of gangs of apprentices come from a somewhat later period, when the apprentice's work and relation to his master may have become more depersonalized. Nevertheless, even in the later Middle Ages, repeated prohibitions in apprenticeship contracts indicate that masters and craft guilds worried, particularly about time spent in taverns, gambling, and consorting with prostitutes. Apprentices' youth meant that the towns and crafts felt a greater need to regulate their behavior than that of other workers. Many guild statutes assumed that allowing apprentices in the streets unsupervised could lead to problems like drinking or gambling, not only to the moral detriment of the apprentice but also to the financial detriment of the master. The Paris chandlers, for example, allowed an apprentice to be sent out to sell candles only after he had served for three years.[92]

The regulations about the drinking, gambling, and sexual activities of apprentices resemble those for university students (see Chapter 3). The concern for social disruption occasioned by young men pervaded many levels of late medieval society. Apprentices, unlike journeymen, would have little opportunity to meet their peers or women at more respectable venues like confraternity functions. The tavern or informal neighborhood groups took their place.

Through these group activities apprentices proved their manhood to each other. In 1339, three Londoners were charged with leading apprentices into the habit of gambling.[93] John Peghen of York dismissed an apprentice for "wasting his goods to the value of six marks and more by playing at dice and cards and other unlawful games contrary to the covenant" they had made.[94] Coventry in 1492 warned tavernkeepers not to receive apprentices (or servants, including journeymen) without their masters' permission, either to spend money or to consort with women of evil fame or anyone of "unsadde" (frivolous) disposition.[95] Masters connected their apprentices' visits to loose women with other crimes, as with John or William Nandy, apprentice to a London apothecary, who his master said went out at night to visit a concubine and also stole twenty pounds' worth of goods.[96]

Apprentices might also become sexually involved with their masters' female servants, particularly problematic for the master because it disrupted the household. In one York case, a cordwainer attempted to force his apprentice to marry a fellow servant whom he had seduced. The apprentice was reluctant to do so unless his master paid him a substantial sum (not stated but presumably enough to set up his own workshop). As Jeremy Goldberg notes, this was a challenge to the master's dominance: "Bown [the master] thus demonstrated his concern was more for his own reputation as a householder than for Margaret Barker, the seduced servant."[97]

Masters wanted their apprentices to accept the model of skill and independence, rather than sexual aggression and male bonding through gambling, which they considered all too typical of youth, as the norm of masculinity for which to struggle. The apprenticeship system worked to control young men by making full masculinity, including heading a household and workshop, a long-term goal for which they had to work, but the young men did not always cooperate.

Skilled Laborers: More than Boys, Less than Men

A young man's completion of his term as apprentice might sometimes suffice for him to become a master and achieve the elusive goal of independence, especially if his father was a master in the same craft. Most former apprentices, however, could not set up their own workshops, but did wage work for a period of time, if not indefinitely. Dependent on another and not in a position to dominate others, they were not full members of the craft or community. Although adult chronologically, many could not achieve the head-of-household status that marked adult masculinity. These skilled wage workers, in their late teens or twenties and up but still in a sense boys, were seen as a disruptive element in medieval society.

They might not stand in the same relation of personal dependence to their masters as servants did, but they were not independent artisans either. Their status varied significantly from region to region, depending in part on the chances of ever becoming a master.

In English, skilled wage laborers were known as journeymen. The term derives from the calculation of their wages by the day or *journée*.[98] The periods of hire often extended to six months or a year for skilled labor, but even if the contract was for a year, the wage was at least originally calculated per day of work. In some places, however, skilled workers were paid a piecework rate.[99] Regulations limiting working hours might benefit either employer or employee depending on the payment method. If the worker was paid by the day, it was in his interest to have a shorter working day, but if he was paid by the piece it was in his interest to work longer and produce more. In either case the method of calculating wages distinguished journeymen from servants, who were hired for an annual wage and were not members of a craft (whereas journeymen might be secondary members).[100]

Because the sources quote wage rates by the day, calculating a journeyman's annual wage is difficult. It is not always easy to determine the number of working days in a year. Regulations of the various guilds include listings of feast days on which members were not supposed to work. Especially in cyclical industries with slack times, there may have been other idle days as well. Most of the data for wage rates come from the building trades, because churches undertaking major building projects kept careful records of how much they paid. Here, of course, the weather made it impossible to work some of the time.

Despite these difficulties scholars have managed to calculate for major cities like Florence and Ghent how much the pay of a journeyman in the building trades and some other crafts amounted to in terms of purchasing power. The results indicate that an unmarried man could live quite comfortably on his wages, and in most years even a married man with children could get by, especially if his wife also brought in some income. However, in some years, including the 1370s in Florence and the 1490s in Ghent, wages dipped well below the subsistence level for a family.[101] Hard times occurred not only when daily wages dropped (or grain prices rose), but also when the number of days of work dropped. In the period from 1484 to 1494, when the southern Netherlands were in economic crisis, the figure of 270 working days per year that scholars usually use to calculate annual wages dropped in Antwerp to somewhere in the 190s. In Ghent from 1321 to 1326, when we have relatively good wage data, a journeyman digger who worked 270 days would have been relatively prosperous, but if he worked only 232 days he would have crossed the threshold of poverty.[102] Even when the wages sufficed to support the family, they did not leave much left over for savings, or to purchase tools or the materials for a masterpiece. The situation worsened in some areas toward the end of the fifteenth century.[103] The masters who paid journeymen these wages were mostly small entrepreneurs. They typically earned about twice as much as journeymen when customers paid both on day rates (as in the building trades); journeymen could look forward to better financial times if they could attain the mastership.

The journeyman working for a master faced other adverse conditions besides low wages. Many crafts severely punished him for leaving his master before his term was up (his master could also be punished for forcing him to go or refusing him his pay, but this provision is found in far fewer guild regulations).[104] In 1366, Thomas de Norhampton, a carpenter in London, complained that he could not fulfill his year's contract with John de Bukstede because he had injured his hand. The master, however, retained four shillings' wages owing to Thomas, as well as his clothing, until the court ruled that he must deliver them and release Thomas from the contract.[105] Another late fourteenth-century London case indicates the length workers might go to to get out of their contracts. John Shrewsbury, a pinner, was contracted for a year to Richard Pynnere of Coventry and agreed to pay forty shillings to get himself and two companions released from their terms.[106] In Florence, if a worker accepted a loan from his employer to tide him over during a slack period when work was not available, he was required to work for that employer when the good times returned.[107] This held wages down and prevented employees from looking for a better deal.

The regulations preventing workers from leaving their master limited employers as well as employees. Many crafts prohibited any master from hiring away the employee of another. Because of this rule, even if a worker wanted to leave his master he might have a hard time finding another who would take him. Gibon Ernald, a fourteenth-century London pouchmaker, found that potential employers took this rule seriously: he complained that for twelve pence his employer released him from about five months of a one-year term, but told other pouchmakers that Ernald was still working for him, so no one would hire him. Even when the worker did find a new job, the punishment could fall on the employee rather than the employer who hired him away. Hubert Cutler left his master to work for a girdler, and blamed the latter for enticing him away, but was nevertheless jailed and fined.[108] These regulations emphasized the subordinated position of the journeyman who could not exercise independence even with regard to choosing a master.

The original justification for rules against leaving one's employer may have been shortages of skilled labor, but this type of provision appears in so many times and places that its retention cannot be due simply to economic needs. It skewed labor relations in favor of the masters, but it also indicates that the crafts understood the relation between masters and workers not simply as economic but also one of personal dependence. The craft organizations regulated the journeyman's behavior, like that of apprentices, with regard to morals, and also specifically prohibited him from working on the side on his own account.[109] In general the master was responsible before the craft for him and his behavior. Masters as guild members had collective responsibility for wage laborers' social and religious lives.[110]

The hiring of a journeyman was more of a straight economic transaction than that of an apprentice, but still couched in the language of service and loyalty. Written contracts from Burgundy required obedience and fidelity from workers rather than specific work. Masters provided clothing and other in-kind payments as well as cash. As members of the household (and in Burgundy many contracts specified that the workers had to live with their masters) the workers were required to do whatever work needed doing, not necessarily only the skilled labor of their trade, although larger households no doubt saved the skilled workers for the more lucrative skilled work. Loyalty to the master was supposed to continue even after the end of the contract: the contracts often did not allow the worker subsequently to work for someone else in the trade without his master's permission. If the worker did not complete his work satisfactorily, not only did he lose his wages and his job, he also incurred judicial penalties.[111] In some places, by contrast, the bonds of household and loyalty were significantly weaker: in some German towns, weavers worked on commission, and the workers got a share of the commission directly from the customer. The master provided the workshop and sometimes lodging. If the master provided food, workers sometimes had to pay extra for it.[112]

As in Burgundy, so too elsewhere unmarried journeymen often lived in the households of the masters, in a quasi-familial situation (especially if they had previously served as apprentices in the same house), but it was also quite common for them to live separately. In 1321, the coopers in several north German towns agreed that journeymen must sleep in the master's house, and guild regulations of many Hanse towns copied this provision; similar regulations were found elsewhere too—for example, several trades in Brussels.[113] In Coventry, however, an ordinance of 1436 required journeymen in most crafts to perform their work in their own houses, not those of their masters, implying both that they lived separately and that they had their own tools.[114] People in the Middle Ages rarely lived by themselves; single people tended to share lodgings if they did not live with their employers. If wealthy enough a single person might have his or her own house, and servants, but the less wealthy who did not have servants did not tend to live alone. Some unmarried workers lodged together.

The tailors of London provide a good example of conflict between masters and workers over living arrangements. In 1415, the London authorities prohibited journeymen tailors from having their own houses where they had apparently lived communally, because the men who lived there, uncontrolled by their masters, "unruly and insolent men without head or governance, often assembled together in great numbers, and held various congregations and conventicles in various places," and had beaten one of their masters. The mayor and aldermen forbade not only such dwelling houses "without any sort of stable governance" but also the liveries or uniforms that the journeymen adopted at their meetings. They attributed the journeymen's instability to their youth.[115]

In 1449, however, the tailors' company required the journeymen to live together if they were not hired out on a yearly contract. Because "divers young men of the said mystery [craft] recently and newly come from their apprenticeship, called chamberholders," were doing tailoring work "in chambers, solars and such other privy and hidden places," continually "moving and leaving from place to place so that no due search and correction should be executed upon their faults," customers risked having their tailoring work done by unqualified workers. The master and wardens required

that every person of the said mystery who has neither shop nor household within the freedom of the said city, and is neither at lot nor scot [i.e., a taxpayer] as other freemen householders are, put himself in service and covenant by the year with another freeman householder of the said mystery . . . or else live in the commons among other servant sewers of the said mystery, under the good rule and governance of the said master and wardens . . . so that other freemen householders at time of need may lawfully require and have such servant sewers for competent wages by the day or by the garment.

Another provision indicated the masters' financial motive: "If any such chamberholder take work to make of any customer of his, that he bring it unto the master by whom he has been employed in other idle and slow times, and that he do the same work there under the rule of his master as he should do other work of his said master's, so that the same master may have the profit thereof that he should have of a customer of his own."[116] Independent living arrangements were anathema because they could lead to independent work and erosion of the craft's monopoly. Instead, the workers were to live under the supervision of the craft so that the masters could retain control of the labor force.

If masters did not treat journeymen properly, the latter might have little recourse to the town judicial system. In many craft guilds complaints and appeals went to the authorities of the craft, although in others they could go to civic authorities. In general, masters' control over their workers went unchallenged except in cases of egregious abuse. Journeymen remained socially as well as economically dependent on their masters, in a sort of perpetual adolescence that conflicted with their chronological age. The tensions this situation created seem to have led relatively infrequently to violence, at least to violence that came to the attention of the authorities.[117]

The wage worker's rights to civic participation varied from place to place. In some Italian towns all but a few magnate families were excluded from participation in government, so masters suffered from the same disability as wage workers. Others, like Florence and Perugia, were guild republics where members of a few major guilds ran things, excluding masters of lesser guilds as well as journeymen.[118] In other regions, men born in the town who had completed an apprenticeship were legally full members of the community. In Paris, for example, they could serve on juries; they did not play a leading role in governance, but neither did masters, as the city was in the hands of royal officials.[119] In London, admission to the freedom of the city, which conferred full political rights, was supposed to come with completion of apprenticeship, although not all masters certified the completion, and not all apprentices took up the freedom. In other English towns, masters who had their own shops were expected to take up (and pay for) the franchise, but in fact did not always do so; wage workers generally did not.[120] In Ghent, journeymen participated actively in protests, to the disapproval of chroniclers, but did not formally participate in the political process.[121]

Participation in craft governance formed an important part of the civic participation that was part of full adult masculinity, and here most crafts severely limited journeymen. In Brussels and Bruges only the fullers' guild allowed a journeyman to be a jurat; in Oudenaarde the fullers, weavers, and shearers; in Courtrai the fullers and weavers; in Ghent the shearers and weavers. [122] In Venice journeymen generally could not vote in guild affairs.[123] The foreign journeymen weavers of London complained to the mayor in 1444 that the masters of their guild had for the last six years usurped the journeymen's right to elect wardens. The mayor ruled that the journeymen should have no voice in the election.[124]

Because of the lack of civic and guild participation, the lack of economic independence, and the regulation of living arrangements, journeymen remained, in a significant sense, still not fully men, no matter what their age. Journeyman status did not always correspond exactly to dependence— some men with the legal status of journeymen did open their own (illicit) shops, to the chagrin of the masters, and in other places masters too were contracted to work for others. For the most part, however, even poor masters were distinguished by their formal recognition within the craft as well as their status as head of household.

Some journeymen could hope that as they grew older their status would rise. In towns other than major industrial centers, where most of the production took place in small artisanal workshops, the number of wage workers was relatively low: masters made do largely with apprentices, family members, and domestic servants. Under these circumstances a worker could relatively easily become a master, facing neither tremendous competition, nor too many onerous requirements for the mastership. This was the case, for example, in Paris in the fourteenth century.[125] It was also the case in some crafts in London in the fifteenth century. In the case of the goldsmiths, where a group of journeymen rebelled against the guild leadership in the 1470s, these seem to have been men well on their way to becoming masters. The issue was one of position in the life cycle rather than permanent subordination or class difference.[126]

In other towns, notably the most populous and industrialized cities in the fourteenth (in Italy) and fifteenth centuries, most wage workers remained in that status for life. In many places, the second half of the fifteenth century brought larger scale production in many crafts, increasing demand for wage laborers but driving small craftsmen out of business and lowering the chances for wage workers to become independent.[127] This diminished horizon of expectations affected their identity as men, even if they did not wait to marry and raise a family until they achieved the mastership that might never come. In this world masculine honor was partly defined by heading a household but also by civic recognition and responsibility, from which these workers were excluded. They had to develop their own sense of masculinity in other ways.

In some towns in the course of the late fourteenth and fifteenth centuries the mastership became quasi-hereditary. A few crafts—notably butchers in some towns—explicitly limited membership to sons of masters.[128] Others fixed the number of masters in the craft, thus limiting openings de facto to one child (or nephew or other relative) per master.[129] More common than an absolute restriction was a high entrance fee for those who were not sons of masters. In the coopers' guild in Bruges, for example, during the first three-quarters of the fifteenth century, new members who were not sons of masters paid 19.5 percent more than the sons of masters for the franchise; in 1478, however, they paid 56.4 percent more.[130] For a builder, the real cost of obtaining the franchise remained constant for a master's son over the course of the fifteenth century, at 5.2 days' work. For someone who was neither the son of a master nor a native of the town, the cost went from 149 to 244 working days.[131] In Ghent in 1414, the fee for a carpenter to become a master was ten pounds, which worked out to 480 days' wages; the son of a master had to pay the equivalent of one day's wages.[132] In the towns of the upper Rhine, too, the cost of entering a craft rose from the end of the fourteenth century through 1480.[133] The closing off of mastership in a craft did not have to be a result of economic decline. David Nicholas argues that in the case of Ghent, it resulted from the increased prosperity of a few large operators who wanted to hire journeymen (who were paid about half as much as a master) rather than small masters.[134]

Even in towns in which the crafts did not favor the children of members with a reduced entry fee, those who were not born into the craft were at a disadvantage. In Douai, for example, marriage contracts reveal that a large number of sons did follow the trades of their fathers. Many daughters married men from their fathers' trades: 42 percent of those whose husbands' trades could be identified from 1441 to 1443. Craft endogamy was not absolute, but the chances of outsiders' marrying into a trade were sharply reduced. A sample from the roll of new citizens shows that 61 percent of children either took up, or married a practitioner of, their father's trade.[135] Douai may be atypical in its rate of craft endogamy.

In Venice, the rate was only 5.5 percent.[136] It is clear, however, that a man whose father or father-in-law was a master would often have a significantly easier time taking up his trade.

Many crafts by the fifteenth century put another obstacle in the way of young men becoming masters: the masterpiece or *chef d'oeuvre*. To be admitted to the mastership, the worker had to demonstrate his skill in all aspects of the craft by creating an object or a series of objects that conformed to specific requirements. Some crafts required that the finished piece be of a particular value.[137] In theory the masterpiece would ensure that a new master had sufficient knowledge of the craft to practice it effectively and to train apprentices. In practice the requirement ensured that anyone without money saved up could not afford to purchase the materials, and therefore could not become a master. For a worker with a family living on the edge of subsistence, purchasing materials could be prohibitive. Again, guilds might exempt sons of masters from the masterpiece as well as from apprenticeship.

These various exclusionary mechanisms, de jure and de facto, ensured that craft members in the later Middle Ages in many Continental towns were disproportionately sons of other members. This process paralleled that by which knighthood came to be treated as hereditary rather than a result of prowess, and that by which the universities began to cater for the aristocracy rather than just the meritorious.

The closing off of opportunities for those without connections was by no means absolute. In some crafts, still only a very small number of the members were sons of masters.[138] In most places young men could retain a possibility, however slim, of advancement. Employees' aspirations kept employers and workers from becoming totally separate classes. Although all journeymen could have harbored the hope of eventually becoming a master, the reality of the situation was that some had much better prospects than others depending on geographical location or family background. In Basel, journeymen in the same craft in which their fathers were masters had a relatively assured career. Journeymen who came from outside the town, however, had little chance of becoming masters there, and their social world focused on the local and regional groups of journeymen rather than kin networks within the town.[139] Elsewhere, as in London, men from the provinces had as good a chance to rise in their chosen crafts as men from the city. Where there was more realistic expectation of advancement, there tended to be less collective conflict.

Worker Solidarities

Where restricted access to mastership built up a class of permanent wage workers, so that many skilled workers spent their lives as journeymen unable to reach full independent householder status, those workers had to develop other ways of demonstrating their masculinity, including the formation of bonds with other men and the taking of collective action. This sort of collective action was stronger and more effective in some regions, such as the Rhineland, than in others, such as England, where it was sporadic and disorganized. This reflects in part the differing degrees of proletarianization of workers, their perceived chances of ever achieving adult manhood according to the traditional craft model.

We cannot read social movements like the Ciompi rebellion in Florence in 1378, in which many wage workers were involved, as generational conflict, younger men frustrated because their opportunities were not opening up soon enough. It might make sense that younger and single workers would more likely become involved in collective action than older men with families to support. But in fact, of those participants in the Ciompi revolt whose ages can be determined from fiscal records, half were between the ages of 28 and 47, and 41.4 percent were between the ages of 37 and 47. In addition, only 11.08 percent of the Ciompi for whom marital status can be determined were unmarried; this indicates that most were mature and established and that the rebellion cannot be taken as an example of youthful defiance, although there may be some who were not heads of households and therefore not discernible in the record.[140] Similarly, although apprentices and young workers were involved in the 1381 revolt in London, it was by no means a revolt of the young or even of wage workers.[141]

Even if it was not age determined, however, wage workers had a good deal of group solidarity. In the Ciompi rebellion, workers from all over the city of Florence acted collectively (as opposed to later unrest in the fifteenth century, in which those who acted together were from the same parish or neighborhood). The uprising itself may have introduced men from different parts of town to each other, but it may be also that worker solidarities already in place contributed to the rebellion. Indeed, chronicle discussions of the Ciompi rebellion indicate that the taverns where clothworkers tended to gather were foci of the interactions that gave rise to rebellion. Some tavernkeepers were involved in the rebellion, although in this rebellion and another in the fifteenth century, 60 percent of those whose occupation could be identified were wage earners in the wool or silk industries.[142]

In some towns in Germany wageworkers expressed their solidarity in more formal ways. Here journeymen in a given craft, not just in one town but across a whole region, joined together for collective action on wages. In the towns of the upper Rhine in the fifteenth century the wage workers (who were less numerous than the masters, making up, for example, 28 percent of the artisanal workforce of Nürnberg in 1449, 25 percent in Straßburg in 1444, and 26 percent in Freiburg im Breisgau in 1497) began to organize themselves separately from the masters. This unrest had roots in the fourteenth century. In Speyer in 1351 journeymen weavers went on strike; a similar conflict over wages broke out in Freiburg in 1365, and in Straßburg in 1398. In some cases the workers were able to play two guilds off against each other. If the master weavers did not pay journeymen weavers enough they could work directly for the drapers or cloth merchants, who were bent on reducing the master weavers to wage worker status. Journeymen millers could work for the bakers instead of for the millers' guild. One scholar has counted thirteen collective actions by textile workers in Germany over the course of the fourteenth and fifteenth centuries, twelve for smiths, seven for bakers, six for tailors, five for shoemakers.[143]

By the fifteenth century, as the German craft guilds were changing from industrial to political organizations, masters and workers no longer shared interests vis-à-vis local authorities. In southern Germany, guilds of master artisans tended to control town councils. In 1407–08, journeymen shoemakers led uprisings across the region against this regime, and by the 1420s workers in many crafts followed. In 1436, all the towns of the upper Rhine prohibited workers from banding together and made them swear an oath to obey the town councils. In a similar regional effort, in 1383 master smiths from nine towns of the middle Rhine had banded together against feared encroachments by journeymen, including formal associations and jurisdictional rights.[144]

Collective action by wage workers in these German towns came about in part through their own guilds or fraternities separate from those of the masters. The German workers' use of the term *Gesellen* (companions) instead of *Knechte* (servants), although the latter also referred to skilled workers, may be a reflection of their attitude toward each other. The journeymen's fraternities had started out subsidiary to the craft guilds but after the Black Death became separate. The labor shortage at that

time gave the journeymen potential economic clout if they could organize to wield it.[145]

Less formal groups also came together for political or economic action. In several English towns journeymen joined together for action
against their employers, indeed sometimes (according to accusations) co-
ordinating strikes or other wage actions; this happened among London
carpenters in 1339, bakers and cordwainers in 1349, shearmen in 1350,
fullers in 1363–64, brewers in 1372. Some of these actions were less organized than others, involving only a few men who demanded higher
wages. The records do not always mention conspiracies and some instances may have been merely individuals dissatisfied with their pay. Other
instances, though, show more collaboration. The shearmen provided in a
1350 ordinance that any dispute between a master and his worker should
be settled by the wardens of the craft, because in the past when a dispute
occurred, the worker had gone to other workers of the craft throughout
the city "and then, by agreement and conspiracy among them made, they
ordered that none of them would work, or serve his master, until the said
master and his servant, or journeyman, had reached an accord, by which
the masters of the said craft were in great mischief, and the people un-
served." The London journeyman cordwainers were also accused of an illegal confederation in 1387.[146] In 1355, Flemish weavers in London joined
together to refuse to work for less than seven pence a day; twelve men
were appointed to agree upon a daily wage, which would apply to both
English and Flemish weavers.[147]

The London saddlers in 1396 objected to a "fraternity" of their workers, with its own meetings and livery. The workers claimed they had had
such an organization as far back as anyone could remember; the masters
said it went back only thirteen years, "under which false color of sanctity,
many of the servants in the trade had stirred up the journeymen among
themselves, and had formed conventicles to raise their wages too exces-
sively," with the result that wages had doubled. (The masters blamed
workers' behavior rather than the post-plague labor shortage.) A group of
six workers and six masters was to meet and reach an agreement, a rare
example of journeymen in a formal position of authority.[148] Other London crafts, too, prohibited workers' "covins or congregations."[149] In
Bristol, the council decreed that masters of any craft could not permit
journeymen to congregate in their guildhalls, an attempt to maintain a
strict delineation and prevent collective action.[150]

Sometimes a craft reached a compromise between masters and workers. In 1415, the "servants and journeymen of the tailors, called yeomen tailors" were denied their request to celebrate the feast of St. John the Baptist because it would cause a disturbance of the peace. These journeymen lived together in groups (as discussed on p. 133) and had "beaten, wounded, and ill-treated" several people, including one of their masters.[151] However, by 1436 the yeomen tailors were allowed to celebrate their feast "under the rule and governance of the master and wardens of the fraternity of St. John the Baptist of tailors of London." They were also to elect their own wardens, "whether they be householders or sewers [i.e., hired workers]," and, if the wardens of the main fraternity approved of the choice, it would stand.[152]

The economic motivation for workers to organize in this manner is obvious: in combination they could put pressure on employers to raise wages (or improve working conditions, but more often the former). The economic incentives for employers to oppose such combinations are apparent as well. The economic reasons, however, are not the only ones. Workers may have identified themselves with their economic interests, but their social identities were also defined by their position in a social hierarchy, not just their labor.[153] The fact that the London journeymen saddlers and tailors assumed their own livery—particular clothing to be worn on special occasions—had no economic motivation but served rather to create a group identity. The master saddlers objected to the livery "against the consent or license of their masters"; the tailors' adoption of a livery showed them to be, in the words of the mayor and aldermen, "a sort of youthful and unstable people."[154] The masters objected because it gave the workers a measure of independence in imitation of the masters, and removed them from their control. In the case of the tailors, by the end of the fifteenth century the yeoman fraternity was highly developed, was renamed the "bachelors' company," and included those masters not important enough to be in the livery company. They had their own livery, and were supervised by the livery company, not in opposition to it.[155] The masters had successfully co-opted the developing solidarity of their workers.

The example of the London tailors demonstrates the complex interaction between political and religious functions of craft guilds and their journeymen branches. In many crafts both masters and journeymen were members of the associated fraternities; but in some large crafts—for example, the cordwainers and tailors of York—the journeymen had their own fraternities for social solidarity.[156] In Denmark there were a number of fraternities especially for skilled wage workers, including those of the bakers, shoemakers, and smiths. These were fraternal and religious organizations, as well as mutual aid societies, but also provided assistance to strangers to the town who belonged to the craft.[157] Dinners given by journeymen's fraternities provided an opportunity not only for socializing but also for serious discussion. In London, four journeymen's guilds held the same feast day, allowing them to drink together and promote communication among workers across craft lines.[158] Some journeymen's guilds allowed masters to join, or at least to remain members after they took up their mastership; this allowed further social contact between the two groups.[159]

In Coventry, the journeymen weavers had their own organization—again, a religious organization closely connected with the craft—that had to pay twelve pence to the head of the master's guild for every member admitted. The masters had to help with the upkeep of the journeymen's memorial candles. The settlement between masters and journeymen recorded in the local Leet book also required journeymen to receive one-third of the payment for cloth they wove.[160]

Some confraternities consisted de facto, not de jure, of wage workers. Where wage workers were concentrated in particular areas of a town, parish guilds would be mainly composed of such workers. In Florence, although authorities tried to keep *sottoposti* from joining the fraternities of guildsmen, they also objected when *sottoposti* had fraternities of their own. The confraternity of San Marco was suppressed in 1317 because it was at risk of becoming a de facto *sottoposto* guild, although the city did permit some other *sottoposto* confraternities in the fifteenth century.[161]

One feature of journeymen's associations, guilds, or organizations within a larger craft guild was the lack of women's involvement. Women could belong to the crafts and associated fraternities, even if only as wives or widows, but they could not be journeymen. Since journeymen for the most part could not marry, women would rarely have been involved in their feasts or ceremonies. Women (not wives) may have been present in more informal meetings at taverns, but these would most likely have been prostitutes or other marginal women, not women who were part of the craft. While there is little evidence of journeymen in the fourteenth or fifteenth century being as vehemently misogynist as what Merry Wiesner describes for Germany in the sixteenth and seventeenth centuries, nevertheless the bonds they formed were homosocial ones. The honor they could gain only through independence was a masculine honor, and the activities they pursued to replace the honor they lost through dependence were masculine activities.[162] Wiesner argues that the opposition to women became part of a new way of defining themselves as masculine once they realized that they themselves would never get to be masters. This process may already have been underway, as we have seen, in the Middle Ages.

Wage workers feasted at taverns both as part of their formal fraternal activity and also less formally. Across Europe, the tavern was an important place for the sociability at all levels, but especially for those who did not have households of their own. Wage workers, and apprentices too, visited taverns together and consorted with prostitutes together. Particular taverns became associated with skilled wage workers, either in general or in a particular craft, similar to the situation in early modern France, when the "tour de France" was an important part of the worker's career and taverns affiliated with the different *compagnonnages* were especially important. Here workers from outside the town could come to meet colleagues, hear news of available jobs, and find lodging; here workers within the town could meet people from outside their workshop to compare working conditions. Restrictive legislation in the towns of the upper Rhine in the fifteenth century forbade such taverns associated with particular journeymen's guilds. Masters who were required by contract or regulation to provide meals to their workers had been sending the food to them in the taverns, an indication that the workers were more in solidarity with each other and less part of the masters' families.[163] The towns did not forbid the workers all forms of sociability, just secret conspiracies, but the taverns were thought to foment such conspiracies.[164]

Even when each craft did not have its own particular tavern, drinking together was an important way of forming bonds. In Paris, in order to join the doubletmakers, a worker had to provide a drinking party for his new brothers.[165] In Denmark, the journeymen smiths of Flensborg in 1425 required that any journeyman hired in the town join their group and drink with them. These drinking sessions were frequent enough among the Danish journeymen that they were strictly regulated: there were penalties for persuading someone to drink more than he wanted to, and for drinking to the point of vomiting.[166] The journeymen also had their own systems of violent redress of grievances; in Basel, for example, the authorities rarely intervened in journeyman-on-journeyman violence, as long as it followed its own norms. Such violence often occurred in taverns, as quarrels between factions or journeymen of different crafts kindled over gambling and other debts. While all these journeymen may not have been young men, the authorities considered youth a major cause of disruptions, and court cases from Basel indicate also that offenses considered typical of youth were committed mainly by and against journeymen.[167] Marjorie McIntosh found that English communities that were particularly concerned with social order, beginning in the 1460s–70s, tended to be those where substantial industrial activity went on and wage laborers were more common.[168]

Communal feasts in guilds or fraternities had provided a social link between masters and workers; when the workers drank together in their own fraternities or in their particular taverns, however, this indicated their independence from the masters.[169] In either setting young wage workers experienced a tension between the model of masculinity embodied by the masters they hoped to emulate and the more immediate gratifications offered by involvement in their peer group.

Marriage and Maturity

The tavern may have been a less important social space to those who had their own households, but young wage workers might have had a hard time establishing them. Having a household meant marrying (or living with a partner without marriage, which amounted to the same thing in economic terms).[170] This could give a man some independence from personal domination by the master, but even where not forbidden (as discussed above) it could be difficult economically. Some journeymen married servants from the household in which they worked, and the couple continued to live in the master's house. These marriages might be strongly encouraged if not forced by masters who were afraid of prosecution for procuring if they allowed nonmarital sex under their roof.[171]

Medieval people thought of wage workers as connected with youth and disruption. Marriage marked an important transition to maturity and stability. This was much more the case for workers than among the social groups discussed in Chapters 2 and 3. University students did not marry while at the university, and if they married later it probably did not change their lives much: a petty aristocrat, lawyer, or royal bureaucrat would not run his own household; he would have servants to do it, whether or not he had a wife to manage them. For knights, marriage might not be possible until a man had inherited his patrimony or had acquired a substantial landholding in some other way, but it was the inheritance rather than the marriage that signified his coming of age. Marriage normally accompanied inheritance and setting up one's own household, but it did not need to.

For the young working man, however, marriage signified independence, one reason why conflicts arose when married journeymen lived in the master's household. Traditionally, marriage marked the setting up of the household and new workshop at the same time. Medieval people assumed that workers could not afford marriage until they had become masters and had their own workshops. As Charles Phythian-Adams puts it, "Marriage in fact represented the most important single step in an individual's career. Not only did it mark the late transition to a socially superior age-group from menial dependency in a household that was not necessarily that of a person's origin, but it also signalised the creation of a new domestic unit that was familial, economic, and social in its implications."[172]

In general, marriage changed women's lives in the Middle Ages more than it changed men's. Women were defined by their marital status, and their working lives depended greatly upon their family situation (whether they lived in their fathers' or their husbands' homes or on their own, whether or not they had young children).[173] Their legal status—whether they had control over their own money and therefore could operate a business—also depended on their marital status. Their connection to a craft—both in terms of gaining a skill and in terms of belonging to a craft organization—often came through marriage.

However, marital status affected men's lives too. A man could do the same kind of work whether married or not, and his legal status did not depend upon his marriage, but his ability to become a master craftsman, and his participation in artisanal masculinity, did depend heavily on it. Marriage could dramatically transform a man's economic situation as well. Not only was it practical to have a wife to run the domestic side of things and help out in the workshop; the idea that a man was not fully adult until he married, and could not be a householder without a family, also pervaded the society.

Marriage and the workshop went together in part because a single man would find it very difficult to manage a workshop. The workshop and the home were connected, and someone had to manage the domestic sphere. A wife could manage the servants (other than those who were primarily employed in the craft), and see to feeding, clothing, and housing all the workers. Often the wife also managed the retail end of the business

while the husband worked in production. Wives (and daughters and domestic servants) also provided extra labor in the workshop when necessary. Even if they did not receive the legally recognized training of
apprenticeship, over a period of time they learned the craft well. In a sense
marriage resembled the hiring of a manager. It also was necessary for the
reproduction of the labor force. Men wished to pass on their workshop
and craft guild membership to their legitimate children, and they could
not acquire those heirs without a wife.

If it was difficult to be a master craftsman without a wife, it was also
difficult to have a wife without being a master craftsman. It was difficult
to support a family on a wage worker's income (and in this period marriage usually meant having a family). The extra labor within the household represented by a wife and children was not especially useful to a
wage worker, who did not have a large group of employees to be fed and
housed, nor a retail business to run. Where the household was not a
workshop, the only way a wife and children could contribute to the family
economy was by seeking wage work themselves.[174] This was not uncommon, although the kinds of work women did were very poorly paid.[175]

The marriage rate in many parts of medieval Europe was unusually
low for a preindustrial society, the number of people marrying late or
never unusually high.[176] This pattern, known as the Western European
Marriage pattern, characterized at least northwestern Europe during the
Middle Ages.[177] In Italy, where there was a larger concentration of urban
areas and therefore a higher proportion of craft workers, the age of marriage for men was even higher than that for northern Europe, but the age
of marriage for women was much younger.

David Herlihy suggests that the late age of marriage for urban areas
in Tuscany can be explained by the fact that there the family did not represent a productive unit, as it did in the countryside (and as it did under
circumstances where marriage was a concomitant of setting up one's own
workshop). For wage workers marriage provided an opportunity for licit
sexual relations and for reproduction, but it did not provide direct economic benefit, as it did in family enterprise.[178] Indeed, having more mouths
to feed might be economically disadvantageous. Furthermore, even if few
workers ever managed to accumulate the capital to establish themselves
independently, many might hope to do so and therefore postpone marriage in order to save. In Florence, Herlihy and Christiane Klapisch-
Zuber found that one man in eight never married; but given that a great
many men never rose above the level of wage workers, many of those

wage workers must have married eventually.[179] For early modern England, scholars have found that nuptiality (rate of marriage) responds to changes in real wages with a fifteen- to twenty-year time lag;[180] in the absence of serial data on marriage for the Middle Ages, we may assume that the pattern was not too different, and that workers were better able to marry when wages were high or the chances of eventual mastership plausible.

The delay of marriage on the part of many craft workers, even if they were not as numerous as agricultural workers, was significant. One effect was the corresponding existence of a large number of unmarried women. The sex ratio in late medieval towns was heavily skewed toward women, in part because of heavy female migration to the towns. For every man who did not marry, an additional one of these women remained single. Because of the limited employment opportunities for women, many of them lived in poverty, doing casual labor of various sorts, including prostitution.

The delay of marriage also meant a demand for prostitution among male craft workers. Even though medieval culture deemed nonmarital sexual activity sinful, prostitution was common and more or less tolerated if not wholeheartedly accepted. Medieval authorities believed that if men did not have the opportunity to direct their sex drive in legitimate ways it would manifest itself in seduction, adultery, and rape.[181] Even as towns fulminated against the disorder caused by prostitution, they also, by establishing official brothels (in southern Germany, the south of France, Italy, and a few jurisdictions in England) or by turning fines for prostitution and brothelkeeping into de facto licensing fees (in the Low Countries, northern France, northern Germany, and England), tacitly tolerated its existence. Apprenticeship regulations, and even those for skilled wage workers generally, often forbade visiting prostitutes, a sign that this was not infrequent. Prostitution, for these men, provided more than just a sexual outlet. Visiting prostitutes was something that the workers did together, like visiting taverns; it was part of having a good time. It also may have substituted in part for the emotional life that they missed out on by not having families.

A concomitant of the late age of marriage for men in Florence—some scholars see it as a result, although some medieval writers saw it as a cause—was the practice of sodomy. Sodomy in Florence had very specific age-related characteristics: up until the age of seventeen or eighteen it was considered somewhat acceptable for boys to play the passive role in homosexual intercourse, while older men were expected to take the active role.[182] The transition from boyhood to manhood was thus marked by a change in sexual behavior. It was most common for young men, rather than older married men, to have sex with these boys, another sign that the period before marriage was a separate life stage (although married men were far from absent from sodomitical gathering places).

Sodomy in Florence was associated to some extent with craft workers. The workshop or bottegha provided a place for young apprentices and older workers to mingle, drinking and gambling together.[183] Dancing and fencing schools also served the same function. Other towns do not seem to have developed such public networks of sodomy, in part because the social life of craft workers may have been less exclusively homosocial elsewhere than it was in Italy.

Young workers often resented their inability to marry. The practice at Dijon of groups of young men demanding high fines when an older man married a young woman, and subjecting the couple to a charivari if they refused, reflected this.[184] Young men who could not themselves marry resented it bitterly when an older man took one of the women whom they considered their potential future partners. This inability to marry—the relegation to prostitutes, the dependence on a master rather than heading one's own household—had significant effects on these young men's concept of their own manhood. Their opportunities for expressing their masculinity were limited to the informal and even illicit, including violence.

This violence was apparent in an epidemic of gang rape in fifteenth-century Dijon. Many of the young men involved were workers—85 percent of attackers were either unmarried journeymen or sons of bourgeois, half between eighteen and twenty-four. They used rape as a tool of social control, directing it especially against women who did not conform to the social roles expected of them, particularly women who had transgressed sexually through fornication or adultery such as priests' partners.[185] By raping these women the young men asserted their wish to participate in the sexual economy of the town from which they were largely excluded. Jacques Rossiaud calls participation in these rapes—in which perhaps half of city youths participated at some time—a rite of passage to manhood.[186] The young men were also asserting their wish to act like the town fathers or authorities: they could not police the women's behavior in any other way so they did so through violence, at the same time dominating the women and challenging the male establishment. It was not a matter just of satisfying sexual needs, but of claiming a place in the community.

These gangs—and similar ones in other towns—took the place of more formal youth organizations. Precisely to remedy this violence, the town of Dijon and others in southeastern France established "youth abbeys" or confraternities, to channel the rebellious energy of men between about eighteen and thirty-six years old. The town authorities controlled the election of the "abbot," and he was generally from one of the leading, established families. Larger towns might have several such organizations corresponding to different social groups. These abbeys celebrated at various festivals, but because they included some married as well as nearly all the unmarried young men, they acted as a restraining force.[187] Such organizations, to which all the young men in a given town belonged, were more common in villages than in towns, and more common in the early modern period than in the late Middle Ages. Where they did exist, they tended to be focused around a religious observance, like the parish guilds, and to consist of young men drawn from the higher levels of society, with craft workers as the lowest level represented.

These organizations concentrated particularly on festive occasions, filling their year with ritual feasts and pageants. In the German towns with fairly well-organized journeymen's fraternities, the latter performed some of the same functions. They had feasts and dances for their own members (sometimes including apprentices), although their participation in larger civic rituals was limited. Some members were married, and indeed there is evidence that women could belong to some of them. However, they explicitly excluded unskilled workers: even though we may view journeymen as part of the working class, they understood themselves as a particularly privileged part of it.[188]

The type of masculinity that the craft workshop was teaching must have been ultimately fairly frustrating to the young men, apprentices or post-apprentice wage workers, who were learning it. They were learning the skills necessary to master a craft, but might never have the opportunity to demonstrate that mastery, remaining subordinate employees indefinitely. They were being trained in a system that no longer worked according to the model they envisioned, where they could expect to set up their own workshop, marry, raise a family, and play a role in guild and even town governance. The honor that came from being a substantial citizen might never be theirs. Even the satisfaction at using their skills to create beautiful and useful objects, which could be a part of masculine achievement, might be absent as well, as especially in the textile trades each guild might perform only one small step of the productive process.

The craft workshop, like the university and the court, was gradually closing and becoming an exclusive milieu in the later Middle Ages (although more so in some regions than in others). Artisanal masculinity involved proving oneself not a woman by having a skill and training available (notionally anyway) only to men, but also proving oneself mature, substantial, honorable, and independent, in competition with other men. The young worker claimed membership in an elite group of men by virtue of his skill, but increasingly could not achieve the independence to which this skill was supposed to entitle him. The masculinity he learned to seek often had to be achieved outside the system established by his elders and social superiors. Not only, then, were there different ideas of masculinity in different sectors of society, but even within the craft sector, there were conflicting ideals.

5

Becoming a Man

MEDIEVAL MEN GREW UP DIFFERENTLY from men of today, but even in the later Middle Ages knights grew up differently from university students, who grew up differently from craft workers. Even a single social context or discourse could contain conflicting ideas about manhood. The variation among models of masculinity in the late Middle Ages is not an obstacle to our finding patterns: rather, it itself constitutes a pattern. Whether in the Middle Ages or any other period, one type of masculinity may predominate at one moment and another type at another, but competing ideas always coexist—even within a single subculture or the mind of a particular individual. Which model dominates depends upon the circumstances of social relations. The three different masculinities this book has discussed share similarities as well as exhibit differences. In all cases young men were training for a share in power, a place in the hierarchy from which they could master other men. In all cases they were learning ways in which they could be unlike women. In all cases they were competing against each other or their elders. The differences, however, show the complexities of such a concept as "medieval masculinity." Depending on the social milieu into which they were born, men sought different ways to demonstrate their manhood.

During the later Middle Ages, the environments of the university, the court, and the workshop produced three different forms of masculinity. The court model rested on physical prowess: one must be a man as opposed to a woman, and demonstrate this through the use of strength in violence. This fundamental opposition between men and women is far from absent in the other two cases, but there are differences of emphasis as we consider other issues besides the opposition to femininity. The predominant model in the university consisted of rationality, self-control, and moderation: the man must be a man as opposed to a beast. The workshop model required sufficiency and independence: he must be a man as opposed to a child. And yet none of these dominant masculinities absolutely determined attitudes or behavior. The immoderate behavior of some university students, attested in their own accounts and their drinking songs as well as in statutes inveighing against it, shows that students had not internalized ideas about manly self-control as thoroughly as university officials might like. In the later Middle Ages, a gentility and refinement that some scholars have labeled feminine moderated the aggressiveness of the ideal knight, even as knights defined themselves by their active role in relation to the passive feminine. The craft worker's independence increasingly became a myth, an unattainable goal.

From a twenty-first century perspective we cannot label one of these models as more masculine than the others. If medieval men behaved in ways that today we tend to code as feminine—the refinement that some texts expected of knights, for example—it means not that they were feminized, but that medieval conceptions of masculine and feminine differed from modern ones. The culture in which these men lived considered them the epitome of manhood, and their sexuality was not in doubt. We cannot assume that men who adhered to modern models of manly behavior were considered manly in the Middle Ages, or that those who did not were not. We need to judge behavior as masculine or feminine based on what people in the Middle Ages said about it or, in the absence of evidence for such discussion, how they treated it.

Masculinity and Medieval Women

Understanding how medieval people constructed masculinity, rather than how well they conformed to modern ideas about masculinity, helps us understand the relation between masculinity and male dominance. Is masculinity—a set of ideas about what it means to be a man—a tool that men use to keep women subordinated? Or is the subordination of women a tool that some men use to dominate others? Are the relations between two sets of men secondary to the domination of women, or are relations between men and women secondary to the domination of some men by others? These questions determine how men's history has been and will be written: as "the history of why men behave the way they do to women" or "the history of how men relate to other men, dominating women in the process."

People's behavior results from a complex mixture of motives, and these alternative ways of approaching men's history complement rather than contradict each other. Discourses representing women as subordinate, inferior, or unimportant except in relation to men functioned to oppress women, but also allowed one man to claim superiority over another because of his control of women. By the later Middle Ages, overt misogynist discourse circulated widely, and women lost some of the political power they had wielded earlier. They remained active in the economy, but never found it as easy as men to accumulate wealth, gain access to the most lucrative or prestigious careers, or gain recognition for their skills.[1] Even when overt polemic was lacking, though, this did not mean an absence of misogyny, but rather a misogyny that treated women as insignificant. Throughout the Middle Ages, men took their domination for granted in ways that did not need to be discussed. The creators of a given discourse about men may not deliberately have used the distinction between masculinity and femininity as a tool for the subjugation of women, but it is inevitably linked to that subjugation.

We must take care not to conclude from women's absence from some discourses that women were not important to medieval men and their homosocial worlds. If medieval men understood masculinity as being about relations among men—who is more and who is less of a man—and women figured only incidentally in this conceptual scheme, that does not mean that the history of masculinity is not an important part of women's history. If men vie to prove to each other that they are more manly, then they prove at the same time that they are not womanly, and this rejection of the feminine is implicit if not explicit in all understandings of masculinity. Femininity is not the only category opposed to masculinity—both childhood and bestiality function as opposites of manhood—but being not-a-woman is always a greater or lesser part of what it means to be a man.

The three case studies discussed here excluded women in different ways, and their absence created different ideas about masculinity. In the universities, women's absence was not a point of discussion or contestation. Masculinity was constructed in the university with little direct reference to femininity. In the court, on the other hand, women remained continuously and necessarily present. The knight was defined by his relation to women as well as by his being not-woman. In chivalric ideology women inspired the knights' great deeds, but they functioned mainly to fill prescribed roles, not to wield real power. Men fought for them or over them, but the battles gave status to the men. Aristocratic women did, in practice, wield a good deal of power in the later Middle Ages. But they usually did so as widows or as regents for their sons or absent husbands. These roles are notably invisible in chivalric texts, which show women wielding power only through the love men have for them. In the world of chivalric discourse women were important as representatives of a category but less so as historical agents.[2]

The reverse held true in the world of the craft workshop, where a woman could make all the difference to the family economy. Running a workshop often required the work of both halves of a couple, and even workers who did not have their own workshops might require two incomes to support a family. The individual woman made a great deal of difference. But the woman who was in effect the co-master of the craft is often invisible in the sources. The man is the guild member, admitted to the mystery. In some places husbands and wives who worked together were both acknowledged as members of the craft. For the most part, though, women were subsumed under their husbands' work, excluded conceptually if not actually.

All of the three institutions excluded women, but their discourses tended not to argue for their exclusion so much as simply to assume it. Some craft regulations that specifically excluded women gave justifications for this; it is not surprising that the arguments about women's incompetence and inferiority were brought to bear precisely in the area in which women were encroaching on male prerogatives. There was less need to argue for the exclusion of women from knighthood or scholarship. The absence of direct confrontation or polemic about femininity in these three contexts suggests that women were securely subordinated and considered unlikely to infringe on masculine prerogatives. This is not to say that there was no antifeminine rhetoric in these institutions—indeed there was, some of it discussed above in the relevant chapters—but the rhetoric did not address the issue of why women could not be knights or university scholars. It was directed against women, and especially women's sexuality, as an ever-present threat, not against women's entry into a particular sphere of activity.

The fact that the exclusion of women from these venues did not require overt justification reveals the depth of misogyny in the culture generally. It also points to the intensely homosocial nature of all three of these institutions, and indeed much of late medieval life. The homosociality of the university is apparent. At the court or within the aristocratic household, men and women participated together in a rich social life, but many aspects even of that life were segregated. The interaction of men and women was highly stylized. When men and women spoke together in groups or alone often they followed a script of convention rather than interacting freely. Nor did knights spend their lives at court. Men traveled in their lords' entourages, for battle or for political and diplomatic reasons. On these trips they certainly did not forego female company, either of their own social class or of servants or prostitutes. They developed closer bonds, however, with the men of the retinue with which they traveled. Other men were their companions and their rivals.

The craft workshop was not an entirely homosocial environment: the master's wife, daughters, and female servants participated in various ways. Nor was the craft worker's world outside the workshop all male. Women who were married to or widows of craft guild members participated in the guilds' social and religious functions. Such women were in the minority, however, and their participation was limited. The guilds of journeymen that began to spring up in some towns, particularly in Germany, did not include women. Composed of unmarried men, they met at taverns and created communities for themselves, communities that sometimes defined themselves explicitly through the exclusion of women.

These three medieval institutions were not alone in their homosociality. In monasticism, the religious were segregated by sex and formed their earthly emotional bonds with their brothers or sisters. Noblewomen had households of women corresponding to their husbands' retinues of men. Peasant men worked together as did peasant women, although peasants of both sexes worked together as well. Marriage was the norm for medieval people who had not chosen a life in religion, but marriage did not necessarily mean forsaking homosociality. Where marriage partners were chosen on the basis of economic or reproductive criteria rather than passion or companionship, the partners' primary bonds would often remain with their friends of the same sex.

The emotional investment of the partners in a marriage could vary by gender. The biggest difference between young manhood and young womanhood was that men were expected to prepare themselves for a variety of careers, whereas women for the most part prepared for only one: marriage. Many different skills went into women's preparation: they needed to learn how to care for children, grow or purchase and prepare food, make clothing, support a husband's economic endeavors in various ways.

Much of women's paid work grew out of these same skills, especially preparing food and drink and working with textiles. Women usually learned these skills, however, not in a workshop—although some young women might be apprenticed in the textile trades—but at home, from their mothers, by way of preparing for marriage. They grew up knowing they would be identified by whom they married rather than by what craft they practiced or what prowess, physical or intellectual, they demonstrated. The various rituals and practices of young womanhood aimed not at creating bonds of solidarity among women, connections that would help them take their places as citizens, but rather at acquiring marriage partners. The main life-cycle ritual for women was the wedding.

Recent scholarship on the role of singlewomen in medieval society has emphasized that many women never married, and many others lived independently for a good part of their adult lives. They built networks of solidarity with other women and formed strong emotional, sometimes romantic bonds with each other.[3] The existence of a sizable number of independent single women, however, does not obviate the fact that marriage was the norm for medieval women. (Some, of course, entered the life of religion rather than marrying; even here, they were metaphorically brides of Christ.) Singlewomen were problematic in medieval society. In rural areas they sometimes controlled their own land, but in other places they depended on a father or brother. Urban singlewomen worked at a variety of jobs, but were always somewhat suspect sexually as well as in other ways. They were generally quite poor, given the low wages for women even in the crafts accessible to them. Marriage remained a choice rather than a mandate, but those who chose to go against the norm did not have an easy time. The records of ecclesiastical courts show the kinds of pressures that could be brought on young women to marry.[4]

Women who did marry young—many aristocratic women, urban women in the Mediterranean regions—spent the period of adolescence or youth, the time when boys were learning how to be men, in childbearing. Women who did not marry young went through a period of maidenhood between childhood and maturity, which Kim Phillips argues was considered the "perfect age" of woman's life.[5] Young women certainly formed their own networks of friendships and bonded together, but these bonds were not as integral to mature feminine identity as were men's homosocial bonds. To become a woman was in most cases to identify with a man, at least in the view of the mainstream culture. Becoming a man, even if it meant marrying, never meant identifying with a woman.

Hierarchies of Men

Just because men socialized with other men, however, does not mean that men as a group had more in common with all other men than they did with any women. The lines of social cleavage that divided noble from peasant, rich from poor, Christian from Jew, and so forth helped construct different forms of masculinity. Those lines of cleavage became sharper in the later Middle Ages. Patriarchy meant not just the dominance of men over women, but the dominance of a small number of men over most men and all women. It is not always possible entirely to disentangle one form of domination from another.

The universities had never been egalitarian institutions. They had no formal regulations about the family background of entrants, but a student could not enter without a basic Latin education that was no more accessible to everyone in the twelfth century than in the fourteenth. In the early years of universities, though, those who attended the universities had been highly motivated, either by learning or by ambition. In the later Middle Ages, university attendance had become a convention among certain groups, a means to acquire credentials, connections, and polish. Aristocrats sent their sons to university (less so in England, where those sons were more likely to attend the Inns of Court, than elsewhere). Students of noble birth might receive special privileges, in addition to bringing their own servants to university or having poorer students serve them. High birth was not a formal qualification, but it became increasingly important.

For knighthood, birth did in some places become a formal qualification. In the German-speaking lands a knight had to have all four grandparents from knightly families. In practice there were few exceptions. In the cities a few crafts accepted only sons or other close relatives of masters. Most did not make so absolute a requirement, but high entrance fees for nonrelatives heavily favored hereditary succession. Once again these preferences were far from absolute, but they were significant.

Particularly after the demographic catastrophe of the Black Death, when in many skilled fields (including the clergy and the aristocracy) the personnel shortage became acute, one might expect that careers would become more open and descent less important, and to a certain extent they did. By the middle of the fifteenth century in many areas, however, population had begun to revive and there was no longer such an acute shortage; furthermore, prolonged depression in many areas meant fewer opportunities than the population size might indicate. Even population shortage, however, does not necessarily mean more openness. The increased social mobility threatened established elites, who tried to undermine it. An overpopulated Europe had excluded people from privilege de facto. There was little room in an overcrowded society for men to rise based on merit without birth. When the demographic situation changed, however, exclusion became more formal or de jure. A general hardening of class lines took place in the later Middle Ages.[6] There were, of course, substantial exceptions. Within particular sectors of society, too—merchants, aristocrats—men and families might rise and fall, but they rarely crossed from one sector to another.

The court, the university, and the workshop—and the masculinities that developed within them—changed over the course of the Middle Ages in other ways besides their exclusivity. In the universities, the twelfth and thirteenth centuries were eras of great intellectual excitement, as opposed to the fourteenth when, in part because of the threat of heresy, intellectual life was more restricted. The students who came to the universities earlier were more likely to have done so for intellectual rather than social reasons. They also remained a good deal more independent. The universities did not act in loco parentis for them in the same way; they were responsible for finding their own lodgings and managing their own lives. By the later Middle Ages the socialization process at the university became more collective. As the intellectual ferment of the universities decreased and university education became more routinized, social formation as opposed to intellectual formation became a more important factor.

The values espoused in chivalric literature of the twelfth century seem quite similar to those of the later Middle Ages. By the fourteenth and fifteenth centuries, ostensibly nonfiction texts had come to accept and include the chivalric and courtly values of twelfth-century writers like Chrétien de Troyes. Nor was this development only textual. Social practice reflected literature, so that later authors and knights adopted an image of chivalry created in the twelfth century by literary ideals. Elements of love and courtliness, which were important values in the twelfth century as well, became more integrated into social practice by the end of the Middle Ages. Seeking the love of a lady constituted a part of a knight's everyday behavior in the later Middle Ages much more than in the twelfth century.[7] Later medieval courts institutionalized the rituals of knighthood. Originally meaning a mounted warrior, *knight* or *miles* had come to mean a man of knightly birth who had undergone a complicated initiation ritual.

A similar institutionalization took place in the crafts. Earlier in the Middle Ages apprenticeship was less formalized. Anyone who wished to become a master craftsman had merely to set up his own shop. In a few cases in the twelfth century, and more widely from the thirteenth century on, stricter definitions of crafts, self-regulation, regulation by the municipality, and stricter control by masters appeared. The developing urban governments played a role in these changes. In the twelfth century the aristocracy and the merchants had struggled for control of the towns. By the later Middle Ages the aristocracy had fallen out of the picture and the more important crafts began to challenge the merchants. Some cities followed a proto-capitalist model, in which a few large entrepreneurs hired even masters to work for them. In other cities, and in some crafts in all cities, individual craftsmen were more independent. Still, all the towns regulated craftsmen in ways that were quite different from the twelfth century. The path that a young man had to follow in acquiring his skills and setting up an independent workshop was regularized and in some cases blocked.

In all three institutions a young man underwent a process of learning and development in the transition from boyhood to mature manhood. That transition marked a distinct stage of life in all three contexts. All segments of medieval society clearly recognized that the age between childhood and manhood, however one labeled it, had its own distinctive features. The way stations in the progression from boy to man became, during the course of the later Middle Ages, more clearly defined and ritualized than before.

Other Paths to Manhood

Other groups in the Middle Ages besides these three acquired their own distinctive masculinities. Neither scholars, knights, nor craft workers comprised the majority of men in the Middle Ages; that distinction goes to agricultural workers, whether peasants (those in possession of their own landholdings, whether they paid rent to their lords in cash or in kind or owned the holding outright) or wage laborers. It is difficult to get at the subjective identities of largely illiterate agricultural workers. There was a gender division of labor, men generally doing the field work (with women helping out at certain times) while women did agricultural work within the family's own holding and much of the preparation of the raw materials into commodities. These lines of division were not absolute, but they were strong.[8] Some literature closely ties agricultural work to masculinity. The story of a peasant husband and wife who argue over who works harder indicates that heavy physical labor formed part of a man's identity.[9] In other places, where young men were involved in transhumance, travel and living away from home was a distinctive part of the masculine experience.[10]

The inheritance of land marked a big step toward mature manhood. As with urban workers, it was difficult for an agricultural worker to marry and support a family until he could claim his inheritance. Inheritance of land did not require the father's death; in England, for example, maintenance agreements allowed sons to take charge of their patrimony and support their fathers in their old age. Inheritance practices in many places worked to exclude women from acquiring land. But they also worked to exclude many men, often through primogeniture (inheritance of the entire holding by the eldest son). If masculinity meant being independent, a head of household, then a large number of men in rural areas never could achieve full adult masculine status or came to it late. One would expect that in regions of partible inheritance the relation of inheritance and landownership to maturity and masculinity would be different than in regions of primogeniture.

Youth abbeys and confraternities in rural areas, particularly in France, provided a way of expressing youthful masculinity in the village. These groups consisted mostly of young unmarried men, who had not yet received their inheritance, but many men remained involved after they were older and married. Robert Muchembled has studied such groups in Flanders and Artois in the sixteenth century and concluded that although considered rowdy and wild, these groups were not really subversive of the social order. Rather, in the acting out that they did in these groups, the young men were preparing to take on civic responsibilities. The bonds they formed with each other would continue after their youth.[11]

The most obvious place where young men formed bonds of brotherhood, of course, was not in rural villages but in monasteries. Most monks made their profession in late boyhood to young manhood.[12] Scholars debate what sort of manhood the novice monk acquired. In taking vows of poverty, chastity, and obedience—renouncing the masculine roles of provider, sexual aggressor, and authority figure—was he in fact rejecting masculinity? Caroline Bynum's classic article "Jesus as Mother and Abbot as Mother" shows that twelfth-century Cistercians saw the abbot as having a maternal, nurturing role.[13] This does not mean, however, that they thought of him as less (or more) than a man. These Cistercian writers used the feminine metaphorically and presented the abbot as combining the good qualities of both men and women. And, while monks rejected certain masculine roles, they also rejected attributes normally connected with femininity, such as love of luxury and comfort, uncontrolled sexuality, and concentration on things of this world. In becoming unsexed, did the monk become ungendered?

R. N. Swanson suggests that the clergy—secular (parish priests) as well as regular (monks)—in the high and later Middle Ages should be seen as "emasculine."[14] Their tonsure and clerical garb made them quasi-transvestites, and their dependence on patronage made them less than masculine. Yet Swanson reaches this conclusion by evaluating the clergy against Vern Bullough's threefold model of masculinity as "impregnating women, protecting dependents, and serving as a provider to one's family." Neither Swanson nor Bullough develops the case that these were universal criteria in the Middle Ages.[15] Patricia Cullum suggests that while fornication and fighting were the two main characteristics of lay masculinity, that does not mean that they were features of all masculinity.[16] She deploys Connell's concept of hegemonic and subordinate masculinities, although religious masculinity cannot quite be seen as subordinate, given the central importance of the church in medieval culture. Of course, the clergy did engage in acts of fornication and of violence; they did not entirely comply with the ideals of their order. This might mean that they accepted the dominant secular ideal of masculinity and attempted to live up to it, but it could also mean that self-control, while also a masculine ideal, was difficult.

Cullum suggests that the clergy were not fully adult because they had not become the heads of their own establishments.[17] Marrying and becoming the head of one's own household was indeed a marker of mature masculinity for the layman. But most laymen, while they might have the opportunity for one kind of independence as head of a household and provider for a family, were dependent in other ways, on a lord or an employer. There were few men in medieval society who could claim full independence, and the clergy's lack of it did not make them either women or boys.

Daniel Boyarin, comparing Jewish with Christian masculinity, agrees with Swanson that monks became ungendered. Boyarin draws a contrast between Jewish and Christian ideals of the spiritual life. In order to become a monk the Christian renounced not only sexuality but genealogy. Even if he illicitly fathered a child, the child could never be recognized, or inherit. Jewish men, however, could be celebrated as husbands and fathers at the same time as they were renowned as scholars.

Boyarin suggests that traditional Jewish society (stretching from the Talmudic era through the western European Middle Ages to the eighteenth century in Eastern Europe) developed its own concept of masculinity. Jews did not view aggression as a masculine ideal or admire fighting back and defending oneself. Physical prowess was for the goyim; knights appeared in a negative context—for example, to symbolize the Wicked Son of the Passover Haggadah.[18] The ideal male was a pale, thin scholar, not a muscular fighter. Nor did the Jewish ideal of masculinity involve independence and the ability to support a household. A man was not to concern himself with such mundane matters but rather to devote his entire life to study. Families considered it an honor to marry a daughter to a promising scholar, so many supported their scholar sons-in-law. In other families wives earned the living. Yet the Jewish community did not see scholars as less than men because they did not support themselves. Thus "femminized" (Boyarin's word) men had a place in the sexual and family life of Jewish culture that monks did not in Christianity. The monk was a binary opposite of the knight, but within Jewish manhood there were no such binary opposites.[19]

For both Christian and Jewish men, growing up involved acquiring the ability to make rational choices, but other aspects differed between the two cultures. For Jews being a man was not a matter of physical prowess or of being admitted into a community based on some sort of esoteric knowledge. Rather, it was the taking on of an obligation: all males older than thirteen were bound by the commandments.[20] The early age of "manhood" in this tradition to some extent reflected marriage practices: Jews tended to marry quite young and did not expect a married couple to be economically independent. Jewish men skipped over a stage of young manhood that medieval Christian men went through, reflecting the difference in the nature of the masculinity they hoped to achieve.

The Middle Ages and the Twenty-first Century

Among the various medieval masculinities, if one had to be identified as hegemonic, it would have to be the knightly model, simply because this model belonged to the group that held political power. However, knightly masculinity was not normative for everyone. The church criticized it, but even its adherents did not urge it on everyone: courtly behavior was only for the elite few.

The sense that different modes of behavior—different ways of being a man—were appropriate to different groups within society is one distinctive feature of the Middle Ages. Certainly in the twenty-first century world there are many different models or views of masculinity, but our recognition of the differences tends to be descriptive rather than prescriptive, and men can to a certain extent pick and choose. The dominant attitude today is not that each subculture should stick to its own appropriate behavior and not get out of place. The hierarchical nature of medieval society, and the idea that each person had a particular status appropriate to him or her, gave the diversity of masculinities a different effect than a comparable diversity today.

The various aspects of masculinity addressed in this book may resonate for twenty-first century readers who recognize components that are present today. Aggressiveness is one such component. But aggressiveness, although it enters into many constructions of masculinity, is not always configured in the same way, and the form it took in the Middle Ages was distinctive. Late medieval chivalric culture did not admire a totally uncontrolled violence. The man who flew off the handle, who reacted with immediate violence to provocation, who did not put up with any disrespect for a moment, was not the ideal.[21] Chivalric literature and tournaments had given the knight of the later Middle Ages the idea of a code of conduct that kept the violence strictly in its place. Reality did not always, or even often, conform to this ideal. Knights did not consistently follow a chivalric code; battle was quite different from the tournament, and they had little compunction about using violence against those not protected by the code of chivalry (or even against those who were). Nevertheless the idea of a code and of knightly behavior remained. While in practice a knight might just as well strike out at someone who insulted him as challenge him to single combat at a later time, late medieval culture most admired a masculinity that could control these aggressive instincts and put them to work for a purpose.

The idea of the knight wooing his lady may have contemporary reso-
nances too, but the man's role in love between the genders in the Middle
Ages is distinctive as well. Medieval men, especially aristocrats, were expected to express the emotions connected with love. In contrast with the
modern cliché of men being unwilling to say the words "I love you," medieval men poured out their feelings of love in a river of poetry and prose.
Of course, we may argue to what extent such productions represent the
true feelings of individuals and to what extent they adhere to convention.
The existence of such a convention in itself, however, shows the permissi-
bility or even desirability of this emotion. The idea of men publicly declaring their love and their willingness to do great deeds for the honor of
their beloved is quite different from the contemporary ideal of the un-
emotional male, who may make such a declaration to his beloved but
hardly to other men.

Involvement with women brought late medieval men more than just
sexual or emotional gratification. In many cases the individual woman was
less important than the place she held or what she represented: the dowry
she brought, the assistance she provided in running a workshop, the success in battle of which she was a marker. Late medieval romances are full
of "trophy wives." Trophy wives may be more than just decorations; their
husbands may well love them deeply, but these relationships also have
symbolic meanings. The woman serves to advertise a man's masculinity to
other men. Attracting or acquiring women was an important part of
becoming a man. In the later Middle Ages, however, while the physical
appearance of one's beloved was important, her social standing, especially
as expressed in terms of property and inheritance, was much more so.
Women's function was very practical as well as symbolic.

Depending on social status, the "provider" aspect of manhood might
not weigh as heavily on a young man growing up in the late Middle Ages
as on one today. For knights this may well have been a real concern, but it
does not emerge prominently in the literature: the pecuniary needs of the
chivalrous seem more or less to take care of themselves. Providing for a
family—or affording to have a family to provide for—came much more to
the forefront in the world of the urban craft workers. Monks, of course,
had no families to provide for, and university students, who might well
end up in the church, do not seem to have concerned themselves very
much about potential families.

In general, material success was less central to medieval masculinities
than to contemporary ones. Some groups, like monks, rejected worldly

measures of achievement. University careers could certainly lead to political power, renown, and a comfortable life, but not to fabulous wealth. Men of the crafts might not become wealthy urban magnates—in most towns merchants rather than artisans more commonly attained that status—but they too could aspire to a comfortable life as the owner of a substantial workshop.

Knights could aspire to more. Not only younger sons who distinguished themselves through military prowess could move up in society; less admired methods, like mercenary service, also enabled men to rise. The English knight John Fastolfe, for example, enriched himself during the Hundred Years War through the taking of ransoms and through payments from the crown to raise mercenary bands.[22] One could not begin with nothing and become a knight, because armor and horses were not cheap. Once equipped with these, however, it was possible to accumulate wealth through tournaments and the ransoming of captives. A boy looking at what it meant to become a man could see the opportunity for both prowess and material success.

Wealth, however, did not measure knightly manhood. It was a by-product of prowess rather than a yardstick. Both romances and chronicles speak of glory rather than wealth; how many jousts or battles a knight had won played a more important part than the riches he acquired. Descriptions in medieval texts of rich garments and caparisons make it clear enough that money was an important part of what it took, and stories of knights marrying widows, although presented in terms of love and romance, reveal another way of gaining wealth, yet as in the other areas of medieval society, wealth was not the most important goal. It was one means of measuring achievement, but not as prominent a means as in other cultures.

Medieval masculinities also took a distinctive form with respect to fatherhood. Lineage, especially patrilineage, was crucial in many medieval contexts. In an era when women had few opportunities other than marriage, and where dowry costs could be onerous, fathering daughters would not seem much of an advantage. Aristocrats wanted sons to pass on their lands: most regions allowed some sort of inheritance by women, but only in default of male heirs. Craftsmen might pass their workshop on to a daughter and her husband, but only if no sons were available. Sons, however, could inherit land, workshop, and to some extent even position. Any boy growing into a man would expect to become a father, unless he went into the clergy, and would hope to father sons. Fathering children became particularly important after the Black Death when people worried about declining population.[23] Changes in the cult of St. Joseph in the later Middle Ages also reflect the great value put on fatherhood.[24]

Reproduction of the population was crucial to the medieval economy, but also to the way people understood gender and sexuality. The sexual economy of the Middle Ages was not predicated on a heterosexual/homosexual binary, but rather on a binary of reproductive/nonreproductive.[25] The church condemned any nonreproductive sex, whether heterosexual or homosexual. Fathering children did not require one to be "a heterosexual." Many men married and nevertheless engaged in sexual relationships with men. Many young men were passive partners in relationships with older men, but still grew up to marry and father children.[26] As long as they reproduced they fulfilled their obligation.

Fatherhood meant more than participating in the conception of a child, since the father also gave the child a name and a social identity. Medieval fatherhood, however, did not mean participating continuously in the upbringing of a child. Mothers and servants commonly took the leading role in childrearing. Even sons who followed in their fathers' footsteps, as knights or as craftsmen, usually trained in a household other than their fathers'. It is hard to know what role paternal love played in fatherhood, because the extant sources (wills, apprenticeship contracts, and so forth) tend to show fathers mainly concerned with getting their children established in life. Fathers did grieve when their children died.[27] But father/son companionship or bonding is not a prominent theme in literary sources. Fathers may be proud of their sons, but do not play a major role in their formation. It was the fact of patrilineal reproduction, rather than the relationship with a son, that contributed to medieval manhood.

The European Middle Ages were characterized by complex lines of dependence and interdependence that meant that standing on one's own—the "sturdy oak" model—could not play the same role in medieval masculinities as in other societies. Total independence is a myth in most cultures, but it was a less important myth in the Middle Ages than in many others. Many university scholars either remained scholars all their lives—which often required them to be members of a religious order, and therefore under vows of obedience and members of a community—or went into the service of a bishop or lord, in a position of dependence, albeit often a powerful one. Knights, even the greatest ones, were dependent on their lord. Craft workers perpetuated the idea of independence, but masters were tightly bound together in guilds by bonds of brotherhood and by regulations; in addition, in many areas the craftsmen were not producing directly for the market but were at the mercy of a large entrepreneur. In this society independence was not as significant an attribute of masculinity as in others.

In young men of the western European Middle Ages we may recognize young men of our own time; certainly many features of medieval masculinities are similar to those of today, in particular the desire to dominate other men and the use of real or metaphorical violence, but they operated quite differently. The privileges, and the burdens that went with them, that a man assumed as he grew up in the later Middle Ages were particular to the time. Medieval society formed men in a variety of ways, and formed a variety of men, always in competition with each other. For a boy to become a man meant testing and proving himself, not only as he came of age but throughout his lifetime.

Notes

Chapter 1

1. James A. Doyle, *The Male Experience*, 2nd ed. (Dubuque, Ia., 1989), 28.

2. Nigel Edley and Margaret Wetherell, *Men in Perspective: Practice, Power, and Identity* (London, 1995), 136–38, citing with approval Paul Hoch, *White Hero, Black Beast: Racism, Sexism, and the Mask of Masculinity* (London, 1979).

3. Sharon Farmer and Carol Braun Pasternack, eds., *Difference and Genders in the Middle Ages* (Minneapolis, forthcoming).

4. This confusion between two senses of "man" or "men" is less in medieval writing, much of which is in Latin, than it is in modern English. Latin has two words which we translate as "man": *homo*, which means "human being" (and from which "homosexual" is *not* derived), and *vir*, which means "adult male human being."

5. Claire Lees with Thelma Fenster and Jo Ann McNamara, eds., *Medieval Masculinities: Regarding Men in the Middle Ages* (Minneapolis, 1994).

6. Some would argue that the male body is not in fact as stable as I suggest here, that my understanding of it as constant is itself a cultural construct. This does not need to be decided here; for purposes of this book we can remain agnostic about the essential nature of biological sex. The key point is that whatever sex may be, gender at least is socially and culturally constructed.

7. This paradigm was seriously challenged by Joseph H. Pleck, *The Myth of Masculinity* (Cambridge, Mass., 1981). For a critique of Pleck's proposed alternative, "sex role strain," as well as the Sex Role Identity paradigm, see R. W. Connell, *Masculinities* (Berkeley, 1995), 22–27; Tim Carrigan, Bob Connell, and John Lee, "Hard and Heavy: Toward a New Sociology of Masculinity," in *Beyond Patriarchy: Essays by Men on Pleasure, Power, and Change*, ed. Michael Kaufman (New York, 1987), 165.

8. Elizabeth Badinter, *XY: On Masculine Identity*, trans. Lydia Davis (New York, 1995), 67–68.

9. Pleck, 129, critiques studies that have shown that masculine initiation rites are more common in societies where male children sleep in their mothers' houses, but fathers do not.

10. The crucial text here is Robert Bly, *Iron John: A Book About Men* (Reading, Mass., 1990). A less archetype-based text, also central to the movement, is Sam Keen, *Fire in the Belly* (New York, 1991).

11. For discussion of flaws in studies of innate difference in behavior between men and women, see Anne Fausto-Sterling, *Myths of Gender: Biological*

Theories about Women and Men (New York, 1985); for psychological differences, Cynthia Fuchs Epstein, *Deceptive Distinctions: Sex, Gender, and the Social Order* (New Haven, Conn., 1988). The literature on primate studies is huge; for a view of the relation between aggression and sexuality among chimpanzees and bonobos in the context of medieval and Renaissance studies, see Frans B. M. de Waal, "The Relation Between Power and Sex in the Simians: Socio-Sexual Appeasement Gestures," in *Gender Rhetorics: Postures of Dominance and Submission in History*, ed. Richard C. Trexler (Binghamton, N.Y., 1994), 15–32.

12. Robert Brannon, "The Male Sex Role: Our Culture's Blueprint of Manhood, and What It's Done for Us Lately," in *The Forty-Nine Percent Majority: The Male Sex Role*, ed. Deborah S. David and Robert Brannon (Reading, Mass., 1976), 12.

13. Michael Kimmel, *Manhood in America: A Cultural History* (New York, 1996), 9 and passim.

14. E. Anthony Rotundo, *American Manhood: Transformations in Masculinity from the Revolution to the Modern Era* (New York, 1993), passim.

15. Elliot J. Gorn, *The Manly Art: Bare-Knuckle Prize Fighting in America* (Ithaca, N.Y., 1986), 141.

16. See Tim Carrigan, Bob Connell, and John Lee, "Toward a New Sociology of Masculinity," in *The Making of Masculinities: The New Men's Studies*, ed. Harry Brod (Boston, 1987), 91, for some examples of subordinated masculinities; see also Andrea Cornwall and Nancy Lindisfarne, "Dislocating Masculinity: Gender, Power, and Anthropology," in *Dislocating Masculinity: Comparative Ethnographies*, ed. Andrea Cornwall and Nancy Lindisfarne (London, 1994), 20.

17. For a critique of the notion of crises of masculinity, see Arthur Brittan, *Masculinity and Power* (Oxford, 1989), 181–85.

18. Badinter, 10–20; Michael S. Kimmel, "The Contemporary 'Crisis' of Masculinity in Historical Perspective," in Brod, 121–53.

19. John MacInnes, *The End of Masculinity* (Buckingham, 1998), 11.

20. Jo Ann McNamara, "The *Herrenfrage*: The Restructuring of the Gender System, 1050–1150," in Lees, 3–12.

21. Michael Kaufman, "Men, Feminism, and Men's Contradictory Experiences of Power," in *Theorizing Masculinities*, ed. Harry Brod and Michael Kaufman (Thousand Oaks, Calif., 1994), 145–46.

22. Barbara Hanawalt, *Growing Up in Medieval London: The Experience of Childhood in History* (New York, 1993), 9–13, discusses the interplay between biology and culture in the understanding of the category "adolescent."

23. Dante Alighieri, *Il Convivio*, 4:24–25, trans. Richard H. Lansing (New York, 1990), 218–28; J. A. Burrow, *The Ages of Man: A Study in Medieval Writing and Thought* (Oxford, 1986), 20–21.

24. Burrow, 23.

25. Burrow, 25–27.

26. Isidore of Seville, *Etymologiarum sive originum libri XX*, 11:2:4–5, ed. W. M. Lindsay, vol. 2, Scriptorum classicorum bibliotheca Oxoniensis (London, 1911) (unpaginated).

27. British Library Additional MS, 37049, from the first half of the fifteenth

century, contains a variety of religious texts, mainly in northern English dialect, as well as an English text of the Book of John Mandeville and extracts from chronicles. It could be either a monastic or a lay devotional collection. *Catalogue of Additions to the Manuscripts in the British Museum in the Years 1900–1905* (London, 1907), 324–32.

28. Burrow, 44–46, 90–92; Madeline Harrison Caviness, *The Early Stained Glass of Canterbury Cathedral circa 1175–1220* (Princeton, N.J., 1977), 127.

29. Hanawalt, 6.

30. Philippe Ariès, *Centuries of Childhood: A Social History of Family Life*, trans. Robert Baldick (New York, 1962), 25.

31. Hanawalt, 108–13.

32. Philippe de Novare says that *jovens* is the most dangerous age for fear of lust, but for him this covers the period that other texts call *adolescentia*. Philippe de Novare, *Les quatre ages de l'homme: Traité moral de Philippe de Navarre*, ed. Marcel de Fréville, Société des anciens textes français (Paris, 1888), 2:33, p. 21.

33. Elizabeth Sears, *The Ages of Man: Medieval Interpretations of the Life Cycle* (Princeton N.J., 1986), 130 and fig. 65.

34. Jean Froissart, *Le joli buisson de jonece*, ed. Anthime Farrier (Geneva, 1975), ll. 1037–1667, pp. 103–4.

35. Frederick J. Furnivall, ed., *Hymns to the Virgin and Christ, The Parliament of Devils, and Other Religious Poems*, Early English Text Society o.s. 24 (London, 1869), 61.

36. British Library Additional MS, 37049, 28v–29r, cited in Burrow 46, 150.

37. Ritchie Girvan, ed., *Ratis Raving and Other Early Scots Poems on Morals*, Scottish Text Society, 3rd ser. 11 (Edinburgh, 1939), ll. 1272–1411, pp. 36–40.

38. James A. Schultz, *The Knowledge of Childhood in the German Middle Ages* (Philadelphia, 1995) 246 and passim; Didier Lett, *L'enfant des miracles: Enfance et société au moyen âge (XIIe–XIIIe siècle)* (Paris, 1997), 198.

39. Lett, 115–37.

40. Fiona Harris Stoertz, *Adolescence in Medieval Culture: The High Medieval Transformation*, Ph.D. dissertation, University of California, Santa Barbara, 1999, has argued that the idea of youth as a stage of life originated in the twelfth century.

41. Mary Dove, *The Perfect Age of Man's Life* (Cambridge, 1986), 15–18.

42. Robert Muchembled, "Die Jugend und die Volkskultur im 15. Jahrhundert: Flandern und Artois," in *Volkskultur des europäischen Spätmittelalters*, ed. Peter Dinzelbacher and Hans-Dieter Mück (Stuttgart, 1987), 35.

43. Michael Mitterauer, *A History of Youth*, trans. Graeme Dunphy (Oxford, 1992), 173.

44. David Herlihy, *Medieval Households* (Cambridge, Mass., 1985), 103–11.

45. Ruth Mazo Karras, "Two Models, Two Standards: Moral Teaching and Sexual Mores," in *Bodies and Disciplines: Intersections of Literature and History in Fifteenth-Century England*, ed. Barbara A. Hanawalt and David Wallace (Minneapolis, 1996), 123–38. But cf. Shannon McSheffrey, "Men and Masculinity in Late Medieval London Civic Culture: Governance, Patriarchy, and Reputation,"

in *Conflicted Identities and Multiple Masculinities: Men in the Medieval West*, ed. Jacqueline Murray (New York, 1999), 257–59.

46. Susan Mosher Stuard, "Burdens of Matrimony: Husbanding and Gender in Medieval Italy," in Lees, 61–63.

47. Although the word "abbot" derives from the Hebrew for "father," and the rhetoric of fatherhood was commonly used for abbot-monk relations, abbots could also be in a motherly position with regard to their monks. Caroline Walker Bynum, *Jesus as Mother: Studies in the Spirituality of the High Middle Ages* (Berkeley, 1982), 110–69, especially 154–59.

48. Connell, *Masculinities*, 186–89.

Chapter 2

1. See discussion in Richard Kaeuper, *War, Justice, and Public Order: England and France in the Later Middle Ages* (Oxford, 1988), 187–88; Richard Kaeuper, *Chivalry and Violence in Medieval Europe* (Oxford, 1999), 47, 143.

2. Pierre Bourdieu, *Masculine Domination*, trans. Richard Nice (Stanford, Calif. 2001), 52.

3. Colin Richmond, *The Paston Family in the Fifteenth Century: Endings* (Manchester, 2000), 147.

4. For a history of the concept, see Joachim Bumke, *The Concept of Knighthood in the Middle Ages*, trans. W. T. H. and Erika Jackson (New York, 1982).

5. Tony Hunt, "The Emergence of the Knight in France and England 1000–1200," in *Knighthood in Medieval Literature*, ed. W. H. Jackson (Woodbridge, Suffolk, 1981), 6–7.

6. For the suggestion that knighthood in Italy was basically moribund at this time, see Elizabeth Crouzet-Pavan, "A Flower of Evil: Young Men in Medieval Italy," in *A History of Young People in the West: Ancient and Medieval Rites of Passage*, ed. Jean-Claude Schmitt and Giovanni Levi, trans. Camille Naish (Cambridge, 1997), 194–96.

7. Michael J. Bennett, *Community, Class, and Careerism: Cheshire and Lancashire Society in the Age of Sir Gawain and the Green Knight* (Cambridge, 1983), 162–91.

8. Frits Pieter van Oostroom, *Court and Culture: Dutch Literature, 1350–1450*, trans. Arnold J. Pomerans (Berkeley, 1992), 159–60.

9. Christine Chism, for example, argues that the alliterative *Morte Arthure* reflects contemporary uneasiness about the court and critiques nostalgia for an era when king and knights had shared goals. Christine Chism, *Alliterative Revivals* (Philadelphia, 2002), 196–208.

10. Beverly Kennedy, *Knighthood in the Morte Darthur* (Rochester, N.Y., 1992), 56–97.

11. Thomas Malory, *The Works of Sir Thomas Malory*, 10:56, ed. Eugène Vinaver, rev. P. J. C. Field, 3rd ed. (Oxford, 1990), 1:108-9; Kennedy, 66-67.

12. Sheila Fisher, "Taken Men and Token Women in *Sir Gawain and the Green Knight*," in *Seeking the Woman in Late Medieval and Renaissance Writings*, ed. Sheila Fisher and Janet E. Halley (Knoxville, 1989), 81–105, uses *Sir Gawain and the Green Knight* as a good example of how literature presents women's apparent dominance only to undermine it.

13. For a good summary of current scholarship on knighthood, including its relation to courtly love, in the high Middle Ages, see Constance Brittain Bouchard, *Strong of Body, Brave and Noble: Chivalry and Society in Medieval France* (Ithaca, N.Y., 1998), 103–44. On troubadour poetry specifically, see Sarah Kay, *Subjectivity in Troubadour Poetry* (Cambridge, 1990), who suggests that the lady in the poems becomes a third gender combining "male feudal images alongside evocations of female sexual attributes" (86).

14. See Oostroom, 275, however, on the lack of popularity of Arthurian literature in Holland, which he attributes to the rise of an administrative nobility who did not identify with it.

15. Maurice Keen, *Chivalry* (New Haven, Conn., 1984), 6–17, for discussion; Kaeuper, *Chivalry and Violence*, 275–97.

16. Michel Stanesco, *Jeux d'errance du chevalier médiéval: Aspects ludiques de la fonction guerrière dans la littérature du moyen âge flamboyant* (New York, 1988), 19–20; Elspeth Kennedy, "The Knight as Reader of Arthurian Romance," in *Culture and the King: The Social Implications of the Arthurian Legend, Essays in Honor of Valerie M. Lagorio*, ed. Martin B. Shichtman and James P. Carley (Albany, 1994). Some of these nonfiction texts are earlier, but heavily read in the later Middle Ages.

17. On Edward III, see Hugh E. L. Collins, *The Order of the Garter 1348–1461: Chivalry and Politics in Late Medieval England* (Oxford, 2000), 8. The later medieval understanding of chivalry drew not only on Arthurian but also on classical models. Especially Italy, but also England, France, Germany, and Burgundy were influenced by Renaissance humanism and its admiration for a pre-Christian ancient chivalry (which, as they depicted it, looked much like the medieval chivalric ethos). The translations of Vegetius were an example of this. It was not only the Renaissance, however, which brought classical models to the fore. Alexander the Great was a chivalric hero all through the Middle Ages. From the fourteenth century the Nine Worthies who served as examples of chivalrous prowess included Joshua, David, and Judah Maccabee from the Old Testament; Hector, Alexander, Julius Caesar from pagan times; and Arthur, Charlemagne, and Godfrey de Bouillon from the Christian era. See Keen, *Chivalry*, 102–24.

18. Stanesco, 94–96; Keen, *Chivalry*, 92.

19. For example, a text entitled "The form that was kept for tournaments and assemblies in the time of King Uther Pendragon and King Arthur," probably by Jacques d'Armagnac for Gaston de Foix (d. 1470), gave 150 paintings of shields of Round Table knights. Edouard Sandoz, "Tourneys in the Arthurian Tradition," *Speculum* 19 (1944): 389–420.

20. Olivier de la Marche, *Mémoires d'Olivier de la Marche*, 4 vols., ed. Henri Beaune and J. d'Arbaumont, Société de l'histoire de France, 71 (Paris, 1883), 3:123.

See also Stanesco, 123–32; Armand Strubel, "Les pas d'armes: Le tournoi entre le romanesque et le théatral," in *Théâtre et spectacles hier et aujourd'hui*, ed. Congrès national des sociétés savantes (Paris, 1991), 273–84.

21. *The Household of Edward IV: The Black Book and the Ordinance of 1478*, ed. A. R. Myers (Manchester, 1959), 129.

22. Not only the court but also the towns of Burgundy were active patrons of chivalric pageantry. Juliet Vale, *Edward III and Chivalry: Chivalric Society and Its Context, 1270–1350* (Woodbridge, Suffolk, 1982), 32–40, discusses civic festivals and jousts in the Burgundian Netherlands in the thirteenth and early fourteenth centuries. See also Thomas Zotz, "Die Stadtgesellschaft und ihre Feste," in *Feste und Feiern im Mittelalter: Paderborner Symposion des Mediävistenverbandes*, eds. Detlef Altenberg, Jörg Jarnut, and Hans-Hugo Steinhoff (Sigmaringen, 1991), 201–13; David Nicholas, "In the Pit of the Burgundian Theater State: Urban Traditions and Princely Ambitions in Ghent, 1360–1420," in *City and Spectacle in Medieval Europe*, ed. Barbara Hanawalt and Kathryn Reyerson (Minneapolis, 1994), 273. For towns elsewhere, see Sheila Lindenbaum, "The Smithfield Tournament of 1390," *Journal of Medieval and Renaissance Studies* 20 (1990): 1–20; Thomas Zotz, "Adel, Bürgertum und Turnier in deutschen Städten vom 13. bis 15. Jahrhundert," in *Das ritterliche Turnier im Mittelallter: Beiträge zu einer vergleichenden Formen- und Verhaltensgeschichte des Rittertums*, ed. Josef Fleckenstein, Veröffentlichungen des Max-Planck-Instituts für Geschichte (Göttingen, 1985), 451–99; Gerard Nijsten, "The Duke and His Towns: The Power of Ceremonies, Feasts, and Public Amusement in the Duchy of Guelders (East Netherlands) in the Fourteenth and Fifteenth Centuries," in Hanawalt and Reyerson, 241; Cecil H. Clough, "Chivalry and Magnificence in the Golden Age of the Italian Renaissance," in *Chivalry in the Renaissance*, ed. Sydney Anglo (Rochester, N.Y., 1990), 32–47.

23. Johan Huizinga, *Men and Ideas: History, the Middle Ages, and the Rensaissance*, trans. James S. Holmes and Hans van Marle (Princton, N.J., 1984), 197.

24. Arthur B. Ferguson, *The Indian Summer of English Chivalry: Studies in the Decline and Transformation of Chivalric Idealism* (Durham, N.C., 1960), 32.

25. Malcolm Vale, *War and Chivalry: Warfare and Aristocratic Culture in England, France, and Burgundy at the End of the Middle Ages* (London, 1981), 1–12 and passim; Keen, *Chivalry*, 219–37.

26. Collins, 153, 234, 284.

27. Larry Benson, *Malory's Morte Darthur* (Cambridge, Mass., 1976), 143.

28. For these women rulers, see Wim Blockmans and Walter Prevenier, *The Promised Lands: The Low Countries Under Burgundian Rule, 1369–1530*, trans. Elizabeth Fackelman, ed. Edward Peters (Philadelphia, 1999).

29. Huizinga, 200.

30. Philippe Contamine, *War in the Middle Ages*, trans. Michael Jones (Cambridge, 1984), 136.

31. Vale, *War and Chivalry*, 101–3.

32. Maurice Keen and Juliet Barker, "The Medieval English Kings and the Tournament," in Maurice Keen, *Nobles, Knights and Men-at-Arms in the Middle Ages* (London, 1996), 93.

33. Alfred T. P. Byles, ed., *The Book of the Ordre of Chyvalry, Translated and Printed by William Caxton from a French Verson of Ramón Lull's "Le libre del ordre de Cauayleria,"* Early English Text Society o.s. 168 (London, 1926), 21.

34. C. M. Woolgar, *The Great Household in Medieval England* (New Haven, Conn. 1999), 34.

35. Madeleine Pelner Cosman, *The Education of the Hero in Arthurian Romance* (Chapel Hill, N.C., 1965), discusses this theme in literary texts.

36. Antoine de la Sale, *Le petit Jehan de Saintré,* ed. Pierre Champion and Fernand Desonay (Paris, 1926), 11–12.

37. Nicholas Orme, "The Education of the Courtier," in *English Court Culture in the Later Middle Ages,* ed. V. J. Scattergood and J. W. Sherborne (London, 1983), 74, 82.

38. Nicholas Orme, *From Childhood to Chivalry: The Education of the English Kings and Aristrocracy 1066–1530* (London, 1984), 133–41, 181–210.

39. Georges Chastellain, "Le livre des faits du bon chevalier Messire Jacques de Lalaing," in *Oeuvres de Georges Chastellain,* ed. Kervyn de Lettenhove (Brussels, 1866), 11.

40. La Marche, 2:203.

41. La Marche, 2:143.

42. Chastellain, ch. 48, 188.

43. Chastellain, 189–97, 201–37.

44. Chastellain, 252ff.

45. Keen, *Chivalry,* 18–19, from an unpublished MS, BN MS Fr 12559.

46. Guttiere Díaz de Games, *El Victorial,* ed. Rafael Beltrán Lavador (Salamanca, 1997), ch. 30, 354.

47. Díaz de Games, ch 37, 375.

48. Díaz de Games, ch. 33–34, 369–678; ch. 83, 585; ch. 86, 593; ch. 92, 676–79.

49. La Marche, 2:124; Chastellain, ch. 48, 189.

50. Josef Fleckenstein, *Ordnungen und formende Kräfte des Mittelalters: Ausgewählte Beiträge* (Göttingen, 1989), 373–74.

51. Keen, *Chivalry,* 163–66

52. Jean Froissart, *Les chroniques de Sire Jean Froissart,* ed. J.-A.-C. Buchon (Paris, 1837), 3:19, vol. 2, p. 428.

53. James F. Powers, *A Society Organized for War: The Iberian Municipal Militias in the Central Middle Ages, 1000–1284* (Berkeley, 1988), 101, discusses *peóns* becoming *caballeros* in the central Middle Ages.

54. Wim Blockmans and Esther Donckers, "Self-Representation of Court and City in Flanders and Brabant in the Fifteenth and Early Sixteenth Centuries," in *Showing Status: Representation of Social Positions in the Late Middle Ages,* ed. Wim Blockmans and Antheun Janse (Turnhout, 1999), 85; Werner Paravicini, "Soziale Schichtung und soziale Mobilität am Hof der Herzöge von Burgund," *Francia* 5 (1977), 138, 148.

55. Antheun Janse, "Marriage and Noble Lifestyle in Holland in the Later Middle Ages," in Blockmans and Janse; Philip of Leyden, *De cura reipublicae et sorte principantis,* cas. 3:20, ed. R. Fruin and P. C. Molhuijsen (The Hague, 1900), 267; P. Leupen, *Philip of Leyden: A 14th-Century Jurist* (The Hague, 1981), 83.

56. La Marche, 1:114. Arthur was conceived, so the story goes, before Uther's and Ygraine's marriage, indeed during her marriage to her first husband. Because his parents later married, however, he would have been legitimate under canon law.

57. Malory, 3:3, vol. 1:99–107.

58. Malory, 2:1, vol. 1:62.

59. Malory, 7:5, vol. 1:299.

60. Malory, 2:16, vol. 1:87.

61. For a history of this process in England, see Anthony Richard Wagner, *Heralds and Heraldry in the Middle Ages: An Inquiry into the Growth of the Armorial Function of Heralds* (London, 1956).

62. Peter Coss, *The Knight in Medieval England 1000–1400* (Stroud, Gloucestershire, 1993), 88; for documents, see N. Harris Nicolas, ed., *The Controversy between Sir Richard Scrope and Sir Robert Grosvenor in the Court of Chivalry, A.D. MCCCLXXXV–MCCCXC*, 2 vols. (London, 1832).

63. Chrétien de Troyes, *Le roman de Perceval ou Le Conte du Graal*, ed. Keith Busby (Tübingen, 1993), 5–26.

64. Geoffroi de Charny, *The Book of Chivalry of Geoffroi de Charny: Text, Context, and Translation*, ed. Richard W. Kaeuper, trans. Elspeth Kennedy (Philadelphia, 1996), 101.

65. *Book of the Ordre of Chyvalry*, 15, 55.

66. Díaz de Games, ch. 8, p. 275, ch. 9, p. 287.

67. Keen, "Some Late Medieval Ideas About Nobility," in *Nobles*, 187–207.

68. John Gough Nichols, ed., *The Boke of Noblesse Addressed to King Edward the Fourth on His Invasion of France in 1475* (London, 1860), 76; Alfred T. P. Byles, ed., *The Book of Fayttes of Armes and of Chyvalrye, Translated and Printed by William Caxton from the French Original by Christine de Pisan*, Early English Text Society o.s. 189 (London, 1937), 29–33.

69. *Knyghthode and Bataile*, st. 23, 10.

70. Malory, 8:1, vol. 1:372.

71. Malory, 9:1, vol. 2:459.

72. Díaz de Games, ch. 23, 334.

73. Charny, *Book of Chivalry*, 33; Kaeuper, *Chivalry and Violence*, 135.

74. See, e.g., Froissart's description of the tournament at London in 1390, 4:16, vol. 3:94ff.; on the other hand, e.g., *Livre de faits de Jacques de Lalaing*, 55–61. On Malory, see Andrew Lynch, *Malory's Book of Arms: The Narrative of Combat in* Le Morte Darthur (Cambridge, 1997), 49–52.

75. Malory, 12:12, vol. 2:841.

76. Malory, 3:15, vol. 1:120.

77. Froissart, 1:1:87, vol. 1:79; Kaeuper, *Chivalry and Violence*, 185.

78. Denis Lalande, ed., *Le livre des fais du bon messire Jehan le Maingre, dit Bouciquaut, Mareschal de France et Gouverneur de Jennes* (Geneva, 1985), 164.

79. *Book of Fayttes and Armes*, 224; Keen, "War, Peace, and Chivalry," in *Nobles*, 9, 17.

80. Andrew Taylor, "Chivalric Conversation and the Denial of Male Fear," in Murray, *Conflicted Identities*, 169–88.

81. *Boke of Noblesse,* 64–65.

82. This issue arose also for Japanese samurai and their commanders: Eiko Ikegami, *The Taming of the Samurai* (Cambridge, Mass., 1995), 99.

83. Chandos Herald, *The Black Prince: An Historical Poem,* trans. Henry Octavius Coxe (London, 1842), 84–85, ll. 2737–40, 2754–56; translation at p. 158.

84. Valerie Krishna, ed., *The Alliterative Morte Arthure: A Critical Edition* (New York, 1976), 92–93, ll. 1922–37; Valerie Krishna, trans., *The Alliterative Morte Arthure: A New Verse Translation* (Washington, D.C., 1983), 50–51.

85. Froissart, 1:2:243, vol. 1:545.

86. Richard Barber, "Chivalry and the Morte Darthur," in *A Companion to Malory,* ed. Elizabeth Archibald and A. S. G. Edwards (Cambridge, 1996), 23.

87. Gilbert de Lannoy, "L'Instruction d'un jeune prince," in *Oeuvres de Ghilebert de Lannoy,* ed. Ch. Potvin (Louvain, 1878), 415; *Book of the Ordre of Chyvalry,* 76.

88. Charny, *Book of Chivalry,* 169.

89. *Book of the Ordre of Chyvalry,* 24.

90. Jean de Bueil, *Le jouvencel par Jean de Bueil,* ed. Camille Favre, 2 vols. (Paris, 1887), 2:21.

91. Malory, 3:2, vol. 1:98.

92. Malory, 13:8, vol. 2:869.

93. Chastellain, 15–25 (quote at 15).

94. La Marche, 2:381–94; G. du Fresne de Beaucourt, ed., *Chronique de Mathieu d'Escouchy* (Paris, 1863), 2:165–222.

95. C. Stephen Jaeger, *The Origins of Courtliness: Civilizing Trends and the Formation of Courtly Ideals 939–1210* (Philadelphia, 1985), passim, has convincingly argued that "courtly" manners had their origin not in knighthood but among clerical statesmen at the court (although he notes, 268, that women may have helped reinforce these ideals).

96. Elizabeth B. Keiser, *Courtly Desire and Medieval Homophobia: The Legitimation of Sexual Pleasure in* Cleanness *and Its Contexts* (New Haven, Conn., 1997), esp. 134–64.

97. Frederick J. Furnivall, ed., *Caxton's Book of Curtesye,* Early English Text Society, Extra Series 3 (London, 1868), 21. Anna Dronzek, *Manners, Models, and Morals: Gender, Status, and Codes of Conduct Among the Middle Classes of Late Medieval England* (Ph.D. dissertation, University of Minnesota, 2001), 113–23, argues that such books were copied (and printed) for and read by primarily the middle classes, but the behavior they describe is clearly arisocratic, even if others did try to emulate it.

98. *Caxton's Book of Curtesye,* 13.

99. Froissart, 1:1:76. vol. 1:68.

100. La Marche, 2:340–80.

101. Charny, *Book of Chivalry,* 29–30.

102. Ruth Harvey, *Moriz von Craûn and the Chivalric World* (Oxford, 1961), 78.

103. E. Jane Burns, *Courtly Love Undressed: Reading Through Clothes in Medieval French Culture* (Philadelphia, 2002).

104. Keiser, 142–43.

105. H. Gérard, ed., *Chronique latine de Guillaume de Nangis de 1113 à 1300 avec les continuations de cette chronique de 1300 à 1368* (Paris, 1843), 2:185, 2:237–38.

106. Charny, *Book of Chivalry,* 193, 189, 191.

107. *Livre des fais de Bouciquaut,* 392, 414.

108. E.g., La Marche, 1:309–10; de la Sale, 81–85.

109. Malory, 8:3, vol. 1:375.

110. S. L. Lee, ed. *The Boke of Huon of Burdeux,* trans. John Bourchier, vol. 1 of 3, Early English Text Society, Extra Series 40–41 (London, 1888), p. 578.

111. Chastellain, 83.

112. Froissart, 1:1:308, vol. 1:256; 1:2:3, vol. 1:288.

113. Charny, *Book of Chivalry,* 113.

114. *The Black Prince,* p. 45, ll. 1510–15, translation, 147–48.

115. René of Anjou, *Le livre des tournois du roi René,* ed. François Avril (Paris, 1986), unpaginated [fols. 76v–77, 97v–98, 100v–101].

116. Díaz de Games, ch. 92, 675.

117. E. F. Kossman, ed. *Die Haager Liederhandschrift* (The Hague, 1940), no. 66, pp. 81–82, trans. in Oostroom, 93–94.

118. Louis Olga Fradenburg, *City, Marriage, Tournament: Arts of Rule in Late Medieval Scotland* (Madison, 1991), 212.

119. See Eric Bousmar, "La place des hommes et des femmes dans les fêtes de cour bourguignonnes (Philippe le Bon-Charles le Hardi)," *Publications du Centre européen d'études bourguignonnes (xivᵉ–xviᵉ s.)* 34 (1994), 123–43.

120. *Livre des tournois,* no pagination [fol. 62v].

121. E.g., Gail Orgelfinger, ed., *The Hystorye of Olyuer of Castylle,* trans. Henry Watson (New York, 1988), 23.

122. *Livre des tournois,* no pagination [fol. 103v]; Helmut Nickel, "The Tournament: An Historical Sketch," in *The Study of Chivalry: Resources and Approaches,* ed. Howell Chickering and Thomas H. Seiler (Kalamazoo, Mich., 1988), 238.

123. *Christine de Pisan's Letter of Othea to Hector,* trans. Jane Chance (Newburyport, Mass., 1990), 75, p. 100.

124. Froissart, 1:1:63, vol. 1:58; cf. also 1:1:69, vol. 1:71.

125. Helen Solterer, "Figures of Female Militancy in Medieval France," *Signs: Journal of Women in Culture and Society* 16 (1991): 532–33, 544–45; Pierre Gencier, "Tournoiement as Dames de Paris," in *Lude e Spettacoli nel Medioevo: I tornei de Dame,* ed. Andrea Pulega (Milan, 1970), 21–63.

126. Solterer, 527.

127. Malory, 2:693. This is Malory's abbreviation of a much longer conversation about love found in the thirteenth-century *Prose Tristan*; see Vinaver's note in Malory, 3:1511–13.

128. J. R. R. Tolkien and E. V. Gordon, eds., *Sir Gawain and the Green Knight,* 2d. ed., rev. Norman Davis (Oxford, 1967), p. 36, ll. 1297–1300.

129. Malory, 10:55, vol. 2:689.

130. La Sale, 20–21.

131. Chastellain, 18, 22–23.

132. Patricia Clare Ingham, *Sovereign Fantasies: Arthurian Romance and the Making of Britain* (Philadelphia, 2001), 153.

133. See R. Howard Bloch, *Medieval Misogyny and the Invention of Western Romantic Love* (Chicago, 1991), 194–97, on "the dialectical relation of the secular denigration and idealization of the feminine."

134. Oostroom, 87, 82.

135. Ikegami, 209–10; Gregory M. Pflugfelder, *Cartographies of Desire: Male-Male Sexuality in Japanese Discourse, 1600–1950* (Berkeley, 1999), 79–73. I am grateful to Luke Roberts for calling this aspect of Japanese culture to my attention.

136. C. Stephen Jaeger, *Ennobling Love: In Search of a Lost Sensibility* (Philadelphia, 1999), argues that it began as an idea of same-sex love.

137. Charny, *Book of Chivalry*, 115.

138. Brussels, KB, MS 1124–26, fols. 80r–81r.

139. Roger Dahood, ed., *The Avowing of Arthur* (New York, 1984), 60–69. The statement that the battle is for the woman's sake is repeated at ll. 295, 318, 362, 502, and 543.

140. Benson, *Malory*, 161–62; Larry D. Benson, "Courtly Love and Chivalry in the Later Middle Ages," in *Fifteenth-Century Studies*, ed. Robert F. Yaeger (Hamden, Conn., 1984), 242–45, 249–51.

141. Stanesco, 103–4; Froissart, 1:1:165–66, vol. 1:145–46; also 1:1:191, vol. 1:164.

142. James Orchard Halliwell, ed., *Palatine Anthology: A Collection of Ancient Poems and Ballads Relating to Lancashire and Cheshire* (London, 1850), 218–21.

143. Keen, "Chivalry and Courtly Love," in *Nobles*, 21–47.

144. Froissart, 1:2:91, vol. 1:401.

145. La Sale, 29.

146. Halliwell, 219.

147. Fleckenstein, *Ordnungen*, 410.

148. *Livre des fais de Bouciquaut*, 27–40.

149. Froissart, 3:99, vol. 2:667.

150. Ingham, *Sovereign Fantasies*, 147–48, makes this point with regard to English literature of the Hundred Years War.

151. Jean-Pierre Jourdan, "Le langage amoureux dans le combat de chevalerie à la fin du moyen âge (France, Bourgogne, Anjou)," *Le moyen âge* 99 (1993): 84–106.

152. La Marche, 2:97; Chastellain, 97, 240.

153. Chastellain, 81, 103–85; Benson, *Malory*, 170–72; "Tournament Between Lord Scales and the Bastard of Burgundy," in *Excerpta historica*, ed. Samuel Bentley (London, 1833), 177–212.

154. Benson, "Courtly Love and Chivalry," 250.

155. For an argument that Andreas's view was never influential, see Henry Ansgar Kelly, *Love and Marriage in the Age of Chaucer* (Ithaca, N.Y., 1975).

156. Chastellain, 30, 105.

157. *Livre des fais de Bouciquaut*, 28.

158. *The Black Prince*, 48, ll. 1587, 1589; translation, p. 148.

159. Christiane Marchello-Nizia, "Amour courtois, société masculine et figures du pouvoir," *Annales E.S.C.* 36 (1981): 979–80.

160. Malcolm G. A. Vale, "Warfare and the Life of the French and Burgundian Nobility in the Late Middle Ages," in *Adelige Sachkultur des Spätmittelalters: internationaler Kongress*, Veröffentlichungen des Instituts für mittelalterliche Realienkunde Österreichs (Vienna, 1982), 178–80; Philippe Contamine, *La noblesse au royaume de France de Philippe le Bel à Louis XII* (Paris, 1997), 281–82.

161. *Book of Fayttes of Armes*, 199–206; Charny, *Book of Chivalry*, 93.

162. See discussion in Keen, *Chivalry*, 228–31.

163. Charny, *Book of Chivalry*, 113.

164. Froissart, 1:2:241, vol. 1:542–43.

165. *Le Jouvencel*, 1:27.

166. Gilbert de Lannoy, 467; Chastellain, 19.

167. Cf. Fradenburg, 223.

168. James L. Gillespie, "Richard II's Knights: Chivalry and Patronage," *Journal of Medieval History* 13 (1987): 143—59.

169. Christine de Pizan, *The Book of the Body Politic*, trans. Kate Langdon Forhan (Cambridge, 1994), 17.

170. I have not used the term "feudalism" because it brings all kinds of controversy with it and does not seem to add anything to this discussion. It is worth noting, however, that although Susan Reynolds, *Fiefs and Vassals: The Medieval Evidence Reinterpreted* (Oxford, 1994), goes to great lengths to demonstrate that the academic and practical "feudal" law did not originate in ancient Germanic custom and was a creation of late twelfth-century lawyers, she by no means denies its existence or importance in the fourteenth and fifteenth centuries (although she dates the ideology of vassalage to the sicteenth century rather than the late Middle Ages: pp. 3–10).

171. E.g., Michael T. Reynolds, "René of Anjou, King of Sicily, and the Order of the *Croissant*," *Journal of Medieval History* 19 (1993): 125–61; Vale, *War and Chivalry*, 35; D'Arcy Jonathan Dacre Boulton, *The Knights of the Crown: The Monarchical Orders of Knighthood in Later Medieval Europe* (New York, 1987).

172. Boulton, 373; see also p. 252.

173. Keen, *Chivalry*, 188–90.

174. William H. Jackson, "The Tournament and Chivalry in German Tournament Books of the Sixteenth Century and in the Literary Works of Emperor Maximilian I," in *The Ideals and Practice of Medieval Knighthood*, ed. Christopher Harper-Bill and Ruth Harvey (Woodbridge, Suffolk, 1986), 56; Jackson, "Tournaments and the German Chivalric *Renovatio*: Tournament Discipline and the Myth of Origins," in Anglo, 84; Werner Meyer, "Turniergesellschaften. Bermerkungen zur sozialgeschichtlichen Bedeutung der Turniere im Spätmittelalter," in Fleckenstein, *Das ritterliche Turnier*, 500–512.

175. Malory, 7:35, vol. 1:360.

176. E.g., Chastellain, ch. 36, 141.

177. *Livre des fais de Bouciquaut*, 87.

178. *Livre des fais de Bouciquaut*, 76.

179. Froissart, 1:1:134, vol. 1:116.

180. *Le jouvencel*, 2:20–21.

181. Pierre Chaplais, *Piers Gaveston: Edward II's Adoptive Brother* (Oxford, 1994), 6–22; see also Keen, "Brotherhood in Arms," in *Nobles*, 43–52.

182. Siegrid Düll, Anthony Luttrell, and Maurice Keen, "Faithful unto Death: The Tomb Slab of Sir William Neville and Sir John Clanvowe, Constantinople 1391," *Antiquaries Journal* 71 (1991): 174–90 (quotation at 185).

183. Elizabeth A. R. Brown and Nancy Freeman Regalado, "*La grant feste*: Philip the Fair's Celebration of the Knighting of His Sons in Paris at Pentecost of 1313," in Hanawalt and Reyerson, 56–86.

184. *Livre des fais de Bouciquaut*, 81.

185. For examples, see Richard Barber and Juliet Barker, *Tournaments: Jousts, Chivalry, and Pageants in the Middle Ages* (New York, 1989), 168; Contamine, 281–83.

186. Stanesco, 66–67.

187. This ritual may owe much to Chrétien de Troyes. See Barbara Sargent-Baur, "Promotion to Knighthood in the Romances of Chrétien de Troyes," *Romance Philology* 37 (1984): 393–408. On the history of dubbing, see Christine Marchello-Nizia, "Courtly Chivalry," in Schmitt and Levi, 131–39.

188. Keen, *Chivalry*, 77–78.

189. Charny, *Book of Chivalry*, 167. Stanesco, 70, suggests it is a symbol of rebirth.

190. *Book of the Ordre of Chyvalry*, 64. Some scholars have also suggested that the immersion in a bath is a symbol of rebirth, akin to baptism. Indeed, the dubbing with the sword has been explained as a symbol of rebirth too, as a knight may be said to be engendered by a sword, cradled in his shield, and so forth. Michel Stanesco, "Chevalerie médiévale et symbolisme guerrier: Le bacheler 'D'Espée engendrez,' " *Littératures* 12 (spring 1985): 7–13.

191. Cf. Stanesco, *Jeux d'errance*, 174.

192. Krishna, 147–48, ll. 3949–92.

193. *Boke of Noblesse*, 77–78.

Chapter 3

1. David Noble, *A World Without Women: The Christian Clerical Culture of Western Science* (New York, 1993), 138–60.

2. Gordon Leff, "The *Trivium* and the Three Philosophies," in *Universities in the Middle Ages*, ed. Hilde de Ridder-Symoens, A History of the University in Europe, 1 (Cambridge, 1992), 308; J. A. Weisheipl, "Curriculum of the Faculty of Arts at Oxford in the Early Fourteenth Century," *Mediaeval Studies* 26 (1964): 143–85.

3. On careers of university students, see Rainer Christoph Schwinges, ed., *Gelehrte im Reich: Zur Sozial- und Wirkungsgeschichte akademischer Eliten des 14. bis 16. Jahrhunderts*, Zeitschrift für historische Forschung, Beiheft 18 (Berlin, 1996).

4. Monika Asztalos, "The Faculty of Theology," in De Ridder-Symoens, 415–16.

5. T. A. R. Evans, "The Number, Origins, and Careers of Scholars," in *The History of the University of Oxford*, vol. 2, ed. J. I. Catto and Ralph Evans (Oxford, 1992), 498.

6. Heinrich Denifle and Emile Chatelain, eds., *Chartularium Universitatis Parisiensis* (Paris, 1889), 1:228, 2:673. The editors question the authenticity or accuracy of the age 14.

7. Owen and Miriam Gingerich, "Matriculation Ages in Sixteenth-Century Wittenberg," *History of Universities* 6 (1986–87): 135–37; John M. Fletcher, "Commentary," *History of Universities* 6 (1986–87): 139–41.

8. Evans, 499–500.

9. Rainer Christoph Schwinges, "Admission," in De Ridder-Symoens, 183; Schwinges, "Student Education, Student Life," in De Ridder-Symoens, 196.

10. Antonio García y García, "The Faculties of Law," in De Ridder-Symoens, 402; Berthe M. Marti, ed., *The Spanish College at Bologna in the Fourteenth Century* (Philadelphia, 1966), 226.

11. Jean Dunbabin, "Meeting the Cost of University Education in Northern France, c. 1240–1340," *History of Universities* 10 (1991): 8–9. On the costs of university study, see A. L. Gabriel, ed., *The Economic and Material Frame of the Medieval University* (Notre Dame, Ind., 1977).

12. Charles Homer Haskins, *Studies in Medieval Culture* (New York, 1965), 7–14.

13. Guy Fitch Lytle, "Patronage Patterns and Oxford Colleges c. 1300–1530," in *The University in Society*, ed. Lawrence Stone, vol. 1 (Princeton, N.J., 1974), 111–49. On the "crisis of patronage" question, see William J. Courtenay, *Schools & Scholars in Fourteenth-Century England* (Princeton, N.J., 1987), 138–40.

14. Dunbabin, 14; Evans, 509; Jacques Pacquet, "Coût des études, pauvreté et labeur: Fonctions et métiers d'étudiants au moyen âge," *History of Universities* 2 (1982): 21–34; Mineo Tanaka, *La nation anglo-allemande de l'Université de Paris à la fin du moyen âge* (Paris, 1990), 79–86.

15. Nicholas Orme, *From Childhood to Chivalry: The Education of the English Kings and Aristocracy 1066–1530* (London, 1984), 66, 71.

16. William J. Courtenay, *Parisian Scholars in the Early Fourteenth Century: A Social Portrait* (Cambridge, 1999), 103.

17. Christoph Fuchs, *Dives, pauper, nobilis, magister, frater, clericus: Sozialgeschichtliche Untersuchungen über Heidelberger Universitätsbesucher des Spätmittelalters (1386–1450)*, Education and Society in the Middle Ages and Renaissance 5 (New York, 1995), 15–17.

18. Rainer Christoph Schwinges, *Deutsche Universitätsbesucher im 14. und 15. Jahrhundert: Studien zur Sozialgeschichte des alten Reiches* (Stuttgart, 1986), 341–465.

19. Dunbabin, 2.

20. Antonio García y García, "The Medieval Students of the University of Salamanca," *History of Universities* 10 (1991): 97, 100. García suggests that the remaining students were drawn from the bourgeoisie, but admits that there is no evidence for this; he does not consider the petty aristocracy. See also Hilde De Ridder-Symoens, "Les origines géographiques et sociales des étudiants de la na-

tion germanique de l'ancien université d'Orléans (1444–1546), Aperçu général," in *The Universities in the Late Middle Ages*, ed. Jozef Ijsewijn and Jacques Pacquet, Medievalia Lovanensia Series 1, Studia 6 (Leuven, 1978), 463.

21. Guy Fitch Lytle, "The Social Origins of Oxford Students in the Late Middle Ages: New College, c. 1380–c.1510," in Ijsewijn and Pacquet, 426–54, esp. 432; Courtenay, *Schools and Scholars*, 13–14. On the south of France, see also Jacques Verger, "L'histoire sociale des universités à la fin du moyen âge: Problèmes, sources, méthodes (à propos des universités du Midi de la France)," in *Die Geschichte der Universitäten und ihre Erforschung*, ed. Siegfried Hoyer and Werner Fläschendräger (Leipzig, 1984), 39–40, who finds the students of the "middling classes," sons of well-off peasant, artisans, merchants, notaries, etc.

22. Rainer Christoph Schwinges, "Studentische Kleingruppen im späten Mittelalter: Ein Beitrag zur sozialgeschichte deutscher Universitäten," in *Politik, Gesellschaft, Geschichtsschreibung: Giessener Festgabe für František Graus zum 60. Geburtstag* (Cologne, 1982), 349; Schwinges, "Student Education, Student Life," 203.

23. Courtenay, *Parisian*, 107–23.

24. Rainer Christoph Schwinges, "Admission," in De Ridder-Symoens, 201.

25. John W. Baldwin, "*Studium et Regnum*: The Penetration of University Personnel into French and English Administration at the Turn of the Twelfth and Thirteenth Centuries," in *L'enseignement en Islam et en occident au moyen âge*, ed. George Makdisi, Dominique Sourdel, and Janine Sourdel-Thomine (Paris, 1977), 199–213.

26. Evans, 532–38; R. N. Swanson, "Learning and Livings: University Study and Clerical Careers in Late Medieval England," *History of Universities* 6 (1987): 95–99.

27. Guy Fitch Lytle, "The Careers of Oxford Students in the Later Middle Ages," in *Rebirth, Reform and Resilience: Universities in Transition 1300–1700*, ed. James M. Kittelson and Pamela J. Transue (Columbus, Ohio, 1984), 217, 229, 247; Peter Moraw, "Careers of Graduates," in De Ridder-Symoens, 244–79; Evans, 519–32; Fuchs, 89–100; Neithard Bulst, "Studium und Karriere im königlichen Dienst in Frankreich im 15. Jahrhundert," in *Schulen und Studium im sozialen Wandel des hohen und späten Mittelalters*, ed. Johannes Fried, Vorträge und Forschungen 30 (Sigmaringen, 1986), 375–405.

28. Evans, 497; Jacques Verger, "Teachers," in De Ridder-Symoens, 147.

29. Rainer Christoph Schwinges, "Sozialgeschichtliche Aspekte spätmittelalterlicher Studentenbursen in Deutschland," in Fried, 530–44. Courtenay, *Parisian*, finds arts students living as *socii* with masters in 1329.

30. A. B. Cobban, "Colleges and Halls 1380–1500," in Catto and Evans, 2:591–92.

31. Gibson Strickland, ed., *Statuta antiqua Universitatis Oxoniensis* (Oxford, 1931), 208–9; Cobban, "Colleges and Halls," 624.

32. Peter Denly, "The Collegiate Movement in Italian Universities in the Late Middle Ages," *History of Universities* 10 (1991): 29–74.

33. Hermann Weissenborn, ed., *Acten der Erfurter Universität* (Halle, 1881), 1:18; Erich Meuthen, "Bursen und Artesfakultät der alten Kölner Universität," in

Philosophy and Learning: Universities in the Middle Ages, ed. J. F. M. Maarten, J. H. Hoenen, Josef Schneider, and Georg Wieland, Education and Society in the Middle Ages and Renaissance 6 (Leiden, 1995), 225–45.

34. Schwinges, "Student Education, Student Life," 218; Cobban, "Colleges and Halls," 624–25.

35. Meuthen, 228.

36. There are a few exceptions. Trota and other midwives may have taught at Salerno in the twelfth century, but certainly there were no women teaching at the university there by the later Middle Ages. See Monica Green, "Women's Medical Practice and Health Care in Medieval Europe," *Signs: Journal of Women in Culture and Society* 14 (1989): 442, for discussion. Novella, the daughter of an eminent jurist, supposedly heard lectures at Bologna from behind a curtain where she would not distract the other students. A possibly apocryphal story from the University of Cracow has a woman enrolling in men's clothing. Michael Shank, "A Female University Student in Late Medieval Kraków," *Signs: Journal of Women in Culture and Society* 12 (1987): 373–80.

37. E.g., for Paris, *Chartularium*, 3:222 (1375), from the medical faculty. See Hastings Rashdall, *The Universities of Europe in the Middle Ages*, ed. F. M. Powicke and A. B. Emden, 2nd ed., 3 vols., (Oxford, 1936), 3:396 and nn. for other examples.

38. Robert Marichal, ed., *Le livre des prieurs de Sorbonne* (Paris, 1987), 272.

39. *Documents Relating to the University and Colleges of Cambridge*, 3 vols. (London, 1852), St. Peter's College, Cambridge, 2:30; King's College, 2:596; J. H. Parker, ed., *Statutes of the Colleges of Oxford*, 3 vols. (Oxford, 1853), vol. 1, Oriel p. 15, All Souls p. 58, vol. 2, Magdalen p. 26.

40. Ruth Mazo Karras, *Common Women: Prostitution and Sexuality in Medieval England* (New York, 1996), 54–55. See also Haskins, *Studies*, 57, 74, on university sermons and handbooks criticizing students' involvement with laundresses.

41. Pseudo-Boethius, *De disciplina scholarium*, ed. Olga Weijers, Studien und Texte zur Geistesgeschichte des Mittelalters (Leiden, 1976), 111.

42. Marcel Fournier, *Les statuts et privilèges des universités françaises depuis leur fondation jusqu'en 1789* (Paris, 1890), 2:490; Marti, 276.

43. Heinrich Denifle and Emile Chatelain, eds., *Liber procuratorum nationis Anglicanae (Alemanniae) in universitate Parisiensi*, vol. 1 of *Auctarium chartularii universitatis Parisiensis* (Paris, 1937), 287; Schwinges, "Student Education, Student Life," 202.

44. Carl I. Hammer, Jr., "The Town-Gown Confraternity of St. Thomas the Martyr in Oxford," *Medieval Studies* 39 (1977): 466–76. See also Schwinges, "Student Education, Student Life," 212, for confraternities in other university towns.

45. *Chartularium*, 1:481.

46. Fournier, 1:22; Jan Pinborg, ed., *Universitas studii Haffnensis: Stiftelsesdokumenter og Stattuter 1479* (Copenhagen, 1979), 117.

47. Marjorie Curry Woods, "Rape and the Pedagogical Rhetoric of Sexual Violence," in *Criticism and Dissent in the Middle Ages*, ed. Rita Copeland (Cambridge, 1996), 56–86.

48. The *Manuale scholarium* is edited in Friedrich Zarncke, *Die deutschen Universitäten im Mittelalter* (Leipzig, 1857), 1–48.

49. Gerhard Ritter, "Über den Quellenwert und Verfasser des sogennanten 'Heidelberger Gesprächbüchleins für Studenten' (Manuale scholarium, um 1490)," *Zeitschrift für die Geschichte des Oberrheins* N.F. 38 (1923): 4–32; Gerhard Streckenbach, "Paulus Niavis, 'Latinum ydeoma pro novellis studentibus'—ein Gesprächsbüchlein aus dem letzten Viertel des 15. Jahrhunderts," *Mittellateinisches Jahrbuch* 6 (1970): 152–91; 7 (1971): 187–251. This is not the place for a full discussion of medieval attitudes toward plagiarism, but it should be noted that it was not at all uncommon for medieval authors to lift large chunks of text from others; authority, rather than originality, was at a premium.

50. Paulus Niavis, 228–29; Zarncke, *Die deutschen Universitäten*, 35–37.

51. Joan Cadden, *Meanings of Sex Difference in the Middle Ages: Medicine, Science, and Culture* (Cambridge, 1993), 175.

52. Paulus Niavis, 231–32; Zarncke, *Die deutschen Universitäten*, 39–40.

53. Paulus Niavis, 229–30; Zarncke, *Die deutschen Universitäten*, 37.

54. Zarncke, *Die deutschen Universitäten*, 67–88.

55. Jacques de Vitry, *The Historia Occidentalis of Jacques de Vitry: A Critical Edition*, ed. John Frederick Hinnebusch, Spicilegium Friburgense 17 (Fribourg, 1972), ch. 7, p. 91.

56. *Chartularium*, 3:53–54.

57. Karras, *Common Women*, 19.

58. Leipzig: Friedrich Zarncke, ed., *Die Statutenbücher der Universität Leipzig aus den ersten 150 Jahren ihres Bestehens* (Leipzig, 1861), 196 (Grosse Fürstenkolleg), 232 (Kleine Fürstenkolleg); Vienna: Rudolf Kink, *Geschichte der kaiserlichen Universität zu Wien*, 2 vols. (Vienna, 1854), 2:253–54, for students who live in *Bursen* or student halls; Johannes Kerer, *Statuta Collegii Sapientiae: The Statutes of the Collegium Sapientiae in Freiburg University, Freiburg, Briesgau 1497*, ed. Josef Hermann Beckmann (Lindau, 1957), 38, 62; Cahors, College of Rodez, 1461 (Fournier, 2:623); Toulouse, College of Foix, 1427 (Fournier, 1:828); Toulouse, College of Mirepoix, 1423–23 (Fournier, 1:790); Angers, 1408, Collège de la Fromagerie (Fournier, 1:353); David Sanderlin, *The Medieval Statutes of the College of Autun in the University of Paris*, Texts and Studies in the History of Medieval Education 13 (Notre Dame, Ind., 1971), 99. Marichal, 106, gives an example of students actually expelled from the Sorbonne for bringing a prostitute in.

59. Zarncke, *Die Statutenbücher*, 271; see also 56, 319, 343, 396, 442.

60. *Statutes of the Colleges of Oxford*, vol. 1, Merton p. 27 (1278), Oriel p. 9 (1326), Queen's p. 20 (1340); *Statuta Antiqua*, 81.

61. *Cartulaire de l'Université de Montpellier*, ed. Université de Montpellier, 2 vols. (Montpellier, 1890), 1:511; Marti, 274.

62. Jacques Le Goff, *Intellectuals in the Middle Ages*, trans. Teresa Lavender Fagan (Cambridge, Mass., 1992), 34, notes the rivalry between clerics and knights for the love of women. This, however, at least as it developed in literature, was mainly a twelfth-century phenomenon, and in any case focused more on sexual favors than reciprocated romantic love.

63. David Lorenzo Boyd and Ruth Mazo Karras, "The Interrogation of a Male Transvestite Prostitute in Fourteenth-Century London," *GLQ: A Journal of Lesbian and Gay Studies* 1 (1994): 459–65.

64. Marichal, 41.

65. H. E. Salter, ed., *Registrum annalium Collegii Meronensis, 1483–1521,* Oxford Historical Society, 76 (Oxford, 1923), 162.

66. Brian Patrick McGuire, "Jean Gerson and Traumas of Masculine Affectivity and Sexuality," in *Conflicted Identities and Multiple Masculinities: Men in the Medieval West,* ed. Jacqueline Murray (New York, 1999), 59; McGuire, "Gerson and Bernard: Languishing with Love," *Cîteaux* 46 (1995): 143; Jean Gerson, *Œuvres complètes,* ed. Palémon Glorieux (Paris, 1963), 5:331.

67. See also Noble, 152–54.

68. Thomas Laqueur, *Making Sex: Body and Gender from the Greeks to Freud* (Cambridge, 1990), esp. 25–62, implies that Aristotelian ideas continued unchanged from Aristotle's own time until the Renaissance. This was by no means the case. While many of the church fathers whose writings were heavily relied on during the Middle Ages were influenced by Greek philosophy, including Aristotle (although not to the same extent as Plato), the influence was neither so direct nor so pervasive before the revival of "The Philosopher" in the universities. On various scholastic views, and Renaissance responses to them, see Ian Maclean, *The Renaissance Notion of Woman: A Study in the Fortunes of Scholasticism and Medical Science in European Intellectual Life* (Cambridge, 1980), esp. 6–19. On the importance of Aristotle in the Middle Ages, see Bernard G. Dod, "Aristoteles Latinus," and C. H. Lohr, "The Medieval Interpretation of Aristotle," in *The Cambridge History of Later Medieval Philosophy: From the Rediscovery of Aristotle to the Disintegration of Scholasticism, 1100–1600,* ed. Norman Kretzmann, Anthony Kenny, and Jan Pinborg (Cambridge, 1982), 45–98. Later scholasticism turned from Aristotle and the Thomist synthesis on many issues. Gordon Leff, *Paris and Oxford Universities in the Thirteenth and Fourteenth Centuries: An Institutional and Intellectual History* (New York, 1968), 238–55, 290–309; Leff, "The Trivium," 319.

69. Cadden, 106. She notes at p. 163 that "although there was no significant disagreement with the belief that women were cooler, weaker, less intellectually competent, and generally less perfect than men, there were, first of all, various ways in which those differences could be played out and understood and, second, numerous dimensions of the procreative process and sexual behavior which had little if anything to do with that central continuum of power, activity, and value."

70. The description of a menstruating woman as poisonous was pervasive enough in medieval culture, though, that it need not have come directly from Aristotle.

71. Cadden, 133–34; Thomas Aquinas, *Summa theologica,* 1:92:1, in *Opera omnia* (Rome, 1889), 5:396. See also Arlene Saxonhouse, *Women in the History of Political Thought, Ancient Greece to Machiavelli* (New York, 1985), 147–50; Kari Elisabeth Børresen, *Subordination and Equivalence: The Nature and Role of Woman in Augustine and Thomas Aquinas,* trans. Charles H. Talbot (Washington, D.C., 1981), 157–78.

72. Cadden, 183–84.

73. Albertus Magnus, *De animalibus libri XXVI*, ed. Hermann Stadler, Beiträge zur Geschichte der Philosophie des Mittelalters, Texte und Untersuchungen, 15–16 (Münster i. Westf., 1916), 15:2:11.

74. There are 83 extant MSS and over 50 fifteenth-century printed editions. Helen Rodnite Lemay, trans., *Women's Secrets: A Translation of Pseudo-Albertus Magnus's* De Secretis Mulierum, *With Commentaries* (Binghamton, N.Y., 1992), Introduction; Lemay, "Some Thirteenth and Fourteenth Century Lectures on Female Sexuality," *International Journal of Women's Studies* 1 (1978): 391–400.

75. Aristotle, *Politics* 1:12, trans. Trevor J. Saunders (Oxford, 1995), 18. The Latin version that medieval scholastics would have known is that of William of Moerbeke: Aristotle, *Politica*, trans. William of Moerbeke, ed. Pierre Michaud-Quantin, Aristoteles Latinus 29 (Bruges, 1961), 21.

76. Albertus Magnus, *Commentarii in octos libros politicorum Aristoteles*, vol. 8, ed. Auguste Borgnet, *Opera omnia* (Paris, 1891), 75.

77. Thomas Aquinas, *Summa contra gentiles*, 4:88, in *Opera omnia* (Rome, 1930), 15:278.

78. Thomas Aquinas, *Sententia libri politicorum*, 1:10, in *Opera omnia* (Rome, 1971), 48:A115–16.

79. Aquinas, *Summa theologica*, 1:92:1, p. 397.

80. Nicole Oresme, *Le livre de politiques d'Aristote*, ed. Albert Douglas Menut, Transactions of the American Philosophical Society, n.s. vol. 60, pt. 6 (Philadelphia, 1970), 73.

81. See Prudence Allen, *The Concept of Woman: The Aristotelian Revolution, 750 BC–AD 1250* (Montreal, 1985).

82. This work, to appear in an article entitled "Using Women to Think With in the Medieval University," is based on the list of quodlibetal questions collected by Palémon Glorieux, *La littérature quodlibétique de 1260 à 1320*, Bibliothèque Thomiste 5 (Le Saulchoir Kain, 1925) and Glorieux, *La littérature quodlibétique II*, Bibliothèque Thomiste 21 (Paris, 1935). I examined all those questions dealing with women or gender that were available in print, or in manuscripts in the Bibliothèque Nationale in Paris.

83. Most of these quodlibetal questions are from the thirteenth century and thus somewhat before the period under examination here. However, later arguments built on these and followed in the same tradition.

84. Durandus of St. Pourçain, Quodlibet, q. 6, Paris, Bibliothèque Nationale (hereafter BN), MS Lat. 14572, fol. 6r. The identification of this and other authors of quodlibets is from Glorieux, *La littérature*. Cf. the treatment of this question by Eustace of Grandcourt (Nicolas de Bar, Quodlibet, q. 125), BN MS Lat. 15850, f. 37r, who says simply that she cannot have the money because it would be a violation of the intention of her father.

85. "R. de Atrebato" (Nicolas de Bar, Quodlibet, q. 56), Paris, BN MS Lat. 15850 fol. 26r.

86. "R. de Atrebato" (Nicolas de Bar, Quodlibet, q. 57), Paris, BN MS Lat. 15850, fol. 26r; cf. Henry of Ghent, *Quodlibeta* (Paris, 1518), Quodlibet 5: q. 38, fol. 214r.

87. Guy de Cluny (Nicolas de Bar, Quodlibet, q. 35), Paris, BN MS Lat. 15850, fol. 20v.

88. Gerard d'Abbeville, Quodlibet 6, q. 8, Paris, BN MS Lat. 16405, fol. 59v. Gerard in fact rejected this argument, determining that in either case the couple should separate.

89. Adenulf of Anagni, Quodlibet, q. 13, Paris, BN MS Lat. 14899, fol. 147v–148r. Cf. the briefer consideration by "R. de Atrebato," (Nicolas de Bar, Quodlibet, q. 55), Paris, BN MS Lat. 15850, vols. 25v–26r.

90. Both Adenulf and Gerard d'Abbeville allow a wife to donate those things that are her *propria*, not marital property; Gerard reached this conclusion based explicitly on natural and civil law. Gerard d'Abbeville, Quodlibet 10, q. 6, Paris, BN MS Lat. 16405, fol. 80v. He did not, however, make any comment about the capacities of women.

91. Glorieux, *La littérature*, 1:318.

92. This passivity may be somewhat noteworthy in light of ideas about feminine lustfulness, but not in light of the pervasive medieval notion of sex as something someone does to someone else rather than as something two people do together.

93. See Kathryn Gravdal, *Ravishing Maidens: Writing Rape in Medieval French Literature and Law* (Philadelphia, 1991).

94. Gervaise of Mont St. Eloi, Quodlibet, q. 4, Paris, BN MS Lat. 15350, fols. 269v–270r. His conclusion was no, based on a distinction between a simple and a solemn vow.

95. Gerard d'Abbeville, Quodlibet 7, q. 17, Paris, BN MS Lat. 16405, fols. 67v–68r.

96. Gerard d'Abbeville, Quodlibet 14, q. 3, Paris, BN MS Lat. 16405, fols. 102v–103r. Even a discussion of prostitution becomes a discussion of the nature of responsibility for actions rather than of prostitution in particular, Quodlibet 5, q. 9, BN MS Lat. 16405, fols. 55v–56v, although this is one place where condemnatory language is used of the women involved.

97. John Marenbon, *Later Medieval Philosophy (1150–1350): An Introduction* (New York, 1987), 20–23; Alfonso Maierù, *University Training in Medieval Europe*, trans. D. N. Pryds (Leiden, 1994), 65–69, 127–37; Courtenay, *Schools and Scholars*, 45; Weisheipl, 147, 153–56, 176–85.

98. They were regulated to keep participants from serving "vanity more than truth" and so that no one would make too long or complex arguments that would prevent others' taking a turn. Decree of the Sorbonne in *Chartularium*, 2:554–56.

99. Maierù, 127 n. 52.

100. On scholastic texts and their relation to lecture and disputation, see Anthony Kenny and Jan Pinborg, "Medieval Philosophical Literature," in Kretzmann et al., 11–42.

101. Walter Ong, *Fighting for Life: Contest, Sexuality, and Consciousness* (Ithaca, N.Y., 1981), 118–48. Ong sees the *agon* primarily as that of the student against the master; but in the medieval university it was also student against student and master (who might also be a student in another faculty) against master.

102. Courtenay, *Schools and Scholars*, 29–30. Cf. Martin Grabmann's description in *Die Geschichte der scholastischen Methode*, vol. 2 (Freiburg im Breisgau, 1911; repr. Graz, 1957), 20–21.

103. John of Garland, *Morale Scolarium*, ed. Louis John Paetow (Berkeley, 1927), ch. 9, p. 160.

104. Jody Enders, "The Theater of Scholastic Erudition," *Comparative Drama* 27 (1993): 341–63. Little evidence has survived as to how the *disputationes* worked in practice. University statutes tell us when they were held, and who could respond or determine, but do not give a picture of the disputation itself. Was it solemn or rowdy, dry or juicy? What model should we have in our minds when we think of the disputation: an academic seminar paper where one person states a thesis and others raise questions? A political debate? For quodlibetal disputations, a press conference where questions may come from the audience on any subject? There is not even a clear agreement among scholars as to how significant a role the master played in the first part of a quodlibet: the second part, the *determinatio*, was all his, but there was a bachelor who responded in the disputational part, and it is not clear how much the master himself said about the questions raised there. See Glorieux, 2:31–36; Wippel, 183–85.

105. A handbook of disputational argument, falsely attributed to Albertus Magnus, gives a good sense of the stylized nature of the argument: Lambert Marie de Rijk, ed., *Die Mittelalterlichen Traktate De Modo Opponendi et Respondendi*, Beiträge zur Geschichte der Philosophie und Theologie des Mittelalters, n.f. 17 (Münster, 1980).

106. Courtenay, *Schools and Scholars*, 258–62.

107. Peter Abelard, *Historia calamitatum*, ed. J. Monfrin (Paris, 1962), 63–64; see comments in Jacques Le Goff, *Time, Work, and Culture in the Middle Ages* (Chicago, 1980), 122–34. Helen Solterer points out that while Abelard considered his intellectual disputes as a form of combat, he invoked the goddess Minerva as his patron, thus incorporating the feminine at least representationally. But the use of a classical goddess figure as metaphor (giving up Mars for Minerva) is not the same thing as constructing an activity as feminine, which Abelard clearly did not do. Helen Solterer, *The Master and Minerva: Disputing Women in French Medieval Culture* (Berkeley, 1995), 29.

108. John of Salisbury, *Metalogicon*, 3:10, ed. J. B. Hall, Corpus Christianorum Continuatio Medievalis, 98 (Turnhout, 1991), 130–39. See also K. S. B. Keats-Rohan, "John of Salisbury and Education in Twelfth-Century Paris from the Account of His *Metalogicon*," *History of Universities* 6 (1986–87): 1–45.

109. *Chartularium*, 1:48.

110. Vincent of Beauvais, *De Eruditione filiorum nobilium*, ed. Arpad Steiner, Medieval Academy of America Publications, 32 (Cambridge, 1938), ch. 20–22, pp. 70–78.

111. Ian P. Wei, "The Self-Image of the Masters of Theology at the University of Paris in the Late Thirteenth and Early Fourteenth Centuries," *Journal of Ecclesiastical History* 46 (1995): 419.

112. R. Howard Bloch, *Medieval French Literature and Law* (Berkeley, 1977), 162–214.

113. Alan M. F. Gunn, "Teacher and Student in the *Roman de la Rose*: A Study in Archetypal Figures and Patterns," in *Esprit Créateur* 2 (1962): 133.

114. See Bloch, *Medieval Misogyny*, 14–22, on the topos of the talkative woman or "woman as riot"; L. R. Poos, "Sex, Lies, and the Church Courts of Pre-Reformation England," *Journal of Interdisciplinary History* 25 (1995): 585–60, on women's speech as reported in church courts.

115. Solterer, 26–35.

116. See, for example, the parodic *quaestiones disputatae* published in Zarncke, *Die deutschen Universitäten*, 49–154.

117. Vienna, 1413: Kink, 251; Freiburg, 1497: Kerer, 58.

118. Although at Nantes in 1461–62, mutual intelligibility was the reason given for the Latin requirement: Fournier, 3:47.

119. Fournier, 1:828.

120. Zarncke, *Die Statutenbücher*, 426; see also Rashdall, 3:375–76.

121. Jaeger, *Ennobling Love*.

122. For examples of newly appointed officials, *Auctarium*, vol. 1, passim, sometimes referring to "paying the *beanium* of his procuratorship" (e.g., p. 278); *Auctarium*, 2:299 for occasions on which the nation was to pay for a feast; 2:411 for the doctorate.

123. *Auctarium*, 1:345.

124. Émile Chatelain, "Notes sur quelques tavernes fréquentés par l'université de Paris au xivᵉ et xvᵉ siècles," *Bulletin de la société de l'histoire de Paris et de l'île de France* 25 (1898): 85–109; Gray Cowan Boyce, *The English-German Nation in the University of Paris During the Middle Ages* (Bruges, 1927).

125. *Auctarium*, 1:363–64; Pearl Kibre, *The Nations in the Mediaeval Universities* (Cambridge, Mass., 1948), 42 for Bologna, 144 for Orléans.

126. *Auctarium*, 5:460.

127. C. H. Lawrence, "The University in State and Church," in Catto, 1:146–47.

128. *Auctarium*, 2:39, 44–45, 50–51, on St. Nicholas Day fight.

129. Marichal, 29.

130. Kerer, 60.

131. Karras, *Common Women*, 71–72.

132. See Lyndal Roper, *The Holy Household: Women and Morals in Reformation Augsburg* (Oxford, 1989), 94.

133. Zarncke, *Die Statutenbücher*, 332; Kerer, 68; Weissenborn, 1:21; Fournier, 1:221 (Orléans); Fournier, 1:381 (Collège de Breuil, Angers); Eduard Winkelmann, ed., *Urkundenbuch der Universität Heidelberg*, 2 vols. (Heidelberg, 1886), 58; Fournier, 3:111 (Dole); Fournier, 2:594 (Cahors, College of St. Nicholas); Fournier, 1:164, 212 (Caen); L. Franchi, ed., *Statuti e ordinamenti della Università de Pavia dall'anno 1361 all'anno 1859* (Pavia, 1925), 22; Alessandro Gherardi, ed., *Statuti della Università e studia fiorentino dell'anno MCCCLXXXVII* (Florence, 1881), 88; *Documents Relating to Cambridge*, 29; Carolo Malagola, ed., *Statuti delle Università e dei collegi dello studio bolognese* (Bologna, 1888), 133, 292; H. Denifle, "Die Statuten der Juristen-Universität Bologna vom J. 1317–1347, und deren Verhältnisse zu jenen Paduas, Perugias, Florenz," *Archiv für Littera-*

tur- und Kirchengeschichte des Mittelalters 3 (1887): 367; Marti, 334; *Statuta antiqua*, 576.

134. A. van Hove, "Statuts de l'université de Louvain antérieurs à l'année 1459," *Bulletin de la commission royale d'histoire* 76 (1907): 597–62.

135. *Liber procuratorum nationis Gallicanae (Franciae)*, ed. Charles Samaran and Emile A. van Moé, vol. 5 of *Auctarium chartularii Universitatis Parisiensis* (Paris, 1942), 387.

136. John North, "The Quadrivium," in De Ridder-Symoens, 343–44.

137. *Statuta antiqua*, 576.

138. Kink, 2:250.

139. Kerer, 66.

140. Marti, 336.

141. Fournier, 2:674 (Perpignan); *Cartulaire de Montpellier*, 1:304; Kink, 2:76 (1384); *Chartularium*, 1:540, also 2:484 (quotation here); Zarncke, *Die Statutenbücher*, 332, 342, 354, 402, 408, 414.

142. Fournier, 1:329.

143. Weissenborn, 1:21; Marti, 336.

144. Van Hove, 636; *Documents Relating to Cambridge*, 1:335; *Libri cancellarii et procuratorum*, in Henry Anstey, ed., *Munimenta academica, or Documents Illustrative of Academical Life and Studies at Oxford*, Rerum Britannicarum Medii Aevi Scriptores 50 (London, 1868), 1:18.

145. Fournier, 1:147, 1:218; Dorothy Mackay Quynn and Harold Sinclair Snellgrove, "Slanderous Comedies at the University of Orléans in 1447," *Modern Language Notes* 57 (1942): 185–88.

146. Kerer, 60.

147. Fournier, 3:330.

148. *Chartularium*, 4:668.

149. Astrik L. Gabriel, *Student Life in Ave Maria College, Medieval Paris. History and Chartulary of the College*, University of Notre Dame, Publications in Mediaeval Studies 14 (Notre Dame, Ind., 1955), 323.

150. Michel Félibien and Guy-Alexis Lobineau, *Histoire de la ville de Paris*, 5 vols. (Paris, 1725), 3:382; Marti, 311; *Statuta antiqua*, 239; for more examples, see Rashdall, 3:385–94; Léo Moulin, *La vie des étudiants au moyen âge* (Paris, 1991), 36–38.

151. Orléans 1447, Fournier, 1:221; Nantes 1461–62, Fournier, 3:48 (also not to make libels on women at Lent); Dole 1424(?), Fournier, 3:115; Pavia 1395, Franchi, 59; Gherardi, 97; *Documents Relating to Cambridge*, 28.

152. H. Ott and J. M. Fletcher, eds., *The Mediaeval Statutes of the University of Freiburg im Breisgau*, Texts and Studies in the History of Medieval Education 10 (Notre Dame, Ind., 1964), 43.

153. *Documents Relating to Cambridge*, 1:29, 2:542; *Statutes of the Colleges of Oxford*, vol. 1, Queen's p. 18, New College p. 48, All Souls p. 55, vol. 2, Magdalen p. 42. For similar prohibitions in Spain, see Schwinges, "Student Education, Student Life," 226.

154. Erfurt 1447: Weissenborn, 1:21; Vienna 1413: Kink, 261; Leipzig 1410: Zarncke, *Die Statutenbücher*, 54.

155. Weissenborn, 1:21; Fournier, 1:73–75 (Orléans), 105; Fournier, 1:453 (Toulouse); Winkelmann, 19; Fournier, 2:615 (Cahors, College of Rodez); Fournier, 3:48 (Nantes), Fournier, 3:111 (Dole), Fournier, 3:164, 212 (Caen), *Cartulaire de Montpellier* 1:305, Malagola 130–31, *Documents Relating to Cambridge,* 319–20; *Statuta antiqua Universitatis Oxoniensis,* 81, 577; *Munimenta academica,* 1:91.

156. J. E. Thorold Rogers, ed., *Oxford City Documents, Financial and Judicial, 1268–1605,* Oxford Historical Society, 18 (Oxford, 1891), 155; see 150ff. for more examples; see also H. E. Salter, ed., *Registrum cancellarii Oxoniensis 1434–1469,* 2 vols., Oxford Historical Society, 93–94 (Oxford, 1936), 2, 3, 5, and passim. Marichal, 221, gives an account of a student drawing a knife on another.

157. Charles Samaran and Emile A. van Moé, eds., *Liber procuratorum nationis Picardiae in Universitatis Parisiensis, Auctarium chartularii Universitatis Parisiensis* vol. 4 (Paris, 1938), 4:58. For more examples, Kibre, 22–23, 35–36, 164–66; Schwinges, "Student Education, Student Life," 227.

158. Fournier, 1:88.

159. Fournier, 2:440–41. Early modern German texts explained the term *beanus* as an acronym: *Beanus Est Animal Nesciens Vitam Studiosorum,* "A *beanus* is an animal that does not know the life of the scholarly." Wilhelm Fabricius, *Die Akademische Deposition* (Frankfurt a.M., 1895), 34. This is, of course, a false etymology. Several people have asked me whether the "beanies" worn by freshmen at some U.S. universities earlier in this century could have any possible relation to "beanus," but the *Oxford English Dictionary,* 2nd edition, derives this from "bean" as slang for "head."

160. Examples abound in *Auctarium,* vol. 1; a Leipzig statute of 1496 provided that "promotion feasts" should be moderate. Zarncke, *Die Statutenbücher,* 20. See also Aix 1420–1440 (Fournier, 3:28); James John, *The College of Prémontré in Mediaeval Paris,* Texts and Studies in the History of Medieval Education, 1 (Notre Dame, Ind., 1953), 30; H. Denifle, "Urkunden zur Geschichte der mittelalterlichen Universitäten," *Archiv für Litteratur- und Kirchengeschichte des Mittelalters* 5 (1888): 297–98 (Register of Procurators of the English Nation in Paris).

161. Franchi, 106.

162. Fournier, 1:125–26; see also *Chartularium,* 2:523–24.

163. Valence 1490–1513, Fournier, 3:395; *Chartularium,* 2:523.

164. Fournier, 1:22.

165. Félibien, 3:170; Fournier, 1:290.

166. Fournier, 2:439–40.

167. Winkelmann, 117. On the sociability of baths, see Georges Duby and Philippe Braunstein, "The Emergence of the Individual," in *A History of Private Life,* vol. 2, ed. Georges Duby, *Revelations of the Medieval World,* trans. Arthur Goldhammer (Cambridge, 1988), 600–610.

168. Fournier, 2:441.

169. Kink, 1:55 (1427). See also Zarncke, *Die Statutenbücher,* 354 (1437): at Leipzig, someone who had just been examined could buy the examiners a beer, but no more.

170. Zarncke, *Die Statutenbücher,* 190, 192.

171. Weissenborn, 18. There are earlier (fragmentary) statutes from the 1370s

or 1380s or perhaps after 1395 that do not include this provision, which may thus be new in the mid-fifteenth century.

172. Kink, 2:77; Zarncke, *Die Statutenbücher*, III, 102; Winkelmann, 183; *Universitas Studii Haffnensis*, 116–17.

173. Zarncke, Die *deutschen Universitäten*, 6.

174. Fabricius, 41–69; Johann Friedrich Hantz, *Geschichte der Universität Heidelberg*, vol. 1 (Mannheim, 1862), 86. Tools for the *depositio*, including knives and pliers, are depicted in Rudolf Kittel, *Die Universität Leipzig und ihre Stellung im Kulturleben* (Dresden, 1924). Luther gave a spiritual interpretation of the *depositio* in one of his *Tischreden* (vol. 4, no. 4714, cited in Almuth Märker, *Geschichte der Universität Erfurt 1392–1816* [Weimar, 1993], 31).

175. Gustav Toepke, ed., *Die Matrikel der Universität Heidelberg* (Heidelberg, 1884; repr. Nendeln, 1976), 1:278.

176. *Goswin Kempgyn de Nussia Trivita Studentium: Eine Einführung in das Universitätsstudium aus dem 15. Jahrhundert;* ed. Michael Bernhard, Münchener Beiträge zur Mediävistik und Renaissance-Forschung, 26 (Munich, 1976), 61–62.

177. Shaving also appears in the records of New College, Oxford, from 1400; it was apparently a "vile and horrible" ritual inflicted upon new masters of arts the night before their inception. *Statutes of the Colleges of Oxford*, vol. 1, New College, p. 47.

178. Johannes Schram of Dachau, as he is identified in the pamphlet, matriculated at Erfurt in 1490 and became a Master of Arts in 1494. The matriculation is in Weissenborn, 435, and the list of masters is in Erich Kleineidam, *Universitas Studii Erffordensis: Überblick über der Universität Erfurt im Mittelalter, 1392–1521* (Leipzig, 1964), 1:386.

179. Johannes Schram, *Monopolium der Schweinezunft*, in Zarncke, *Die deutschen Universitäten*, III.

180. Alexander Murray, *Reason and Society in the Middle Ages* (Oxford, 1978), 237–44.

181. Le Goff, *Intellectuals in the Middle Ages*, 80.

182. Karras, "Separating the Men from the Goats: Masculinity, Civilization, and Identity Formation in the Medieval University," in Jacqueline Murray, *Conflicted Identities*, 199.

183. Fuchs, 17, 75–76.

184. Albertus Magnus, *De Animalibus*, 22:2:1, p. 1369.

185. Vincent of Beauvais, *Speculum Naturale* (Nuremberg, 1485), 19:31, fol. 124r.

186. This use of excrement for male ailments contrasts sharply with Hippocratic writings that associate excrement with the ailments of women. Heinrich von Staden, "Women and Dirt," *Helios* 19 (1992): 7–30.

187. Or perhaps their use was merely threatened or implied. Contemporary fraternity initiation rituals (although with their emphasis on alcohol, they tend to focus on vomiting more than on excreting) sometimes involve making the initiate believe that he is eating feces and drinking urine, when this is not actually the case. The purpose, according to Sanday, is to build trust and teach the initiate to obey unquestioningly. Peggy Reeves Sanday, *Fraternity Gang Rape: Sex, Brotherhood,*

and Privilege on Campus (New York, 1990), 160, 169; Larry Colton, *Goat Brothers* (New York, 1993), 48.

188. L. Wehrhahn-Stauch, "Bock," in *Lexikon der Christlichen Ikonographie,* ed. Engelbert Kirschbaum (Rome, 1968), 314–15.

189. Isidore, 12:1:14, vol. 2 (unpaginated).

190. Florence McCulloch, *Medieval Latin and French Bestiaries* (Chapel Hill, N.C., 1962), 121–23; Le Clerc, Guillaume, *Le Bestiare: Das Thierbuch des normannischen Dichters Guillaume le Clerc,* ed. Robert Reinsch, Altfranzösische Bibliothek 14 (Leipzig, 1892; repr. New York, 1973), 298.

191. Richard Barber, trans., *Bestiary* (Woodbridge, 1993), 82.

192. William M. Voelkle, "Moran Manuscript M. 1001: The Seven Deadly Sins and the Seven Evil Ones," in *Monsters and Demons in the Ancient and Medieval Worlds,* ed. Anne E. Farkas, Prudence O. Harper and Evelyn B. Harrison (Mainz, 1987), 106; Wehrhahn-Stauch, 316; Beryl Rowland, *Blind Beasts: Chaucer's Animal World* (Kent, Ohio, 1971), 19.

193. Albertus Magnus, *De animalibus,* 22:2:1, p. 1369.

194. Samuel Kinser, "Presentation and Representation: Carnival at Nuremberg, 1450–1550,"*Representations* 13 (1986): 6.

195. Joshua Trachtenberg, *The Devil and the Jew: The Medieval Conception of the Jew and Its Relation to Modern Antisemitism* (Philadelphia, 1961), 46–47. See also Ruth Mellinkoff, *The Horned Moses in Medieval Art and Thought* (Berkeley, 1970), 121–37.

196. Many modern goats are dehorned or bred for hornlessness, but this was not the case in the Middle Ages.

197. Zarncke, *Die deutschen Universitäten,* 111.

198. I am not suggesting that the "civilizing process" going on in this initiation ritual is the same thing described by Norbert Elias: *The Civilizing Process,* vol. 1, *The History of Manners,* trans. Edmund Jephcott (New York, 1978); vol. 2, *Power and Civility,* trans. Edmund Jephcott (New York, 1982). Elias is talking about the process of civilization on a societal rather than on an individual level. Elias suggests that "civilized" behavior became important at the time of the Renaissance and the rise of the state, as a centralized monopoly on violence replaced a system in which the individual nobleman could basically do as he pleased. But the story here about university initiation has little directly to do with state power.

199. John W. Baldwin, *The Language of Sex: Five Voices from Northern France Around 1200* (Chicago, 1994), 184–86; Cadden, 273–76; Danielle Jacquart and Claude Thomasset, *Sexuality and Medicine in the Middle Ages,* trans. Matthew Adamson (Princeton, N.J., 1988), 136.

200. Joyce E. Salisbury, *The Beast Within: Animals in the Middle Ages* (New York, 1994), 78–80.

201. The literature on the connection of femininity and lasciviousness is vast. I have discussed it in various places, including "Gendered Sin and Misogyny in John of Bromyard's 'Summa Predicantium,' " *Traditio* 47 (1992): 233–57. See also Bloch, *Medieval Misogyny.* Joyce Salisbury, 155–58, discusses the association of women with animals.

Chapter 4

1. On the normative "cursus honorum" and its long life despite its variance from social reality, see Geoffrey Crossick, "Past Masters: In Search of the Artisan in European History," in *The Artisan and the European Town*, ed. Geoffrey Crossick (Aldershot, 1997), 7.

2. Bronislaw Geremek, *The Margins of Society in Late Medieval Paris*, trans. Jean Birrell (Cambridge, 1987), 252.

3. Knut Schulz, *Handwerksgesellen und Lohnarbeiter: Untersuchungen zur oberrheinischen und oberdeutschen Stadtgeschichte des 14. bis 17. Jahrhunderts* (Sigmaringen, 1985), 220–21. Anyone born in an urban environment would be free, but even in the later Middle Ages some rural dwellers who came to towns to work were of servile status.

4. André Gouron, *La réglementation des métiers en Languedoc au moyen âge*, Etudes d'histoire économique, politique et sociale, 22 (Geneva, 1958), 241–42; Kathryn L. Reyerson, personal communication, December 2001.

5. Gervase Rosser, "Crafts, Guilds and the Negotiation of Work in the Medieval Town," *Past and Present* 154 (February 1997): 1–31.

6. Heather Swanson, "The Illusion of Economic Structure: Craft Guilds in Late Medieval English Towns," *Past and Present* 121 (1988): 29–48, argues that rather than guilds playing a role in government, the guilds could be a tool of the civic authorities to control the workforce, masters and employees alike. George Unwin, *The Gilds and Companies of London*, 4th ed. (London, 1963), 65ff., is a good exponent of the traditional view of English guilds.

7. Marc Boone, "Les métiers dans les villes flamandes au bas moyen âge (XIVe–XVIe siècles): Images normatives, réalitiés socio-politiques et économiques," in *Les métiers au moyen âge: aspects économiques et sociaux*, ed. Pascale Lambrechts and Jean-Pierre Sosson (Louvain-la-Neuve, 1994), 12.

8. Ronald F. E. Weissman, *Ritual Brotherhood in Renaissance Florence* (New York, 1982), 4.

9. Charles de la Roncière, *Prix et salaires à Florence au XIVe siècle* (Rome, 1982), 259–60.

10. Samuel Kline Cohn, Jr., *The Laboring Classes in Renaissance Florence* (New York, 1980), 9–11.

11. E.g., Brian Tierney and Sidney Painter, *Western Europe in the Middle Ages, 300–1475*, 5th ed. (New York, 1992), 281.

12. Heather Swanson, *Medieval Artisans: An Urban Class in Late Medieval England* (Oxford, 1989), 111.

13. Matthew Davies, "Artisans, Guilds and Government in London," in *Daily Life in the Late Middle Ages*, ed. Richard Britnell (Frome, Somerset, 1998), 130.

14. Steven A. Epstein, *Wage Labor and Guilds in Medieval Europe* (Chapel Hill, N.C., 1991), 115, 122–23, 137, 231; Maryanne Kowaleski and Judith M. Bennett, "Crafts, Gilds, and Women in the Middle Ages: Fifty Years After Marian K. Dale," *Signs: Journal of Women in Culture and Society* 14 (1989): 474–88. For an important theoretical statement on women's work, see Judith M. Bennett, *Ale,*

Beer, and Brewsters in England: Women's Work in a Changing World, 1300–1600 (New York, 1996), 145–57.

15. Benjamin R. McRee, "Unity or Division? The Social Meaning of Guild Ceremony in Urban Communities," in *City and Spectacle in Medieval Europe,* ed. Barbara A. Hanawalt and Kathryn L. Reyerson (Minneapolis, 1994), 191 (dealing with religious and not specifically craft fraternities); Noël Coulet, "Les confréries de métier en Provence au moyen âge," in *Travail et travailleurs en Europe au moyen âge et au début des temps modernes,* ed. Claire Dolan, Papers in Mediaeval Studies (Toronto, 1991), 37; Carmen Battle, "Le travail à Barcelone vers 1300: Les métiers," in Dolan, 82.

16. Audrey Douglas, "Midsummer in Salisbury: The Tailors' Guild and Confraternity 1444–1642," *Renaissance and Reformation/Renaissance et réforme* n.s. 13 (1989): 37.

17. Gervase Rosser, "Solidarités et changement social: Les fraternités urbaines anglaises à la fin du moyen âge," *Annales: Économies, sociétés, civilisations* 48 (1993): 1129–31.

18. Hanawalt, *Growing Up,* 139–40.

19. The discussion of apprenticeship in this section, as far as it relates to London, covers some of the same ground as Hanawalt, *Growing Up.* A number of the examples that I have used are the same ones that she used, because we consulted the same sources. I have not cited her work each time I use a source that she also used. Nevertheless I am indebted to her account, especially for pointing me to the Mayor's Court Bills as a source.

20. "The Book of Ordinances 1478–83," trans. Lorna E. M. Walker, in *The Early History of the Goldsmiths' Company 1327–1509,* by T. F. Reddaway (London, 1975), 248. Swanson, "Illusion," has questioned whether the apprenticeship system in England was really as important as it appears in guild statutes, since it was not required for admission to the freedom of the city (citizenship). It still remained a key stage, however, in the training of skilled workers.

21. In Languedoc, the beginning age could be from fourteen to twenty-five; in Burgundy, twelve to fifteen with an occasional exception as high as thirty (Philippe Didier, "L'apprentissage médiéval en France: Formation professionelle, entretien ou emploi de la main-d'oeuvre juvenile?" *Zeitschrift der Savigny-Stiftung für Rechtsgeschichte, Germanistische Abteilung* 101 [1984]: 237); in Sweden, typically eight or nine (A. A. Svanidze, "Town Handicraft and Hired Labour in Mediaeval Sweden in the 13th to Early 15th Centuries," in *Forme ed evoluzione del lavoro in Europa: XIII–XVIII secc.* [Prato, 1991], 582). Apprenticeship contracts from Tournai show some boys entering into the contract themselves and some parents doing so on behalf of their sons, an indication that some were above and some below the age of fourteen: Léo Verriest, *Les luttes sociales et le contrat d'apprentissage à Tournai jusqu'en 1424* (Brussels, 1912), 33; cf. Kathryn L. Reyerson, "The Adolescent Apprentice/Worker in Medieval Montpellier," *Journal of Family History* 17:4 (1992): 356. In London, apprentices who brought claims against their masters sometimes did so on their own, but sometimes their parents brought the claim on their behalf, indicating either that they were still minors or that family ties remained strong: Corporation of London Records Office (here-

after CLRO), MC 1/1/18; MC 1/2A/1; CLRO, Plea and Memoranda Roll A10 m. 4d; Plea and Memoranda Roll A22a m. 5. In the latter case, the boy had served for eight years, so it is not likely he was still under fourteen.

22. Epstein, 104.

23. Dennis Menjot, "Les métiers en Castille au bas moyen âge: Approche des vécus socio-économiques," in Lambrechts and Sosson, 219; Verriest, 34–35.

24. Among apprentice artists in Palermo in the fourteenth and fifteenth centuries, for example, contracts for boys who began at twelve usually specified a term of six years; at fifteen, three years; and at eighteen, one year (Geneviève Bresc-Bautier, *Artistes, patriciens et confréries: Production et consommation de l'oeuvre d'art à Palerme et en Sicile occidentale (1348–1460)* [Rome, 1979], 8).

25. Epstein, 141–42, suggests otherwise. See his table of different periods of apprenticeship in different crafts in Paris and Genoa. Reyerson, 356, for Montpellier, finds neither an inverse nor a direct relation between length of apprenticeship and difficulty of the craft.

26. At Nîmes, for example, where periods of apprenticeship ranged from eight months for textile workers to six years for barber-surgeons, a notarial register of 1381 included contracts with a one-year apprenticeship for a physician and a four-year apprenticeship for a farrier. Gouron, 270.

27. Didier, "L'apprentissage," 250–55. See also Didier, "Le contrat d'apprentissage en Bourgogne aux XIVe et XVe siècles," *Revue historique de droit français et étranger* 54 (1976): 35–57. In the guilds of the cuirass-makers and smiths of Florence, an apprentice had to serve three years if he were paying his own expenses, and eight years if the master were paying his expenses. In Marseille and in the German towns of the upper Rhine, too, shorter contracts required higher fees. In Brussels the sons of poor families, exempt from payment for apprenticeship fees, had to serve longer. In England apprenticeship fees varied according to the family's means, but lower payments do not seem to have occasioned longer periods of apprenticeship. Giulia Camerani Marri, ed., *Statuti delle arti dei corazzai, dei chiavaioli, ferraioli e calderai e dei fabbri di Firenze (1321–1344)*, Fonti sulle corporazioni medioevali, 6 (Florence, 1957), 30, 159; Francine Michaud, "Apprentissage et salariat à Marseille avant la peste noire," *Revue historique* 291 (1994): 25–26; Schulz, *Handwerkgesellen*, 249; G. Des Marez, *L'organisation du travail à Bruxelles au XVe siècle* (Brussels, 1904), 49.

28. Boone, "Les métiers," 17.

29. Public Record Office (hereafter PRO), C1/64/358, C1/64/978, C1/97/65, C1/141/99.

30. In Paris, the apprentice might receive a small wage after a few years' experience, or a lump sum upon completion of his term. If the master hired out his apprentice to work for someone else, the apprentice could get a portion of the payment (Gustave Fagniez, *Etudes sur l'industrie et la classe industrielle à Paris au XIIIe et XIVe siècles* [Paris, 1877], 69–71). In Coventry apprenticeship contracts from the 1490s set out wages to be paid amounting to around twelve shillings a year (Mary Dormer Harris, ed., *The Coventry Leet Book* [London, 1907–1908], 560).

31. Didier, "L'apprentissage," 245–46.

32. Michaud, "Apprentissage," 31–32; Françoise Michaud-Fréjaville, "Crise urbaine et apprentissage à Orléans, 1475–1500," in *Villes, bonnes villes, cités et capitales: Études d'histoire urbaine (XIIe–XVIIIe siècle)*, ed. Monique Bourin (Caen, 1993), 16–18.

33. Matthew Davies, ed., *The Merchant Taylors' Company of London: Court Minutes, 1486–1493* (Stamford, 2000), 336–37.

34. Epstein, 109; Didier, "L'apprentissage," 218. On the blurring of the line between apprentice and servant in Venice, see Dennis Romano, *Housecraft and Statecraft: Domestic Service in Renaissance Venice, 1400–1600* (Baltimore, 1996), 47.

35. Verriest, 88; see also 37–38.

36. CLRO, Plea and Memoranda Roll A10, m. 7; Plea and Memoranda Roll A11, m. 5d; PRO C1/155/43; CLRO, MC 1/2/5, 1/2/116, 1/2A/1. See also PRO C1/19/33.

37. On parental involvement, see Reyerson, 357.

38. In Orléans in the fifteenth century, as many as two-thirds of the apprentices may have been orphans. Françoise Michaud-Fréjaville, "Enfants orphelins, enfants séparés, enfants élevés: Gardes et des mineurs d'âge à Orléans au XVe siècle," in *Education, apprentissages, initiation au moyen âge* (Montpellier, 1991), 2:301.

39. Didier, "L'apprentissage," 224–25. This provision did not serve solely to keep up family ties, however: the money the apprentice earned by working at the harvest may have helped him pay his apprenticeship fees.

40. PRO C1/66/215.

41. Sylvia Thrupp, *The Merchant Class of Medieval London 1300–1500* (Ann Arbor, 1962), 214–16; leprosy was also a disqualification. Unfree birth was a disqualification in Norwich too: William Hudson and John Cottingham Tingey, eds., *The Records of the City of Norwich* (Norwich, 1906), 2:291.

42. CLRO, Letter-Book I, fol. 259.

43. Walter Sherburne Prideaux, ed., *Memorials of the Goldsmiths' Company, being Gleanings from their Records Between the Years 1335 and 1815* (London, 1896), 17.

44. One apprentice vintner of London, who borrowed money in his master's name but without the latter's knowledge, said he had done so because his master had in his keeping charters relating to the apprentice's lands and tenements, and he was afraid of not getting them back. Other apprentices, too, ran into problems over masters' seizure of their wealth, or, if they kept control of their own money, found themselves accused of stealing their masters' goods. CLRO, Plea and Memoranda Roll A30, m. 5; PRO, C1/39/221, C1/47/52, C1/12/159.

45. Davies, *Merchant Taylors*, 32–34; Thrupp, 206–22, 389–92.

46. Verriest, 32.

47. Philippe Bernardi, "Apprentissage et transmission du savoir dans les métiers du bâtiment à Aix-en-provence à la fin du moyen âge," in *Education, apprentissages, initiation au moyen âge* (Montpellier, 1991), 1:72.

48. For some London cases about who assumed responsibility for the apprentice under various circumstances, see PRO C1/45/96, C1/61/413, C1/64/415.

49. Marc Boone, "Les métiers," 1–21, at 17.

50. Didier, "L'apprentissage," 221; Reyerson, 363.

51. Verriest, 37.

52. "The Book of Ordinances," 261–62.

53. Didier, "L'apprentissage," 221, 215–17.

54. PRO, C1/19/491; CLRO, Plea and Memoranda Roll A45 m. 2d; PRO, C1/19/33.

55. Verriest, 64.

56. Epstein, 109; Fagniez, *Etudes,* 65.

57. David Nicholas, *The Metamorphosis of a Medieval City: Ghent in the Age of the Arteveldes, 1302–1390* (Lincoln, 1987), 164.

58. Thrupp, 168. One mercer's apprentice who broke his indenture by marrying, Anthony Pontisbury, claimed to the chancellor that an anti-marriage clause "is contrary to the laws of God and causes much fornication and adultery." PRO, C1/154/60.

59. In one London case, an apprentice goldsmith died and his master had his fiancée arrested, claiming the apprentice had given her jewels belonging to the master. PRO, C1/166/45.

60. CLRO, Plea and Memoranda Roll A9, m. 1d.

61. CLRO, Plea and Memoranda Roll A21, m. 9; PRO C1/61/353; PRO C1/6/7; CLRO MC 1/1/11. John Bruhern, apprentice to the vintner Richard Manton of London, came up with a very creative excuse for running away. He claimed that because of his loyalty to the temporarily ousted king Edward IV and "certain language" that he used about Henry VI, he had to go into hiding. This story was clearly calculated to win the sympathy of the reinstated Edward's chancellor. PRO C1/46/169.

62. E.g., for London, CLRO MC1/1/17, 1/1/18.

63. Didier, "L'apprentissage," 228–31; René Lespinasse, *Les métiers et corporations de la ville de* Paris (Paris, 1886), 3:383, nos. 6–7, 2:625 no. 3, 2:642 no. 27. But cf. Jean-Pierre Leguay, "Les métiers de l'artisanat dans les villes du duché de Bretagne aux XIVe et XVe siècles," in Lambrechts and Sosson, 187.

64. E.g., Giovanni Monticolo, ed., *I capitolari delle arti veneziane* (Rome, 1896–1914), 2:313 no. 16; 2:497 no. 19–20; 3:169 no. 38; for London, PRO C1/28/171.

65. In the London Goldsmiths' Company, a 1386 regulation provided that if an apprentice bought himself out of his term, he had to bind himself to a new master (Prideaux, 7). The Merchant Taylors' company recorded a number of cases of apparently voluntary transfer of an apprentice from one master to another; presumably substantial negotiation had gone on before the parties appeared in court, and a payment was usually involved (Davies, *Merchant Taylors,* 93, 101, 104, 138, 153, 176, 216, 225). John Sutton, grocer of Bristol, was accused of having his apprentice (who had served two years of a nine-year term) imprisoned in order to extort from the boy's father eight pounds to buy him out of his term (PRO, C1/15/165). In other cases, apprentices who bought themselves out of their term might find that if they prospered their former master might claim them back (PRO, C1/38/40).

66. Gustave Fagniez, ed., *Documents relatifs à l'histoire de l'industrie et du commerce en France,* vol. 2, *XIVe et XVe siècles* (Paris, 1900), 221; Reyerson, 361–62,

for cancellation by mutual consent in Montpellier; Hudson and Tingey, 2:154, in which the apprentice wished to become a priest; CLRO, Plea and Memoranda Roll A16, m. 5d.

67. CLRO, Plea and Memoranda Roll A9 m. 4b; Plea and Memoranda Roll A28, m. 135; CLRO, MC1/3/231, MC1/3/290; PRO, C1/48/11, C1/61/342, C1/64/110, C1/64/1108. For disputes over the sufficiency of instruction, see PRO C/51/105. For fines for failing to enroll apprentices, see Davies, *Merchant Taylors*, 94 and passim; for petitions from apprentices who claim that they have not been enrolled, taught, or provided for, see CLRO MC1/2A/2–5, 1/2A/46–53, 1/2A/62–72, 1/3/339. In one case, the court transferred an apprentice because his master was unable to train him because of mental illness (CLRO, Plea and Memoranda Roll A43, m. 8).

68. PRO, C1/10/68.

69. CLRO, Plea and Memoranda Roll A20, m. 12.

70. Fagniez, *Documents*, 170; Didier, "L'apprentissage," 222.

71. CLRO, Plea and Memoranda Roll A16, m. 5. For other cases involving beatings, see CLRO, Plea and Memoranda Roll A11, m. 2d; PRO C1/66/236; Fagniez, *Etudes*, 67–69.

72. Davies, *Merchant Taylors*, 96, 197–98, 228. Bowman found out and had the warden arrested; the tailors fined Bowman ten shillings.

73. This could lead to problems, as with apprentice mason Geoffrey Denby, whose dead master's heir sold the remaining three years of his term to a master he found unsuitable (PRO, C1/11/367).

74. See, e.g., Lespinasse 1:455 no. 8; 1:378 no. 14; 1:537 no. 5; and passim.

75. Didier, "L'apprentissage," 215, 218; Leonard Ennen and Gottfried Eckertz, *Quellen zur Geschichte der Stadt Köln*, 6 vols. (Aalen, 1970), 6:516 (Cologne saddlers).

76. Fagniez, *Documents*, 173.

77. E.g., CLRO, Plea and Memoranda Roll A57, m. 5d; PRO, C1/107/27.

78. Prideaux, 12. One of them did marry her but refused to carry out the agreement.

79. Barbara Hanawalt, " 'The Childe of Bristowe' and the Making of Middle-class Adolescence," in *Bodies and Disciplines: Intersections of Literature and History in Fifteenth Century England*, ed. Barbara Hanawalt and David Wallace (Minneapolis, 1996), 163; P. J. P. Goldberg, "Masters and Men in Later Medieval England," in *Masculinity in Medieval Europe*, ed. Dawn M. Hadley (London, 1999), 62.

80. PRO C1/124/34; C1/221/37.

81. Gervase Rosser, "Workers' Associations in English Medieval Towns," in Lambrechts and Sosson, 295.

82. Davies, "Artisans, Guilds," 137–38. Those who became free of the craft through redemption (buying their way in), however, had an even better chance.

83. Jean-Pierre Sosson, "Die Körperschaften in den Niederlanden und Nordfrankreich: Neue Forschungsperspektiven," in *Gilde und Korporation in den nordeuropäischen Städten des späten Mittelalters*, ed. Klaus Friedland (Cologne, 1984), 84; Swanson, "Illusion," 46; Nicholas, *Metamorphosis*, 172. Of course, the

reasons varied. Not all of these apprentices finished their term; others did but could not afford to set up in business or chose not to.

84. See, e.g., Svanidze, 577.

85. Battle, 91; Hanawalt, *Growing Up*, 171 (case of Thomas Wood).

86. C. Nyrop, ed., *Danmarks Gilde- og Lavskraaer fra Middelalderen* (Copenhagen, 1895–1904), 2:88–89, nos. 12, 16; Marri, 92 no. 48.

87. Francesca Morandini, *Statuti delle arti degli oliandoli e pizzicagnoli e dei beccai di Firenze (1318–1346)*, Fonti sulle corporazioni medioevali 9 (Florence, 1961), 210 no. 7.

88. Ennen and Eckertz, 6:21, 540, 548.

89. PRO, C1/64/313.

90. Prideaux, 22; Hanawalt, *Growing Up*, 165.

91. Jacques Rossiaud, "Fraternités de jeunesse et niveaux de culture dans les villes du Sud-Est à la fin du moyen âge," *Cahiers d'histoire* 21 (1976), 72.

92. Didier, "L'apprentissage," 219; Lespinasse, 1:547 no. 2.

93. CLRO, Plea and Memoranda Roll A3, m. 8.

94. PRO, C1/67/319.

95. *Coventry Leet Book*, 545.

96. CLRO, MC1/1/7 and 1/2/120. The name given is John in one bill and William in the other, and the first is undated, but they clearly refer to the same apprentice.

97. Goldberg, 58–60. On the responsibility of men in positions of authority over the sexual behavior of others in the urban setting, see McSheffrey, 256.

98. This term might seem to derive from the necessity of their going from town to town to find work. By analogy to the Tour de France required of skilled workers in early modern France, one scholar has claimed the term as evidence that traveling was the salient feature in England, whereas the French *compagnon* shows that the bonding among them was the salient feature. Cynthia Marie Truant, *The Rites of Labor: Brotherhoods of Compagnonnage in Old and New Regime France* (Ithaca, N.Y., 1994), 57. This, however, is a false etymology.

99. Frances Consitt, *The London Weavers' Company* (Oxford, 1933), 77–78; Charles Phythian-Adams, *Desolation of a City: Coventry and the Urban Crisis of the Late Middle Ages* (Cambridge, 1979), 106. They were still, however, called journeymen.

100. There might, however, be a good deal of overlap between skilled workers and servants both in what they did and in how they were viewed. On the distinction between wage workers and servants in Venice, see Romano, *Housecraft and Statecraft*, esp. 105–6, 186.

101. Charles de la Roncière, "La condition des salariés à Florence au XIVe siècle," in *Il Tumulto dei Ciompi: Un momento di storia fiorentina ed europea* (Florence, 1981), 20–21; for more detail, de la Roncière, *Prix et salaires*, esp. 397–421; Beatrix Baillieul and Anne Duhameeuw, *Een Stad in Opbouw: Gent voor 1540* (Tielt, 1989), 210–11.

102. W. P. Blockmans and W. Prevenier, "Poverty in Flanders and Brabant from the Fourteenth to the Mid-Sixteenth Century: Sources and Problems,"

Acta historica neerlandicae 10 (1978), 24–26. A more detailed version of this article in Dutch is available in *Tijdschrift voor Geschiedenis* 88 (1975), 501–38.

103. Schulz, *Handwerksgesellen*, 430–32.

104. E.g., Luigi Simeoni, ed., *Gli antichi statuti delle arti veronesi, secundo la revisione scaligera del 1319* (Venice, 1914), 146 no. 143, 167 no. 53, 181 n. 63, and passim, for apprentices as well as journeymen.

105. CLRO, Plea and Memoranda Roll A11, m. 2.

106. CLRO, MC1/1/83.

107. John M. Najemy, "*Audiant Omnes Artes*: Corporate Origins of the Ciompi Revolution," in *Il tumulto dei Ciompi*, 73; Anna Maria Agnoletti, ed., *Statuto dell'arte della lana di Firenze (1317–19)*, Fonte e studi sulle corporazioni artigiane del medio evo, Fonti 1 (Florence, 1940–58), 148 no. 3:2.

108. Gouron, 261–62; other examples in Nyrop, 2:27 no. 8, 2:67 no. 8, 2:74 nos. 16–18, and passim; Francesco Sartini, ed., *Statuti dell'arte dei rigattiei e linaioli di Firenze (1296–1340)*, Fonti e studi sulle corporazioni artigiane del medio evo, Fonti 2 (Florence, 1940–58), 73 no. 47, 125 no. 48, and passim; Henry Thomas Riley, ed., *Liber Custumarum, Munimenta Gildhallae Londoniensis*, 2 (London, 1860), 81 no. 7, 101 no. 6, 129; Monticolo, 1:30 no. 8, 2:71 no. 24, and passim; Lespinasse, 2:328 no. 4 and passim; CLRO, Letter-Book F, fol. 147, fol. 155, fol. 159, fol. 184; *The Little Red Book of Bristol* (Bristol, 1900), 2:60; CLRO, MC1/2/51 and 1/2A/8.

109. For violation of this rule, see CLRO MC1/1/112. Regulations also protected the journeymen in some respects, for instance by forbidding masters from hiring workers who were not members of the craft company in that city (although sometimes the wardens of the craft could give special permission for this). CLRO, MC1/2A/19. For fines for hiring "foreigners" (those from outside the city), see Davies, *Merchant Taylors*, 52 and passim.

110. Epstein, 115.

111. Philippe Didier, "Les contrats de travail en Bourgogne aux XIVe et XVe siècles d'après les archives notariales," *Revue historique de droit français et étranger* 50 (1972), 18–31, 44–46.

112. Knut Schulz, "Die Stellung der Gesellen in der spätmittelalterlichen Stadt," in *Haus und Familie in der spätmittelalterlichen Stadt*, ed. Alfred Haverkamp (Cologne, 1984), 311–12.

113. Rolf Sprandel, "Der handwerkliche Familienbetrieb des Spätmittelalters und seine Probleme," in Haverkamp, 330–31; Des Marez, 65.

114. *Coventry Leet Book*, 185 (see also 115, 183).

115. CLRO, Letter-Book I, fol. 151r–151v.

116. Guildhall Library, MS 34003, fol. 10r–10v. This is the same MS cited by Davies, *Merchant Taylors*, under its previous designation of Guildhall Library, Merchant Taylors' Company Miscellaneous Documents 2A.

117. Katharina Simon-Muscheid, "Gewalt und Ehre im spätmittelalterlichen Handwerk am Beispiel Basels," *Zeitschrift für historische Forschung* 18 (1991): 13–14. The tensions occasionally broke out in nonviolent ways. The London dyer John Fissh complained that his journeyman John Halliwell ran off

with his wife and goods worth £200. Halliwell admitted the adultery but not the theft, and the court found for the plaintiff. CLRO, Plea and Memoranda Roll A13 m. 4d.

118. Epstein, 190–206.

119. Raymond Cazelles, *Nouvelle histoire de Paris de la fin du règne de Phlippe Auguste à la mort de Charles V, 1323–1380* (Paris, 1994), 84.

120. Henry Thomas Riley, trans., *Liber Albus: The White Book of the City of London* (London, 1861), 237; Swanson, *Medieval Artisans*, 110.

121. Peter Arnade, *Realms of Ritual: Burgundian Ceremony and Civic Life in Late Medieval Ghent* (Ithaca, N.Y., 1996), 147.

122. Des Marez, 62; Hans van Werveke, "De medezeggenschap van de knapen (gezellen) in de middeleewsche ambachten," *Mededelingen van de Koninklijke Vlaamsche Academie voor Wetenschappen, Letteren en Schoone Kunsten van België, Klasse der Letteren,* 5:3 (1943): 13–14.

123. Richard Mackenney, *Tradesmen and Traders: The World of the Guilds in Venice and Europe, c. 1250–c. 1650* (Totowa, N.J., 1987), 22–23.

124. Consitt, 76–77; CLRO, Letter-Book K, fol. 216.

125. Fagniez, *Etudes*, 90–92.

126. Rosser, "Crafts, Guilds," 17–18.

127. For England, see Marjorie Keniston McIntosh, *Controlling Misbehavior in England, 1370–1600* (Cambridge, 1998), 161.

128. Lespinasse, 1:270 no. 23; Hans van Werveke, "Ambachten en erfe-lijkheid," *Mededelingen van de Koninklijke Vlaamsche Academie voor Wetenschappen, Letteren en Schoone Kunsten van België, Klasse der Letteren* (1942): no. 1, 12–16.

129. For Paris, see Bronislaw Geremek, *Le salariat dans l'artisanat parisien aux XIIIe–XVe siècles,* trans. Anna Posner and Christiane Klapisch-Zuber, Industrie et Artisanat 5 (Paris, 1968), 45ff., and Lespinasse, passim; for Spain, Emiliano Fernandez de Pinedo, "Structure économique et conflits sociaux: corporations et marchands dans la monarchie espagnole (XIIIe au XVIIIe siècles)," in *Forme ed evoluzione,* 457; for Brussels, Jean-Pierre Sosson, "L'artisanat Bruxellois du metal: hierarchie sociale, salaires et puissance economique (1360–1500)," *Cahiers Bruxellois* 7 (1962): 227–32; Des Marez, 53ff.

130. Jean-Pierre Sosson, "La structure sociale de la corporation médiévale: l'exemple des tonneliers de Bruges de 1350 à 1500," *Revue belge de philologie et d'histoire* 44 (1966): 460.

131. Sosson, "Die Körperschaften," 84; Jean-Pierre Sosson, "Les métiers: Norme et réalité. L'exemple des anciens pays-bas méridionaux aux XIVe et XVe siècles," in *Le travail au moyen âge: une approche interdisciplinaire: Actes du colloque international de Louvain-la-Neuve, 21–23 mai 1987,* ed. Jacqueline Hamesse and Colette Muraille-Samaran (Louvain-la-Neuve, 1990), 345.

132. Baillieul, 216. For Italian examples on easier admission of sons to the guilds, see Simeoni, passim.

133. Schulz, *Handwerksgesellen*, 211–26.

134. Nicholas, *Metamorphosis*, 289.

135. Martha Howell, *The Marriage Exchange: Property, Social Place, and Gender in Cities of the Low Countries, 1300–1550* (Chicago, 1998), 191–92. The absolute numbers are rather small in these samples.

136. Dennis Romano, *Patricians and Popolani: The Social Foundations of the Venetian Renaissance State* (Baltimore, 1987), 77.

137. The guilds of Paris in the fifteenth century mostly had requirements for masterpieces, which can be found in Lespinasse, passim (for example, brewers 1:621 no. 1).

138. In Bruges, only 21 percent of master coopers from 1375 to 1500 were sons of masters, despite much higher entrance fees for those who were not. Sosson, "Körperschaften," 84; Sosson, "Structure sociale," 463–85. In Basel in the fifteenth century, 20 to 30 percent of masters overall were the sons of masters in the same craft. Schulz, *Handwerksgesellen*, 312. The numbers of sons who took up the trade of their fathers could vary greatly from guild to guild within a single town. Oscar Itzcovich, "Masters and Apprentices in Genoese Society, 1450–1535," in *History and Computing II*, ed. Peter Denley, Stefan Fogelvik, and Charles Harvey (Manchester, 1989), 214.

139. Simon-Muscheid, "Gewalt und Ehre," 6–7.

140. Alessandro Stella, *La révolte des Ciompi: les hommes, les lieux, le travail* (Paris, 1993), 95–96.

141. Paul Strohm, *Theory and the Premodern Text* (Minneapolis, 2000), 54, and Andrew Prescott, "London in the Peasants' Revolt: A Portrait Gallery," *London Journal* 7 (1981): 131, discuss the involvement of servants and apprentices, although it can be difficult to identify them in the records.

142. Cohn, 82, 89, 147.

143. Rainer Schröder, *Zur Arbeitsverfassung des Spätmittelalters* (Berlin, 1984), 177.

144. Schulz, *Handwerksgesellen*, 37–97; see also Wilfried Reininghaus, *Die Entstehung der Gesellengilden im Spätmittelalter*, Vierteljahrschrift für Sozial- und Wirtschaftsgeschichte, Beihefte, 71 (Wiesbaden, 1981), 49.

145. Reininghaus, 44–46, 61–70.

146. Rosser, "Workers' Associations," 293; CLRO, Plea and Memoranda Roll A3, m. 4 (carpenters); A6 m. 1d (bakers); A6 m. 5d (shearmen); A17 m. 10 (brewers); Letter-Book F fol. 173 (shearmen); Letter-Book H fol. 219 (cordwainers).

147. CLRO, Plea and Memoranda Roll A7 m. 4.

148. CLRO, Letter-Book H, fol. 309v. For an earlier (1380) case involving saddlers, see CLRO, Plea and Memoranda Roll A23 m. 4d.

149. Ordinances of the Fullers, CLRO Letter-Book G, fol. 116r–116v.

150. Swanson, *Medieval Artisans*, 115.

151. CLRO, Letter-Book I, fol. 151; Charles M. Clode, *The Early History of the Guild of Merchant Taylors of Fraternity of St. John the Baptist* (London, 1888), 1:61. Matthew Davies, the historian of the Merchant Taylors' Company (pers. comm., July 26, 2001), suggests that the phrase "servientes et allocate Cissorum dicte civitatis yomen taillours nuncupat" should rather be translated "the servants and journeymen of those tailors who are called yeoman tailors"—in other words, that "yeoman tailors" refers to the masters and not to the rebellious journeymen

themselves. From the language it is not clear to me that this is the case; the journeymen or "allocate" (hired men) could be free of the city and yeomen members of the craft who had not set up their own workshops.

152. Guildhall Library, MS 34003, fol. 8v–9r.

153. James Farr, *Artisans in Europe 1300–1914* (Cambridge, 2000), 5.

154. CLRO, Letter-Book H, fol. 309v; Letter-Book I, fol. 151.

155. Davies, *Merchant Taylors*, 23–25.

156. Swanson, *Medieval Artisans*, 115.

157. Christoph Anz, *Gilden im mittelalterlichen Skandinavien* (Göttingen, 1998), 228–35.

158. Gervase Rosser, "Going to the Fraternity Feast: Commensality and Social Relations in Late Medieval England," *Journal of British Studies* 33 (1994): 442.

159. Schulz, *Handwerksgesellen*, 167.

160. *Coventry Leet Book*, 93–94.

161. Weissman, 63–66.

162. Merry Wiesner, "Guilds, Male Bonding, and Women's Work in Early Modern Germany," *Gender and History* 1 (1989): 125–37; "*Wandervogels* and Women: Journeymen's Concepts of Masculinity in Early Modern Germany," *Journal of Social History* 24 (1991): 767–82.

163. Schulz, "Die Stellung," 315.

164. Schulz, *Handwerksgesellen*, 94–96; see also 166, 171, 177.

165. Fagniez, *Etudes*, 78.

166. Nyrop, 2:51–52, nos. 6–7, 12–13.

167. Simon-Muscheid, "Gewalt und Ehre," 12–13, 27, 29–31.

168. McIntosh, *Controlling Misbehavior*, 176–77.

169. Reininghaus, 66.

170. Living together without marriage was increasingly strictly condemned in south German towns at the end of the fifteenth and beginning of the sixteenth century, and correspondingly legitimate birth became an important requirement for craft guild membership and inclusion in the community. Schulz, *Handwerksgesellen*, 223–24.

171. Simon-Muscheid, "Gewalt und Ehre," 8–9.

172. Phythian-Adams, 86.

173. Grethe Jacobsen, "Economic Progress and the Sexual Division of Labor: The Role of Guilds in the Late-Medieval Danish City," *Alltag und Fortschritt im Mittelalter*, Veröffentlichungen des Instituts für mittelalterliche Realienkunde Österreichs, 8 (Vienna, 1986), 223–36, discusses this issue very helpfully.

174. On the household as *not* a workshop, see Peter Laslett, "Family and Household as Work Group and Kin Group: Areas of Traditional Europe Compared," in *Forme ed evoluzione del lavaro in Europa, XIII–XVIII secc.*, 289–333.

175. Geremek, 97–98.

176. Maryanne Kowaleski, "Singlewomen in Medieval and Early Modern Europe: The Demographic Perspective," in *Singlewomen in the European Past 1250–1800*, ed. Judith M. Bennett and Amy M. Froide (Philadelphia, 1999), 38–81, is an up-to-date summary of medieval demographics with relation to marriage.

177. The model was originally designed to describe modern society. For medieval data, see P. J. P. Goldberg, *Women, Work and the Life Cycle in a Medieval Economy: Women in York and Yorkshire c. 1300–1520* (New York, 1992), 203–32.

178. David Herlihy and Christiane Klapische-Zuber, *Tuscans and Their Families: A Study of the Florentine Catasto of 1427* (New Haven, Conn., 1985), 221.

179. Herlihy and Klapische-Zuber, *Tuscans*, 216.

180. Kowaleski, "Singlewomen," 55.

181. Ruth Mazo Karras, *Common Women: Prostitution and Sexuality in Medieval England* (New York, 1996), 32, 133–34.

182. Michael Rocke, *Forbidden Friendships: Homosexuality and Male Culture in Renaissance Florence* (New York, 1996), esp. 88, 158, 187.

183. Bernardino of Siena preached repeatedly and vigorously against sodomy in Florence, but was more concerned with the elites than with workers, claiming that idleness was a contributing factor. Franco Mormando, *The Preacher's Demons: Bernardino of Siena and the Social Underworld of Early Renaissance Italy* (Chicago, 1999), 109–63, esp. 133.

184. Jacques Rossiaud, *Medieval Prostitution* (Oxford, 1988), 11–37.

185. Rossiaud, *Medieval Prostitution*, 28–29.

186. Rossiaud, *Medieval Prostitution*, 21. For rape in Basel, see Simon-Muscheid, "Gewalt und Ehre," 20–21.

187. Rossiaud, "Fraternités," 71–75. For discussion of ritual culture related to the crafts and to carnival in the early modern period, see Peter Burke, *Popular Culture in Early Modern Europe* (New York, 1978).

188. Reininghaus, 188–227.

Chapter 5

1. Judith M. Bennett, *Ale, Beer, and Brewsters in England: Women's Work in a Changing World, 1300–1600* (New York, 1996), 144–57, provides a good statement of this.

2. Joan of Arc, the most famous female soldier of the Middle Ages, may be the exception that proves the rule: she was not an aristocrat or a knight, and although she was an inspirational leader, she was not of a social class that would ever wield power. A recent introduction to the voluminous literature on Joan may be found in *Fresh Verdicts on Joan of Arc*, ed. Bonnie Wheeler and Charles T. Wood (New York, 1996).

3. Judith M. Bennett and Amy M. Froide, "A Singular Past," in *Singlewomen in the European Past, 1250–1800*, ed. Bennett and Froide (Philadelphia, 1999), 1–37; Judith M. Bennett, " 'Lesbian-Like' and the Social History of Lesbianisms," *Journal of the History of Sexuality* 9 (2000): 1–24, at 23–24.

4. R. H. Helmholz, *Marriage Litigation in Medieval England* (Cambridge, 1974), 90–94.

5. Kim M. Phillips, "Maidenhood as the Perfect Age of Woman's Life," in *Young Medieval Women*, ed. Katherine J. Lewis, Noël James Menuge, and Kim M. Phillips (New York, 1999), 1–24.

6. For England, see, e.g., S. H. Rigby, *English Society in the Later Middle Ages: Class, Status, and Gender* (New York, 1995), 324–25.

7. On the twelfth century, see Constance Brittain Bouchard, *Strong of Body, Brave and Noble: Chivalry and Society in Medieval France*, (Ithaca, N.Y., 1998), 129–44.

8. Judith M. Bennett, *Women in the Medieval English Countryside: Gender and Household in Brigstock Before the Plague* (New York, 1986), 115–20; Barbara A. Hanawalt, *The Ties That Bound: Peasant Families in Medieval England* (New York, 1986), 141–55.

9. "Ballad of a Tyrannical Husband," in *Reliquiae antiquae*, ed. Thomas Wright and James Orchard Halliwell (London, 1843, repr. New York, 1966), 2:196–99.

10. Emmanuel Le Roy Ladurie, *Montaillou: The Promised Land of Error*, trans. Barbara Bray (New York, 1978), 69–88.

11. Robert Muchembled, "Die Jugend und die Volkskultur im 15. Jahrhundert: Flandern und Artois," in *Volkskultur des europäischen Spätmittelalters*, ed. Peter Dinzelbacher and Hans-Dieter Mück (Stuttgart, 1987), 35–58.

12. Benedictine monks were supposed to be nineteen at profession, but boys could enter as novices at a younger age. Barbara Harvey, *Living and Dying in England, 1100–1540: The Monastic Experience* (Oxford, 1993), 118.

13. Caroline Walker Bynum, *Jesus as Mother: Studies in the Spirituality of the High Middle Ages* (Berkeley, 1982), 110–69.

14. R. N. Swanson, "Angels Incarnate: Clergy and Masculinity from Gregorian Reform to Reformation," in *Masculinity in Medieval Europe*, ed. D. M. Hadley (New York, 1999), 160–77.

15. Vern L. Bullough, "On Being a Male in the Middle Ages," in *Medieval Masculinities: Regarding Men in the Middle Ages*, ed. Clare A. Lees with Thelma Fenster and Jo Ann McNamara (Minneapolis, 1994), 34. Bullough acknowledges that manhood is defined in varied ways and labels this triad as "the most simplistic way of defining it."

16. P. H. Cullum, "Clergy, Masculinity, and Transgression in Late Medieval England," in Hadley, 186.

17. Cullum, 194–95.

18. Daniel Boyarin, *Unheroic Conduct: The Rise of Heterosexuality and the Invention of the Jewish Man* (Berkeley, 1997), 53.

19. Boyarin, 26.

20. John Cooper, *The Child in Jewish History* (Northvale, N.J., 1996), 185. This is, of course, the age marked by the Bar Mitzvah ceremony; see Leopold Löw, *Die Lebensalter in der jüdischen Literatur* (Szegedin, 1875), 210, on its history in Europe, as well as Ivan Marcus, *Rituals of Childhood: Jewish Acculturation in Medieval Europe* (New Haven, Conn., 1996), 18–34, 117, 215–26.

21. Many of the articles in *Anger's Past: The Social Uses of an Emotion in the Middle Ages* (Ithaca, N.Y., 1998), ed. Barbara H. Rosenwein, address the question of the ideal of self-control and different types of anger, justified or not.

22. K. B. McFarlane, "The Investment of Sir John Fastolfe's Profits of War," *Transactions of the Royal Historical Society*, 5th ser. 7 (1957), 91–116.

23. Richard Trexler, "La prostitution florentine au XVe siècle: Patronages et clientèles," *Annales: Economies, sociétés, civilizations* 36 (1981): 983–84.

24. Rosemary Drage Hale, "Joseph as Mother: Adaptation and Appropriation in the Construction of Male Virtue," in *Medieval Mothering*, ed. John Carmi Parsons and Bonnie Wheeler (New York, 1996), 101–16.

25. Karma Lochrie, *Covert Operations: The Medieval Uses of Secrecy* (Philadelphia, 1999), 194–205. There was also an important binary distinction between active and passive, which, however, applied to persons rather than acts.

26. Michael Rocke, *Forbidden Friendships: Homosexuality and Male Culture in Renaissance Florence* (New York, 1996), 87–111.

27. See, e.g., Didier Lett, *L'enfant des miracles: Enfance et société au moyen âge (XIIe–XIIIe siècle)* (Paris, 1997), 144–47.

Bibliography

MANUSCRIPT SOURCES

Brussels, Bibliothèque royale/Koninklijke Bibliotheek
    MS 1124–26
Kew (London), Public Record Office (PRO)
    Early Chancery Petitions (C1)
London, Corporation of London Records Office (CLRO)
    Letter-Books (L-B)
    Mayor's Court, Original Bills (MC)
    Plea and Memoranda Rolls (PMR)
London, Guildhall Library
    MS 34003
Paris, Bibliothèque nationale
    MS Lat. 14572
    MS Lat. 14899
    MS Lat. 15350
    MS Lat. 15850
    MS Lat. 16405

PUBLISHED PRIMARY SOURCES

Abelard, Peter. *Historia calamitatum.* Ed. J. Monfrin. Paris, 1962.
Agnoletti, Anna Maria, ed. *Statuto dell'arte della lana di Firenze (1317–19).* Fonte e studi sulle corporazioni artigiane del medio evo, Fonte 1. Florence, 1940–58.
Albertus Magnus. *Commentarii in octos libros politicorum Aristoteles.* Ed. Auguste Borgnet. *Opera omnia* vol. 8. Paris, 1891.
———. *De animalibus libri XXVI.* Ed. Hermann Stadler. Beiträge zur Geschichte der Philosophie des Mittelalters, Texte und Untersuchungen, 15–16. Münster i. Westf., 1916.
Alighieri, Dante. *Il Convivio.* Trans. Richard H. Lansing. New York, 1990.
Anstey, Henry, ed. *Munimenta academica, or Documents Illustrative of Academical Life and Studies at Oxford.* 2 vols. Rerum Britannicarum Medii Aevi Scriptores, 50. London, 1868.
Aquinas, Thomas. *Opera omnia.* Rome, 1882–.
Aristotle. *Politica.* Trans. William of Moerbeke. Ed. Pierre Michaud-Quantin. Aristoteles Latinus 29. Bruges, 1961.

———. *Politics.* Trans. Trevor J. Saunders. Oxford, 1995.

"Ballad of a Tyrannical Husband." In *Reliquiae antiquae,* ed. Thomas Wright and James Orchard Halliwell, 196–99. London, 1843, repr. New York, 1966.

Barber, Richard, trans. *Bestiary.* Woodbridge, 1993.

"The Book of Ordinances 1478–83." Trans. Lorna E. M. Walker. In *The Early History of the Goldsmiths' Company 1327–1509,* ed. T. F. Reddaway, 209–74. London, 1975.

Boyd, David Lorenzo, and Ruth Mazo Karras. "The Interrogation of a Male Transvestite Prostitute in Fourteenth-Century London." *GLQ: A Journal of Gay and Lesbian Studies* 1 (1994): 459–65.

Bueil, Jean de. *Le jouvencel par Jean de Bueil.* Ed. Camille Favre. 2 vols. Paris, 1887.

Byles, Alfred T. P., ed. *The Book of Fayttes of Armes and of Chyvalrye, Translated and Printed by William Caxton from the French Original by Christine de Pisan.* Early English Text Society, o.s. 189. London, 1937.

———, ed. *The Book of the Ordre of Chyvalry, Translated and Printed by William Caxton from a French Version of Ramón Lull's "Le libre del ordre de Cauayleria."* Early English Text Society, o.s. 168. London, 1926.

Cartulaire de l'Université de Montpellier. Ed. Université de Montpellier. 2 vols. Montpellier, 1890.

Chandos Herald. *The Black Prince: An Historical Poem.* Trans. Henry Octavius Coxe. London, 1842.

Charny, Geoffroi de. *The Book of Chivalry of Geoffroi de Charny: Text, Context, and Translation.* Trans. Elspeth Kennedy. Ed. Richard W. Kaeuper. Philadelphia, 1996.

Chastellain, Georges. "Le livre des faits du bon chevalier Messire Jacques de Lalaing." In *Oeuvres de Georges Chastellain,* ed. Kervyn de Lettenhove, 1–259. Brussels, 1866.

Chrétien de Troyes. *Le roman de Perceval ou Le conte du graal.* Ed. Keith Busby. Tübingen, 1993.

Christine de Pisan. *The Book of the Body Politic.* Trans. Kate Langdon Forhan. Cambridge, 1994.

———. *Christine de Pisan's Letter of Othea to Hector.* Trans. Jane Chance. Newburyport, Mass., 1990.

Dahood, Roger, ed. *The Avowing of Arthur.* New York, 1984.

Davies, Matthew, ed. *The Merchant Taylors' Company of London: Court Minutes, 1486–1493.* Stamford, 2000.

Denifle, Heinrich. "Die Statuten der Juristen-Universität Bologna vom J. 1317–1347, und deren Verhältnisse zu jenen Paduas, Perugias, Florenz." *Archiv für Litteratur- und Kirchengeschichte des Mittelalters* 3 (1887): 196–408.

———. "Urkunden zur Geschichte der mittelalterlichen Universitäten." *Archiv für Litteratur- und Kirchengeschichte des Mittelalters* 5 (1888): 167–348.

———, and Emile Chatelain, eds. *Liber procuratorum nationis Anglicanae (Alemanniae) in Universitate Parisiensi.* 2 vols. Vols. 1 and 2 of *Auctarium chartularii Universitatis Parisiensis.* Paris, 1937.

————, eds. *Chartularium Universitatis Parisiensis.* Vols. 1 and 2. Paris, 1889.

De Rijk, Lambert Marie, ed. *Die Mittelalterlichen Traktate De modo opponendi et respondendi.* Beiträge zur Geschichte der Philosophie und Theologie des Mittelalters, n.f. 17. Münster, 1980.

Díaz de Games, Guttiere. *El Victorial.* Ed. Rafael Beltrán Lavador. Salamanca, 1997.

Documents Relating to the University and Colleges of Cambridge. 3 vols. London, 1852.

Ennen, Leonard, and Gottfried Eckertz, eds. *Quellen zur Geschichte der Stadt Köln.* 6 vols. Aalen, 1970.

Fagniez, Gustave, ed. *Documents relatifs à l'histoire de l'industrie et du commerce en France.* Vol. 2, *XIVe et XVe siècles.* Paris, 1900.

Félibien, Michel, and Guy-Alexis Lobineau. *Histoire de la ville de Paris.* 5 vols. Paris, 1725.

Fournier, Marcel. *Les statuts et privilèges des universités françaises depuis leur fondation jusqu'en 1789.* Paris, 1890.

Franchi, L., ed. *Statuti e ordinamenti della Università di Pavia dall'anno 1361 all'anno 1859.* Pavia, 1925.

Fresne de Beaucourt, G. du, ed. *Chronique de Mathieu d'Escouchy.* Paris, 1863.

Froissart, Jean. *Le joli buisson de jonece.* Ed. Anthime Farrier. Geneva, 1975.

————. *Les chroniques de Sire Jean Froissart.* Ed. J.-A.-C. Buchon. 3 vols. Paris, 1837.

Furnivall, Frederick J., ed. *Caxton's Book of Curtesye.* Early English Text Society, Extra Series 3. London, 1868.

————, ed. *Hymns to the Virgin and Christ, The Parliament of Devils, and Other Religious Poems.* Early English Text Society, o.s. 24. London, 1869.

Gabriel, Astrik L. *Student Life in Ave Maria College, Medieval Paris. History and Chartulary of the College.* University of Notre Dame Publications in Mediaeval Studies, 14. Notre Dame, Ind., 1955.

Gérard, H., ed. *Chronique latine de Guillaume de Nangis de 1113 à 1300 avec les continuations de cette chronique de 1300 à 1368.* Paris, 1843.

Gerson, Jean. *Œuvres complètes.* Ed. Palémon Glorieux. Vol. 5. Paris, 1963.

Gherardi, Alessandro, ed. *Statuti della Università e studia fiorentino dell'anno MCCCLXXXVII.* Florence, 1881.

Girvan, Ritchie, ed. *Ratis Raving and Other Early Scots Poems on Morals.* Scottish Text Society, 3rd series, 11. Edinburgh, 1939.

Halliwell, James Orchard, ed. *Palatine Anthology: A Collection of Ancient Poems and Ballads Relating to Lancashire and Cheshire.* London, 1850.

Harris, Mary Dormer, ed. *The Coventry Leet Book.* 3 vols. Early English Text Society, o.s. 134, 135, 138. London, 1907–13.

Henry of Ghent. *Quodlibeta.* Paris, 1518.

Hudson, William, and John Cottingham Tingey, eds. *The Records of the City of Norwich.* 2 vols. Norwich, 1906.

Isidore of Seville. *Etymologiarum sive originum libri XX.* 2 vols. Ed. W. M. Lindsay. London, 1911–18.

Jacques de Vitry. *The Historia Occidentalis of Jacques de Vitry: A Critical Edition.* Spicilegium Friburgense 17. Ed. John Frederick Hinnebusch. Fribourg, 1972.

John of Garland. *Morale scolarium*. Ed. Louis John Paetow. Berkeley, 1927.

John of Salisbury. *Metalogicon*. Ed. J. B. Hall. Corpus Christianorum Continuatio Medievalis 98. Turnhout, 1991.

Kempgyn, Goswin. *Goswin Kempgyn de Nussia Trivita Studentium: Eine Einführung in das Universitätsstudium aus dem 15. Jahrhundert*. Ed. Michael Bernard. Münchener Beiträge zur Mediävistik und Renaissance-Forschung, 26. Munich, 1976.

Kerer, Johannes. *Statuta Collegii Sapientiae: The Statutes of the Collegium Sapientiae in Freiburg University, Freiburg, Breisgau 1497*. Ed. Josef Hermann Beckmann. Lindau, 1957.

Kink, Rudolf. *Geschichte der kaiserlichen Universität zu Wien*. 2 vols. Vienna, 1854.

Kossman, E. F., ed. *Die Haager Liederhandschrift*. The Hague, 1940.

Krishna, Valerie, ed. *The Alliterative Morte Arthure: A Critical Edition*. New York, 1976.

———, trans. *The Alliterative Morte Arthure: A New Verse Translation*. Washington, D.C., 1983.

Lalande, Denis, ed. *Le livre des fais du bon messire Jehan le Maingre, dit Bouciquaut, Mareschal de France et Gouverneur de Jennes*. Geneva, 1985.

La Marche, Olivier de. *Mémoires d'Olivier de la Marche*. Ed. Henri Beaune and J. d'Arbaumont. 4 vols. Société de l'histoire de France, 71. Paris, 1883.

Lannoy, Gilbert de. "L'instruction d'un jeune prince" and "Les enseignements paternels." In *Oeuvres de Ghilebert de Lannoy*, ed. Ch. Potvin, 327–472. Louvain, 1878.

La Sale, Antoine de. *Le petit Jehan de Saintré*. Ed. Pierre Champion and Fernand Desonay. Paris, 1926.

Le Clerc, Guillaume. *Le Bestiare: Das Thierbuch des normannischen Dichters Guillaume le Clerc*. Ed. Robert Reinsch. Altfranzösische Bibliothek, 14. Leipzig, 1892, repr. New York, 1973.

Lee, S. L., ed. *The Boke of Huon of Burdeux*. Trans. John Bourchier. 3 vols. Early English Text Society, Extra Series 40–41. London, 1888.

Lemay, Helen Rodnite, trans. *Women's Secrets: A Translation of Pseudo-Albertus Magnus's De Secretis Mulierum, with Commentaries*. Binghamton, N.Y., 1992.

Lespinasse, René. *Les métiers et corporations de la ville de Paris*. 3 vols. Paris, 1886.

The Little Red Book of Bristol. 2 vols. Bristol, 1900.

Malagola, Carolo, ed. *Statuti delle Università e dei collegi dello studio bolognese*. Bologna, 1888.

Malory, Thomas. *The Works of Sir Thomas Malory*. Ed. Eugène Vinaver. Rev. P. J. C. Field. 3rd ed. Oxford, 1990.

Marichal, Robert, ed. *Le livre des prieurs de Sorbonne*. Paris, 1987.

Marri, Giulia Camerani, ed. *Statuti delle arti dei corazzai, dei chiavaioli, ferraioli e calderai e dei fabbri di Firenze (1321–1344)*. Fonti sulle corporazioni medioevali, 6. Florence, 1957.

Monticolo, Giovanni, ed. *I capitolari delle arti veneziane*. 3 vols. Fonti per la storia d'Italia, 26–28. Rome, 1896–1914.

Morandini, Francesca. *Statuti delle arti degli oliandoli e pizzicagnoli e dei beccai di Firenze (1318–1346).* Fonti sulle corporazioni medioevali, 9. Florence, 1961.

Myers, A. R., ed. *The Household of Edward IV: The Black Book and the Ordinance of 1478.* Manchester, 1959.

Nichols, John Gough, ed. *The Boke of Noblesse Addressed to King Edward the Fourth on His Invasion of France in 1475.* London, 1860.

Nicolas, N. Harris, ed. *The Controversy between Sir Richard Scrope and Sir Robert Grosvenor in the Court of Chivalry,* A.D. *MCCCLXXXV–MCCCXC.* 2 vols. London, 1832.

Nyrop, C., ed. *Danmarks Gilde- og Lavskraaer fra Middelalderen.* 2 vols. Copenhagen, 1895–1904.

Oresme, Nicole. *Le livre de politiques d'Aristote.* Ed. Albert Douglas Menut. Transactions of the American Philosophical Society, n.s. vol. 60, pt. 6. Philadelphia, 1970.

Orgelfinger, Gail, ed. *The Hystorye of Olyuer of Castylle.* Trans. Henry Watson. New York, 1988.

Ott, H., and J. M. Fletcher, eds. *The Mediaeval Statutes of the University of Freiburg im Breisgau.* Texts and Studies in the History of Medieval Education, 10. Notre Dame, Ind., 1964.

Parker, J. H., ed. *Statutes of the Colleges of Oxford.* 3 vols. Oxford, 1853.

Philip of Leyden. *De cura reipublicae et sorte principantis.* Ed. R. Fruin and P. C. Molhuijsen. The Hague, 1900.

Philippe de Novare. *Les quatre âges de l'homme: Traité moral de Philippe de Navarre.* Ed. Marcel de Fréville. Société des anciens textes français. Paris, 1888.

Pinborg, Jan, ed. *Universitas studii Haffnensis: Stiftelsesdokumenter og Stattuter 1479.* Copenhagen, 1979.

Prideaux, Walter Sherburne, ed. *Memorials of the Goldsmiths' Company, Being Gleanings from Their Records Between the Years 1335 and 1815.* 2 vols. London, 1896.

Pseudo-Boethius. *De disciplina scholarium.* Ed. Olga Weijers. Studien und Texte zur Geistesgeschichte des Mittelalters. Leiden, 1976.

René of Anjou. *Le livre des tournois du roi René.* Ed. François Avril. Paris, 1986.

Riley, Henry Thomas, ed. *Liber Custumarum.* Vol. 2 of *Munimenta Gildhallae Londoniensis.* London, 1860.

———, trans. *Liber Albus: The White Book of the City of London.* London, 1861.

Rogers, J. E. Thorold, ed. *Oxford City Documents, Financial and Judicial, 1268–1605.* Oxford Historical Society, 18. Oxford, 1891.

Salter, H. E., ed. *Registrum annalium Collegii Mertonensis, 1483–1521.* Oxford Historical Society, 76. Oxford, 1923.

———, ed. *Registrum cancellarii Oxoniensis 1434–1469.* 2 vols. Oxford Historical Society, 93–94. Oxford, 1936.

Samaran, Charles, and Emile A. van Moé, eds. *Liber procuratorum nationis Picardiae in Universitatis Parisiensis.* Vol. 4 of *Auctarium chartularii Universitatis Parisiensis.* Paris, 1938.

————. *Liber procuratorum nationis Gallicanae (Franciae)*. Vol. 5 of *Auctarium chartularii Universitatis Parisiensis*. Paris, 1942.

Sartini, Francesco, ed. *Statuti dell'arte dei rigattiei e linaioli di Firenze (1296–1340)*. Fonti e studi sulle corporazioni artigiane del medio evo, Fonti 2. Florence, 1940–58.

Simeoni, Luigi, ed. *Gli antichi statuti delle arti veronesi, secundo la revisione scaligera del 1319*. Venice, 1914.

Streckenbach, Gerhard. "Paulus Niavis, 'Latinum ydeoma pro novellis studentibus'—ein Gesprächsbüchlein aus dem letzten Viertel des 15. Jahrhunderts." *Mittellateinisches Jahrbuch* 6 (1970): 152–91, 7 (1971): 187–251.

Strickland, Gibson, ed. *Statuta antiqua Universitatis Oxoniensis*. Oxford, 1931.

Toepke, Gustav, ed. *Die Matrikel der Universität Heidelberg*. Heidelberg, 1884, repr. Nendeln, 1976.

Tolkien, J. R. R., and E. V. Gordon, eds. *Sir Gawain and the Green Knight*. 2d ed. Rev. Norman Davis. Oxford, 1967.

"Tournament Between Lord Scales and the Bastard of Burgundy." In *Excerpta historica*, ed. Samuel Bentley, 171–212. London, 1833.

van Hove, A. "Statuts de l'université de Louvain antérieurs à l'année 1459." *Bulletin de la commission royale d'histoire* 76 (1907): 597–662.

Vincent of Beauvais. *De Eruditione filiorum nobilium*. Ed. Arpad Steiner. Medieval Academy of America Publications, 32. Cambridge, 1938.

————. *Speculum naturale*. Nuremberg, 1485.

Weissenborn, Hermann, ed. *Acten der Erfurter Universität*. Halle, 1881.

Winkelmann, Eduard, ed. *Urkundenbuch der Universität Heidelberg*. 2 vols. Heidelberg, 1886.

Zarncke, Friedrich, ed. *Die deutschen Universitäten im Mittelalter*. Leipzig, 1857.

————, ed. *Die Statutenbücher der Universität Leipzig aus den ersten 150 Jahren ihres Bestehens*. Leipzig, 1861.

SECONDARY SOURCES

Allen, Prudence. *The Concept of Woman: The Aristotelian Revolution, 750 BC–AD 1250*. Montreal, 1985.

Anz, Christoph. *Gilden im mittelalterlichen Skandinavien*. Göttingen, 1998.

Ariès, Philippe. *Centuries of Childhood: A Social History of Family Life*. Trans. Robert Baldick. New York, 1962.

Arnade, Peter. *Realms of Ritual: Burgundian Ceremony and Civic Life in Late Medieval Ghent*. Ithaca, N.Y., 1996.

Asztalos, Monika. "The Faculty of Theology." In *Universities in the Middle Ages*, ed. Hilde de Ridder-Symoens, 409–41. Cambridge, 1992.

Badinter, Elizabeth. *XY: On Masculine Identity*. Trans. Lydia Davis. New York, 1995.

Baillieul, Beatrix, and Anne Duhameeuw. *Een Stad in Opbouw: Gent voor 1540*. Tielt, 1989.

Baldwin, John W. *The Language of Sex: Five Voices from Northern France Around 1200*. Chicago, 1994.

———. "*Studium et Regnum*: The Penetration of University Personnel into French and English Administration at the Turn of the Twelfth and Thirteenth Centuries." In *L'enseignement en Islam et en occident au moyen âge*, ed. George Makdisi, Dominique Sourdel, and Janine Sourdel-Thomine, 199–213. Paris, 1977.

Barber, Richard. "Chivalry and the Morte Darthur." In *A Companion to Malory*, ed. Elizabeth Archibald and A. S. G. Edwards, 19–35. Cambridge, 1996.

Barber, Richard, and Juliet Barker. *Tournaments: Jousts, Chivalry, and Pageants in the Middle Ages*. New York, 1989.

Battle, Carmen. "Le travail à Barcelone vers 1300: Les métiers." In *Travail et travailleurs en Europe au moyen âge et au début des temps modernes*, ed. Claire Dolan, 79–102. Toronto, 1991.

Bennett, Judith M. *Ale, Beer, and Brewsters in England: Women's Work in a Changing World, 1300–1600*. New York, 1996.

———. " 'Lesbian-Like' and the Social History of Lesbianisms." *Journal of the History of Sexuality* 9 (2000): 1–24.

———. *Women in the Medieval Countryside: Gender and Household in Brigstock Before the Plague*. New York: 1987.

Bennett, Judith M., and Amy M. Froide. "A Singular Past." In *Singlewomen in the European Past, 1250–1800*, ed. Judith M. Bennett and Amy M. Froide, 1–37. Philadelphia, 1999.

Bennett, Michael J. *Community, Class and Careerism: Cheshire and Lancashire Society in the Age of Sir Gawain and the Green Knight*. Cambridge, 1983.

Benson, Larry. *Malory's Morte Darthur*. Cambridge, Mass., 1976.

Benson, Larry D. "Courtly Love and Chivalry in the Later Middle Ages." In *Fifteenth-Century Studies*, ed. Robert F. Yaeger, 237–57. Hamden, Conn., 1984.

Bernardi, Philippe. "Apprentissage et transmission du savoir dans les métiers du bâtiment à Aix-en-Provence à la fin du moyen âge." In *Education, apprentissages, initiation au moyen âge*, 69–79. Montpellier, 1991.

Bloch, R. Howard. *Medieval French Literature and Law*. Berkeley, 1977.

———. *Medieval Misogyny and the Invention of Western Romantic Love*. Chicago, 1991.

Blockmans, W. P., and W. Prevenier. "Poverty in Flanders and Brabant from the Fourteenth to the Mid-Sixteenth Century: Sources and Problems." *Acta historica neerlandicae* 10 (1978): 20–57.

Blockmans, Wim, and Esther Donckers. "Self-Representation of Court and City in Flanders and Brabant in the Fifteenth and Early Sixteenth Centuries." In *Showing Status: Representation of Social Positions in the Late Middle Ages*, ed. Wim Blockmans and Antheun Janse, 81–111. Turnhout, 1999.

Blockmans, Wim, and Walter Prevenier. *The Promised Lands: The Low Countries Under Burgundian Rule, 1369–1530*. Trans. Elizabeth Fackelman. Ed. Edward Peters. Philadelphia, 1999.

Bly, Robert. *Iron John: A Book About Men.* Reading, Mass., 1990.

Boone, Marc. "Les métiers dans les villes flamandes au bas moyen âge (XIVe–XVle siècles): Images normatives, réalités socio-politiques et économiques." In *Les métiers au moyen âge: aspects économiques et sociaux,* ed. Pascale Lambrechts and Jean-Pierre Sosson, 1–21. Louvain-la-Neuve, 1994.

Børresen, Kari Elisabeth. *Subordination and Equivalence: The Nature and Role of Woman in Augustine and Thomas Aquinas.* Trans. Charles H. Talbot. Washington, D.C., 1981.

Bouchard, Constance Brittain. *Strong of Body, Brave and Noble: Chivalry and Society in Medieval France.* Ithaca, N.Y., 1998.

Boulton, D'Arcy Jonathan Dacre. *The Knights of the Crown: The Monarchical Orders of Knighthood in Later Medieval Europe.* New York, 1987.

Bourdieu, Pierre. *Masculine Domination.* Trans. Richard Nice. Stanford, Calif., 2001.

Bousmar, Eric. "La place des hommes et des femmes dans les fêtes de cour bourguignonnes (Philippe le Bon-Charles le Hardi)." *Publications du Centre européen d'études bourguignonnes (xive–xvie s.)* 34 (1994): 123–43.

Boyarin, Daniel. *Unheroic Conduct: The Rise of Heterosexuality and the Invention of the Jewish Man.* Berkeley, 1997.

Boyce, Gray Cowan. *The English-German Nation in the University of Paris During the Middle Ages.* Bruges, 1927.

Brannon, Robert. "The Male Sex Role: Our Culture's Blueprint of Manhood, and What It's Done for Us Lately." In *The Forty-Nine Percent Majority: The Male Sex Role,* ed. Deborah S. David and Robert Brannon, 1–45. Reading, Mass., 1976.

Bresc-Bautier, Geneviève. *Artistes, patriciens et confréries: Production et consommation de l'oeuvre d'art à Palerme et en Sicile occidentale (1348–1460).* Rome, 1979.

Brittan, Arthur. *Masulinity and Power.* Oxford, 1989.

Brown, Elizabeth A. R., and Nancy Freeman Regalado. "*La grant feste*: Philip the Fair's Celebration of the Knighting of His Sons in Paris at Pentecost of 1313." In *City and Spectacle in Medieval Europe,* ed. Barbara Hanawalt and Kathryn Reyerson, 56–86. Minneapolis, 1994.

Bullough, Vern L. "On Being a Male in the Middle Ages." In *Medieval Masculinities: Regarding Men in the Middle Ages,* ed. Clare A. Lees with Thelma Fenster and Jo Ann McNamara, 31–45. Minneapolis, 1994.

Bulst, Neithard. "Studium und Karriere im königlichen Dienst in Frankreich im 15. Jahrhundert." In *Schulen und Studium im sozialen Wandel des hohen und späten Mittelalters,* ed. Johannes Fried, 375–405. Vorträge und Forschungen 30. Sigmaringen, 1986.

Bumke, Joachim. *The Concept of Knighthood in the Middle Ages.* Trans. W. T. H. and Erika Jackson. New York, 1982.

Burke, Peter. *Popular Culture in Early Modern Europe.* New York, 1978.

Burns, E. Jane. *Courtly Love Undressed: Reading Through Clothes in Medieval French Culture.* Philadelphia, 2002.

Burrow, J. A. *The Ages of Man: A Study in Medieval Writing and Thought*. Oxford, 1986.

Bynum, Caroline Walker. *Jesus as Mother: Studies in the Spirituality of the High Middle Ages*. Berkeley, 1982.

Cadden, Joan. *Meanings of Sex Difference in the Middle Ages: Medicine, Science, and Culture*. Cambridge, 1993.

Carrigan, Tim, Bob Connell, and John Lee. "Hard and Heavy: Toward a New Sociology of Masculinity." In *Beyond Patriarchy: Essays by Men on Pleasure, Power, and Change*, ed. Michael Kaufman, 139–92. New York, 1987.

———. "Toward a New Sociology of Masculinity." In *The Making of Masculinities: The New Men's Studies*, ed. Harry Brod, 63–100. Boston, 1987.

Catalogue of Additions to the Manuscripts in the British Museum in the Years 1900–1905. London, 1907.

Caviness, Madeline Harrison. *The Early Stained Glass of Canterbury Cathedral circa 1175–1220*. Princeton, N.J., 1977.

Cazelles, Raymond. *Nouvelle histoire de Paris de la fin du règne de Philippe Auguste à la mort de Charles V, 1323–1380*. Paris, 1994.

Chaplais, Pierre. *Piers Gaveston: Edward II's Adoptive Brother*. Oxford, 1994.

Chatelain, Émile. "Notes sur quelques tavernes fréquentés par l'université de Paris au xive et xve siècles." *Bulletin de la Société de l'histoire de Paris et de l'île de France* 25 (1898): 85–109.

Chism, Christine. *Alliterative Revivals*. Philadelphia, 2002.

Clode, Charles M. *The Early History of the Guild of Merchant Taylors of Fraternity of St. John the Baptist*. 2 vols. London, 1888.

Clough, Cecil H. "Chivalry and Magnificence in the Golden Age of the Italian Renaissance." In *Chivalry in the Renaissance*, ed. Sydney Anglo, 32–47. Rochester, N.Y., 1990.

Cobban, A. B. "Colleges and Halls 1380–1500." In *The History of the University of Oxford*, vol. 2, ed. J. I. Catto and Ralph Evans, 581–633. Oxford, 1992.

Cohn, Samuel Kline, Jr. *The Laboring Classes in Renaissance Florence*. New York, 1980.

Collins, Hugh E. L. *The Order of the Garter 1348–1461: Chivalry and Politics in Late Medieval England*. Oxford, 2000.

Colton, Larry. *Goat Brothers*. New York, 1993.

Congrès national des sociétiés savantes, ed. *Théâtre et spectacles hier et aujourd'hui*. Paris, 1991.

Connell, R. W. *Masculinities*. Berkeley, 1995.

Consitt, Frances. *The London Weavers' Company*. Vol. 1. Oxford, 1933.

Contamine, Philippe. *La noblesse au royaume de France de Philippe le Bel à Louis XII*. Paris, 1997.

———. *War in the Middle Ages*. Trans. Michael Jones. Cambridge, 1984.

Cooper, John. *The Child in Jewish History*. Northvale, N.J., 1996.

Cornwall, Andrea, and Nancy Lindisfarne. "Dislocating Masculinity: Gender, Power, and Anthropology." In *Dislocating Masculinity: Comparative Ethnographies*, ed. Andrea Cornwall and Nancy Lindisfarne, 11–47. London, 1994.

Cosman, Madeleine Pelner. *The Education of the Hero in Arthurian Romance.* Chapel Hill, N.C., 1965.

Coss, Peter. *The Knight in Medieval England 1000–1400.* Stroud, Gloucestershire, 1993.

Coulet, Noël. "Les confréries de métier en Provence au moyen âge." In *Travail et travailleurs en Europe au moyen âge et au début des temps modernes,* ed. Claire Dolan, 21–46. Papers in Mediaeval Studies. Toronto, 1991.

Courtenay, William J. *Parisian Scholars in the Early Fourteenth Century: A Social Portrait.* Cambridge, 1999.

———. *Schools and Scholars in Fourteenth-Century England.* Princeton, N.J., 1987.

Crossick, Geoffrey. "Past Masters: In Search of the Artisan in European History." In *The Artisan and the European Town,* ed. Geoffrey Crossick, 1–40. Aldershot, 1997.

Crouzet-Pavan, Elizabeth. "A Flower of Evil: Young Men in Medieval Italy." In *A History of Young People in the West: Ancient and Medieval Rites of Passage,* ed. Jean-Claude Schmitt and Giovanni Levi, trans. Camille Naish. 173–221. Cambridge, 1997.

Cullum, P. H. "Clergy, Masculinity and Transgression in Late Medieval England." In *Masculinity in Medieval Europe,* ed. Dawn M. Hadley, 178–96. New York, 1999.

Davies, Matthew. "Artisans, Guilds and Government in London." In *Daily Life in the Late Middle Ages,* ed. Richard Britnell, 125–50. Frome, Somerset, 1998.

De la Roncière, Charles. "La condition des salariés à Florence au XIVe siècle." In *Il tumulto dei Ciompi: Un momento di storia fiorentina ed europea,* 13–40. Florence, 1981.

———. *Prix et salaires à Florence au XIVe siècle.* Rome, 1982.

Denly, Peter. "The Collegiate Movement in Italian Universities in the Late Middle Ages." *History of Universities* 10 (1991): 29–74.

De Ridder-Symoens, Hilde. "Les origines géographiques et sociales des étudiants de la nation germanique de l'ancien université d'Orléans (1444–1546), Aperçu général." In *The Universities in the Late Middle Ages,* ed. Jozef Ijsewijn and Jacques Pacquet, 455–74. Medievalia Lovanensia Series 1, Studia 6. Leuven, 1978.

Des Marez, G. *L'organisation du travail à Bruxelles au XVe siècle.* Brussels, 1904.

De Waal, Frans B. M. "The Relation Between Power and Sex in the Simians: Socio-Sexual Appeasement Gestures." In *Gender Rhetorics: Postures of Dominance and Submission in History,* ed. Richard C. Trexler, 15–32. Binghamton, N.Y., 1994.

Didier, Philippe. "L'apprentissage médiéval en France: Formation professionelle, entretien ou emploi de la main-d'oeuvre juvénile?" *Zeitschrift der Savigny-Stiftung für Rechtsgeschichte, Germanistische Abteilung* 101 (1984): 200–255.

———. "Le contrat d'apprentissage en Bourgogne aux XIVe et XVe siècles." *Revue historique de droit français et étranger* 54 (1976): 35–57.

———. "Les contrats de travail en Bourgogne aux XIVe et XVe siècles d'après les archives notariales." *Revue historique de droit français et étranger* 50 (1972): 13–69.

Dod, Bernard G. "Aristoteles Latinus." In *The Cambridge History of Later Me-*

dieval Philosophy: From the Rediscovery of Aristotle to the Disintegration of Scholasticism, 1100–1600, ed. Norman Kretzmann, Anthony Kenny, and Jan Pinborg, 45–79. Cambridge, 1982.

Douglas, Audrey. "Midsummer in Salisbury: The Tailor's Guild and Confraternity 1444–1642." *Renaissance and Reformation/Renaissance et réforme* n.s. 13 (1989): 35–51.

Dove, Mary. *The Perfect Age of Man's Life*. Cambridge, 1986.

Doyle, James A. *The Male Experience*. 2nd ed. Dubuque, Ia., 1989.

Dronzek, Anna. *Manners, Models, and Morals: Gender, Status, and Codes of Conduct Among the Middle Classes of Late Medieval England*. Ph.D. Dissertation, University of Minnesota, 2001.

Duby, Georges, and Philippe Braunstein. "The Emergence of the Individual." In *A History of Private Life*. vol. 2, *Revelations of the Medieval World*, ed. Georges Duby, trans. Arthur Goldhammer, 507–630. Cambridge, 1988.

Düll, Siegrid, Anthony Luttrell, and Maurice Keen. "Faithful unto Death: The Tomb Slab of Sir William Neville and Sir John Clanvowe, Constantinople 1391." *Antiquaries Journal* 71 (1991): 174–90.

Dunbabin, Jean. "Meeting the Cost of University Education in Northern France, c. 1240–1340." *History of Universities* 10 (1991): 1–28.

Edley, Nigel, and Margaret Wetherell. *Men in Perspective: Practice, Power, and Identity*. London, 1995.

Elias, Norbert. *The Civilizing Process*. Trans. Edmund Jephcott. 2 vols. New York, 1978–82.

Enders, Jody. "The Theater of Scholastic Erudition." *Comparative Drama* 27 (1993): 341–63.

Epstein, Cynthia Fuchs. *Deceptive Distinctions: Sex, Gender, and the Social Order*. New Haven, Conn., 1988.

Epstein, Steven A. *Wage Labor and Guilds in Medieval Europe*. Chapel Hill, N.C., 1991.

Evans, T. A. R. "The Number, Origins, and Careers of Scholars." In *The History of the University of Oxford*, vol. 2, ed. J. I. Catto and Ralph Evans, 485–538. Oxford, 1992.

Fabricius, Wilhelm. *Die Akademische Deposition*. Frankfurt am Main, 1895.

Fagniez, Gustave. *Etudes sur l'industrie et la classe industrielle à Paris au XIIIe et XIVe siècles*. Paris, 1877.

Farmer, Sharon, and Carol Braun Pasternack, eds. *Difference and Genders in the Middle Ages*. Minneapolis, forthcoming.

Farr, James. *Artisans in Europe 1300–1914*. Cambridge, 2000.

Fausto-Sterling, Anne. *Myths of Gender: Biological Theories about Women and Men*. New York, 1985.

Ferguson, Arthur B. *The Indian Summer of English Chivalry: Studies in the Decline and Transformation of Chivalric Idealism*. Durham, N.C., 1960.

Fernandez de Pinedo, Emiliano. "Structure économique et conflits sociaux: Corporations et marchands dans la monarchie espagnole (XIIIe au XVIIIe siècles)." In *Forme ed evoluzione del lavoro in Europa: XIII–XVIII secc.*, 449–66. Prato, 1991.

Fisher, Sheila. "Taken Men and Token Women in *Sir Gawain and the Green Knight.*" In *Seeking the Woman in Late Medieval and Renaissance Writings,* ed. Sheila Fisher and Janet E. Halley, 71–105. Knoxville, 1989.

Fleckenstein, Josef. *Ordnungen und formende Kräfte des Mittelalters: Ausgewählte Beiträge.* Göttingen, 1989.

Fletcher, John M. "Commentary." *History of Universities* 6 (1986–87): 139–41.

Fradenburg, Louise Olga. *City, Marriage, Tournament: Arts of Rule in Late Medieval Scotland.* Madison, 1991.

Fuchs, Christoph. *Dives, pauper, nobilis, magister, frater, clericus: Sozialgeschichtliche Untersuchungen über Heidelberger Universitätsbesucher des Spätmittelalters (1386–1450).* Education and Society in the Middle Ages and Renaissance 5. New York, 1995.

Gabriel, A. L., ed. *The Economic and Material Frame of the Medieval University.* Notre Dame, Ind., 1977.

García y García, Antonio. "The Faculties of Law." In *Universities in the Middle Ages,* ed. Hilde de Ridder-Symoens, 388–408. Cambridge, 1992.

———. "The Medieval Students of the University of Salamanca." *History of Universities* 10 (1991): 93–115.

Gencier, Pierre. "Tournoiement as Dames de Paris." In *Lude e Spettacoli nel Medioevo: I Tornei de Dame,* ed. Andrea Pulega, 21–63. Milan, 1970.

Geremek, Bronislaw. *The Margins of Society in Late Medieval Paris.* Trans. Jean Birrell. Cambridge, 1987.

———. *Le salariat dans l'artisanat parisien aux XIIIe–XVe siècles.* Trans. Anna Posner and Christiane Klapisch-Zuber. Industrie et Artisanat 5. Paris, 1968.

Gillespie, James L. "Richard II's Knights: Chivalry and Patronage." *Journal of Medieval History* 13 (1987): 143–59.

Gingerich, Owen and Miriam. "Matriculation Ages in Sixteenth-Century Wittenberg." *History of Universities* 6 (1986–87): 135–37.

Glorieux, Palémon. *La littérature quodlibétique de 1260 à 1320.* Bibliothèque Thomiste 5. Le Saulchoir Kain, 1925.

———. *La litterature quodlibetique, II.* Bibliothèque Thomiste 21. Paris, 1935.

Goldberg, P. J. P. "Masters and Men in Later Medieval England." In *Masculinity in Medieval Europe,* ed. Dawn M. Hadley, 56–70. London, 1999.

———. *Women, Work, and the Life Cycle in a Medieval Economy: Women in York and Yorkshire c. 1300–1520.* New York, 1992.

Gorn, Elliott J. *The Manly Art: Bare-Knuckle Prize Fighting in America.* Ithaca, N.Y., 1986.

Gouron, André. *La réglementation des métiers en Languedoc au moyen âge.* Etudes d'histoire économique, politique et sociale, 22. Geneva, 1958.

Grabmann, Martin. *Die Geschichte der scholastischen Methode.* Vol. 2. Freiburg im Breisgau, 1911, repr. Graz, 1957.

Gravdal, Kathryn. *Ravishing Maidens: Writing Rape in Medieval French Literature and Law.* Philadelphia, 1991.

Green, Monica. "Women's Medical Practice and Health Care in Medieval Europe." *Signs: Journal of Women in Culture and Society* 14 (1989): 434–73.

Gunn, Alan M. F. "Teacher and Student in the *Roman de la Rose*: A Study in Archetypal Figures and Patterns." *Esprit créateur* 2 (1962): 126–34.

Hale, Rosemary Drage. "Joseph as Mother: Adaptation and Appropriation in the Construction of Male Virtue." In *Medieval Mothering*, ed. John Carmi Parsons and Bonnie Wheeler, 101–16. New York, 1996.

Hammer, Carl I., Jr. "The Town-Gown Confraternity of St. Thomas the Martyr in Oxford." *Medieval Studies* 39 (1977): 466–76.

Hanawalt, Barbara. " 'The Childe of Bristowe' and the Making of Middle-class Adolescence." In *Bodies and Disciplines: Intersections of Literature and History in Fifteenth Century England*, ed. Barbara Hanawalt and David Wallace, 155–78. Minneapolis, 1996.

———. *Growing Up in Medieval London: The Experience of Childhood in History.* New York, 1993.

———. *The Ties That Bound: Peasant Families in Medieval England.* New York, 1986.

Hantz, Johann Friedrich. *Geschichte der Universität Heidelberg.* Vol. 1. Mannheim, 1862.

Harvey, Barbara. *Living and Dying in England, 1100–1540: The Monastic Experience.* Oxford, 1993.

Harvey, Ruth. *Moriz von Craûn and the Chivalric World.* Oxford, 1961.

Haskins, Charles Homer. *Studies in Medieval Culture.* New York, 1965.

Helmholz, R. H. *Marriage Litigation in Medieval England.* Cambridge, 1974.

Herlihy, David. *Medieval Households.* Cambridge, Mass. 1985.

———, and Christiane Klapische-Zuber. *Tuscans and Their Families: A Study of the Florentine Catasto of 1427.* New Haven, Conn., 1985.

Howell, Martha. *The Marriage Exchange: Property, Social Place, and Gender in Cities of the Low Countries, 1300–1550.* Chicago, 1998.

Huizinga, Johan. *Men and Ideas: History, the Middle Ages, and the Renaissance.* Trans. James S. Holmes and Hans van Marle. Princeton, N.J., 1984.

Hunt, Tony. "The Emergence of the Knight in France and England 1000–1200." In *Knighthood in Medieval Literature*, ed. W. H. Jackson, 1–22. Woodbridge, Suffolk, 1981.

Ikegami, Eiko. *The Taming of the Samurai.* Cambridge, Mass., 1995.

Ingham, Patricia Clare. *Sovereign Fantasies: Arthurian Romance and the Making of Britain.* Philadelphia, 2001.

Itzcovich, Oscar. "Masters and Apprentices in Genoese Society, 1450–1535." In *History and Computing II*, ed. Peter Denley, Stefan Fogelvik, and Charles Harvey, 209–18. Manchester, 1989.

Jackson, William H. "The Tournament and Chivalry in German Tournament Books of the Sixteenth Century and in the Literary Works of Emperor Maximilian I." In *The Ideals and Practice of Medieval Knighthood*, ed. Christopher Harper-Bill and Ruth Harvey, 19–73. Woodbridge, Suffolk, 1986.

———. "Tournaments and the German Chivalric *Renovatio*: Tournament Discipline and the Myth of Origins." In *Chivalry in the Renaissance*, ed. Sydney Anglo, 77–91. Rochester, N.Y., 1990.

Jacobsen, Grethe. "Economic Progress and the Sexual Division of Labor: The Role of Guilds in the Late-Medieval Danish City." In *Alltag und Fortschritt im Mittelalter*, 223–36. Veröffentlichungen des Instituts für mittelalterliche Realienkunde Österreichs, 8. Vienna, 1986.

Jacquart, Danielle, and Claude Thomasset. *Sexuality and Medicine in the Middle Ages*. Trans. Matthew Adamson. Princeton, N.J., 1988.

Jaeger, C. Stephen. *Ennobling Love: In Search of a Lost Sensibility*. Philadelphia, 1999.

———. *The Origins of Courtliness: Civilizing Trends and the Formation of Courtly Ideals 939–1210*. Philadelphia, 1985.

Janse, Antheun. "Marriage and Noble Lifestyle in Holland in the Later Middle Ages." In *Showing Status: Representation of Social Positions in the Late Middle Ages*, ed. Wim Blockmans and Antheun Janse, 113–38. Turnhout, 1999.

John, James. *The College of Prémontré in Mediaeval Paris*. Texts and Studies in the History of Medieval Education, 1. Notre Dame, Ind., 1953.

Jourdan, Jean-Pierre. "Le langage amoureux dans le combat de chevalerie à la fin du Moyen Age (France, Bourgogne, Anjou)." *Le moyen âge* 99 (1993): 84–106.

Kaeuper, Richard W. *Chivalry and Violence in Medieval Europe*. Oxford, 1999.

———. *War, Justice, and Public Order: England and France in the Later Middle Ages*. Oxford, 1988.

Karras, Ruth Mazo. *Common Women: Prostitution and Sexuality in Medieval England*. New York, 1996.

———. "Gendered Sin and Misogyny in John of Bromyard's 'Summa Predicantium.' " *Traditio* 47 (1992): 233–57.

———. "Separating the Men from the Goats: Masculinity, Civilization, and Identity Formation in the Medieval University." In *Conflicted Identities and Multiple Masculinities: Men in the Medieval West*, ed. Jacqueline Murray, 189–213. New York, 1999.

———. "Two Models, Two Standards: Moral Teaching and Sexual Mores." In *Bodies and Disciplines: Intersections of Literature and History in Fifteenth-Century England*, ed. Barbara A. Hanawalt and David Wallace, 123–38. Minneapolis, 1996.

Kaufman, Michael. "Men, Feminism, and Men's Contradictory Experiences of Power." In *Theorizing Masculinities*, ed. Harry Brod and Michael Kaufman, 142–63. Thousand Oaks, Calif., 1994.

Kay, Sarah. *Subjectivity in Troubadour Poetry*. Cambridge, 1990.

Keats-Rohan, K. S. B. "John of Salisbury and Education in Twelfth-Century Paris from the Account of His *Metalogicon*." *History of Universities* 6 (1986–87): 1–45.

Keen, Maurice. *Chivalry*. New Haven, Conn., 1984.

———, and Juliet Barker. "The Medieval English Kings and the Tournament." In Maurice Keen, *Nobles, Knights, and Men-at-Arms in the Middle Ages*, 83–89. London, 1996.

Keen, Sam. *Fire in the Belly*. New York, 1991.

Keiser, Elizabeth B. *Courtly Desire and Medieval Homophobia: The Legitimation of Sexual Pleasure in* Cleanness *and Its Contexts*. New Haven, Conn., 1997.

Kelly, Henry Ansgar. *Love and Marriage in the Age of Chaucer.* Ithaca, N.Y., 1975.

Kennedy, Beverly. *Knighthood in the Morte Darthur.* Rochester, N.Y., 1992.

Kennedy, Elspeth. "The Knight as Reader of Arthurian Romance." In *Culture and the King: The Social Implications of the Arthurian Legend, Essays in Honor of Valerie M. Lagorio,* ed. Martin B. Shichtman and James P. Carley, 70–90. Albany, 1994.

Kenny, Anthony, and Jan Pinborg. "Medieval Philosophical Literature." In *The Cambridge History of Later Medieval Philosophy: From the Rediscovery of Aristotle to the Disintegration of Scholasticism, 1100–1600,* ed. Norman Kretzmann, Anthony Kenny, and Jan Pinborg, 11–42. Cambridge, 1982.

Kibre, Pearl. *The Nations in the Mediaeval Universities.* Cambridge, Mass., 1948.

Kimmel, Michael S. "The Contemporary 'Crisis' of Masculinity in Historical Perspective." In *The Making of Masculinities: The New Men's Studies,* ed. Harry Brod, 121–53. Boston, 1987.

———. *Manhood in America: A Cultural History.* New York, 1996.

Kinser, Samuel. "Presentation and Representation: Carnival at Nuremberg, 1450–1550." *Representations* 13 (1986): 1–41.

Kittel, Rudolf. *Die Universität Leipzig und ihre Stellung im Kulturleben.* Dresden, 1924.

Kleineidam, Erich. *Universitas Studii Erffordensis: Überblick über der Universität Erfurt im Mittelalter, 1392–1521.* Leipzig, 1964.

Kowaleski, Maryanne. "Singlewomen in Medieval and Early Modern Europe: The Demographic Perspective." In *Singlewomen in the European Past 1250–1800,* ed. Judith M. Bennett and Amy M. Froide, 38–81. Philadelphia, 1999.

———, and Judith M. Bennett. "Crafts, Gilds, and Women in the Middle Ages: Fifty Years After Marian K. Dale." *Signs: Journal of Women in Culture and Society* 14 (1989): 474–88.

Ladurie, Emmanuel Le Roy. *Montaillou: The Promised Land of Error.* Trans. Barbara Bray. New York, 1978.

Laqueur, Thomas. *Making Sex: Body and Gender from the Greeks to Freud.* Cambridge, 1990.

Laslett, Peter. "Family and Household as Work Group and Kin Group: Areas of Traditional Europe Compared." In *Forme ed evoluzione del lavoro in Europa: XIII–XVIII secc.,* 289–333. Prato, 1991.

Lawrence, C. H. "The University in State and Church." In *The History of the University of Oxford,* vol. 1, ed. J. I. Catto, 97–150. Oxford, 1984.

Lees, Clare A., with Thelma Fenster and Jo Ann McNamara, ed. *Medieval Masculinities: Regarding Men in the Middle Ages.* Minneapolis, 1994.

Leff, Gordon. *Paris and Oxford Universities in the Thirteenth and Fourteenth Centuries: An Institutional and Intellectual History.* New York, 1968.

———. "The *Trivium* and the Three Philosophies." In *Universities in the Middle Ages,* ed. Hilde de Ridder-Symoens, 307–36. A History of the University in Europe, 1. Cambridge, 1992.

Le Goff, Jacques. *Time, Work, and Culture in the Middle Ages.* Chicago, 1980.

———. *Intellectuals in the Middle Ages.* Trans. Teresa Lavender Fagan. Cambridge, Mass., 1992.

Leguay, Jean-Pierre. "Les métiers de l'artisanat dans les villes du duché de Bretagne aux XIVe et XVe siècles." In *Les métiers au moyen âge: Aspects économiques et sociaux*, ed. Pascale Lambrechts and Jean-Pierre Sosson, 157–204. Louvain-la-Neuve, 1994.

Lemay, Helen Rodnite. "Some Thirteenth and Fourteenth Century Lectures on Female Sexuality." *International Journal of Women's Studies* 1 (1978): 391–400.

Lett, Didier. *L'enfant des miracles: Enfance et société au moyen âge (XIIe–XIIIe siècle)*. Paris, 1997.

Leupen, P. *Philip of Leyden: A 14th-Century Jurist*. The Hague, 1981.

Lindenbaum, Sheila. "The Smithfield Tournament of 1390." *Journal of Medieval and Renaissance Studies* 20 (1990): 1–20.

Lochrie, Karma. *Covert Operations: The Medieval Uses of Secrecy*. Philadelphia, 1999.

Lohr, C. H. "The Medieval Intepretation of Aristotle." In *The Cambridge History of Later Medieval Philosophy: From the Rediscovery of Aristotle to the Disintegration of Scholasticism, 1100–1600*, ed. Norman Kretzmann, Anthony Kenny, and Jan Pinborg, 80–98. Cambridge, 1982.

Löw, Leopold. *Die Lebensalter in der jüdischen Literatur*. Szegedin, 1875.

Lynch, Andrew. *Malory's Book of Arms: The Narrative of Combat in* Le Morte Darthur. Cambridge, 1997.

Lytle, Guy Fitch. "The Careers of Oxford Students in the Later Middle Ages." In *Rebirth, Reform and Resilience: Universities in Transition 1300–1700*, ed. James M. Kittelson and Pamela J. Transue, 213–53. Columbus, Ohio, 1984.

———. "Patronage Patterns and Oxford Colleges c. 1300–1530." In *The University in Society*, vol. 1, ed. Lawrence Stone, 111–49. Princeton, N.J., 1974.

———. "The Social Origins of Oxford Students in the Late Middle Ages: New College, c. 1380–c. 1510." In *The Universities in the Late Middle Ages*, ed. Jozef Ijsewijn and Jacques Pacquet, 426–54. Leuven, 1978.

MacInnes, John. *The End of Masculinity*. Buckingham, 1998.

Mackenney, Richard. *Tradesmen and Traders: The World of the Guilds in Venice and Europe, c. 1250–c. 1650*. Totowa, N.J., 1987.

Maclean, Ian. *The Renaissance Notion of Woman: A Study in the Fortunes of Scholasticism and Medical Science in European Intellectual Life*. Cambridge, 1980.

Maierù, Alfonso. *University Training in Medieval Europe*. Trans. D. N. Pryds. Leiden, 1994.

Marchello-Nizia, Christiane. "Amour courtois, société masculine et figures du pouvoir." *Annales: Économies, sociétés, civilisations* 36 (1981): 969–81.

———. "Courtly Chivalry." In *A History of Young People in the West: Ancient and Medieval Rites of Passage*, ed. Jean-Claude Schmitt, and Giovanni Levi, trans. Camille Naish, 120–72. Cambridge, Mass., 1997.

Marcus, Ivan. *Rituals of Childhood: Jewish Acculturation in Medieval Europe*. New Haven, Conn., 1996.

Marenbon, John. *Later Medieval Philosophy (1150–1350): An Introduction*. New York, 1987.

Märker, Almuth. *Geschichte der Universität Erfurt 1392–1816*. Weimar, 1993.

Marti, Berthe M., ed. *The Spanish College at Bologna in the Fourteenth Century*. Philadelphia, 1966.

McCulloch, Florence. *Medieval Latin and French Bestiaries*. Chapel Hill, N.C., 1962.

McFarlane, K. B. "The Investment of Sir John Fastolfe's Profits of War." *Transactions of the Royal Historical Society* 5th ser. 7 (1957): 91–116.

McGuire, Brian Patrick. "Gerson and Bernard: Languishing with Love." *Citeaux* 46 (1995): 127–56.

————. "Jean Gerson and Traumas of Masculine Affectivity and Sexuality." In *Conflicted Identities and Multiple Masculinities: Men in the Medieval West*, ed. Jacqueline Murray, 45–72. New York, 1999.

McIntosh, Marjorie Keniston. *Controlling Misbehavior in England, 1370–1600*. Cambridge, 1998.

McNamara, Jo Ann. "The *Herrenfrage*: The Restructuring of the Gender System, 1050–1150." In *Medieval Masculinities: Regarding Men in the Middle Ages*, ed. Clare A. Lees, with Thelma Fenster and Jo Ann McNamara, 3–29. Minneapolis, 1994.

McRee, Benjamin R. "Unity or Division? The Social Meaning of Guild Ceremony in Urban Communities." In *City and Spectacle in Medieval Europe*, ed. Barbara A. Hanawalt and Kathryn L. Reyerson, 189–207. Minneapolis, 1994.

McSheffrey, Shannon. "Men and Masculinity in Late Medieval London Civic Culture: Governance, Patriarchy, and Reputation." In *Conflicted Identities and Multiple Masculinities: Men in the Medieval West*, ed. Jacqueline Murray, 243–78. New York, 1999.

Mellinkoff, Ruth. *The Horned Moses in Medieval Art and Thought*. Berkeley, 1970.

Menjot, Dennis. "Les métiers en Castille au bas moyen âge: Approche des vécus socio-économiques." In *Les métiers au moyen âge: Aspects économiques et sociaux*, ed. Pascale Lambrechts and Jean-Pierre Sosson, 205–27. Louvain-la-neuve, 1994.

Meuthen, Erich. "Bursen und Artesfakultät der alten Kölner Universität." In *Philosophy and Learning: Universities in the Middle Ages*, ed. J. F. M. Maarten, J. H. Hoenen, Josef Schneider, and Georg Wieland, 225–45. Education and Society in the Middle Ages and Renaissance 6. Leiden, 1995.

Meyer, Werner. "Turniergesellschaftern. Bemerkungen zur sozialgeschichtlichen Bedeutung der Turniere im Spätmittelalter." In *Das ritterliche Turnier im Mittelalter: Beiträge zu einer vergleichenden Formen- und Verhaltensgeschichte des Rittertums*, ed. Josef Fleckenstein, 500–512. Göttingen, 1985.

Michaud, Francine. "Apprentissage et salariat à Marseille avant la peste noire." *Revue historique* 291 (1994): 3–36.

Michaud-Fréjaville, Françoise. "Crise urbaine et apprentissage à Orléans, 1475–1500." In *Villes, bonnes villes, cités et capitales: Études d'histoire urbaine (XIIe–XVIIIe siècle)*, ed. Monique Bourin, 13–23. Caen, 1993.

————. "Enfants orphelins, enfants séparés, enfants élevés: Gardes et des mineurs d'âge à Orléans au XVe siècle." In *Education, apprentissages, initiation au moyen âge*, 297–308. Montpellier, 1991.

Mitterauer, Michael. *A History of Youth*. Trans. Graeme Dunphy. Oxford, 1992.

Moraw, Peter. "Careers of Graduates." In *Universities in the Middle Ages*, ed. Hilde de Ridder-Symoens, 244–79. Cambridge, 1992.

Mormando, Franco. *The Preacher's Demons: Bernardino of Siena and the Social Underworld of Early Renaissance Italy*. Chicago, 1999.

Moulin, Léo. *La vie des étudiants au moyen âge*. Paris, 1991.

Muchembled, Robert. "Die Jugend und die Volkskultur im 15. Jahrhundert: Flandern und Artois." In *Volkskultur des europäischen Spätmittelalters*, ed. Peter Dinzelbacher and Hans-Dieter Mück, 35–58. Stuttgart, 1987.

Murray, Alexander. *Reason and Society in the Middle Ages*. Oxford, 1978.

Najemy, John M. "*Audiant Omnes Artes:* Corporate Origins of the Ciompi Revolution." In *Il tumulto dei Ciompi: Un momento di storia fiorentina ed europea*, 59–93. Florence, 1981.

Nicholas, David. "In the Pit of the Burgundian Theater State: Urban Traditions and Princely Ambitions in Ghent, 1360–1420." In *City and Spectacle in Medieval Europe*, ed. Barbara Hanawalt and Kathryn Reyerson, 271–95. Minneapolis, 1994.

———. *The Metamorphosis of a Medieval City: Ghent in the Age of Arteveldes, 1302–1390*. Lincoln, 1987.

Nickel, Helmut. "The Tournament: An Historical Sketch." In *The Study of Chivalry: Resources and Approaches*, ed. Howell Chickering and Thomas H. Seiler, 213–53. Kalamazoo, Mich., 1988.

Nijsten, Gerard. "The Duke and His Towns: The Power of Ceremonies, Feasts, and Public Amusement in the Duchy of Guelders (East Netherlands) in the Fourteenth and Fifteenth Centuries." In *City and Spectacle in Medieval Europe*, ed. Barbara Hanawalt and Kathryn Reyerson, 235–70. Minneapolis, 1994.

Noble, David. *A World Without Women: The Christian Clerical Culture of Western Science*. New York, 1993.

North, John. "The Quadrivium." In *Universities in the Middle Ages*, ed. Hilde de Ridder-Symoens, 307–36. Cambridge, 1992.

Ong, Walter. *Fighting for Life: Contest, Sexuality, and Consciousness*. Ithaca, N.Y., 1981.

Oostrom, Frits Pieter van. *Court and Culture: Dutch Literature, 1350–1450*. Trans. Arnold J. Pomerans. Berkeley, 1992.

Orme, Nicholas. "The Education of the Courtier." In *English Court Culture in the Later Middle Ages*, ed. V. J. Scattergood, and J. W. Sherborne, 63–85. London, 1983.

———. *From Childhood to Chivalry: The Education of the English Kings and Aristocracy 1066–1530*. London, 1984.

Pacquet, Jacques. "Coût des études, pauvreté et labeur: Fonctions et métiers d'étudiants au moyen âge." *History of Universities* 2 (1982): 21–34.

Paravicini, Werner. "Soziale Schichtung und soziale Mobilität am hof der Herzöge von Burgund." *Francia* 5 (1977): 127–82.

Pflugfelder, Gregory M. *Cartographies of Desire: Male-Male Sexuality in Japanese Discourse, 1600–1950*. Berkeley, 1999.

Phillips, Kim M. "Maidenhood as the Perfect Age of Woman's Life." In *Young*

Medieval Women, ed. Katherine J. Lewis, Noël James Menuge, and Kim M. Phillips, 1–24. New York, 1999.

Phythian-Adams, Charles. *Desolation of a City: Coventry and the Urban Crisis of the Late Middle Ages.* Cambridge, 1979.

Pleck, Joseph H. *The Myth of Masculinity.* Cambridge, Mass. 1981.

Poos, L. R. "Sex, Lies, and the Church Courts of Pre-Reformation England." *Journal of Interdisciplinary History* 25. (1995): 585–607.

Powers, James F. *A Society Organized for War: The Iberian Municipal Militias in the Central Middle Ages, 1000–1284.* Berkeley, 1988.

Prescott, Andrew. "London in the Peasants' Revolt: A Portrait Gallery." *London Journal* 7 (1981): 125–43.

Quynn, Dorothy Mackay, and Harold Sinclair Snellgrove. "Slanderous Comedies at the University of Orléans in 1447." *Modern Language Notes* 57 (1942): 185–88.

Rashdall, Hastings. *The Universities of Europe in the Middle Ages.* Ed. F. M. Powicke and A. B. Emden, 2nd ed. 3 vols. Oxford, 1936.

Reininghaus, Wilfried. *Die Entstehung der Gesellengilden im Spätmittelalter.* Vierteljahrschrift für Sozial- und Wirtschaftsgeschichte, Beihefte 71. Wiesbaden, 1981.

Reyerson, Kathryn L. "The Adolescent Apprentice/Worker in Medieval Montpellier." *Journal of Family History* 17 (1992): 353–70.

Reynolds, Michael T. "René of Anjou, King of Sicily, and the Order of the *Croissant.*" *Journal of Medieval History* 19 (1993): 125–61.

Reynolds, Susan. *Fiefs and Vassals: The Medieval Evidence Reinterpreted.* Oxford, 1994.

Richmond, Colin. *The Paston Family in the Fifteenth Century: Endings.* Manchester, 2000.

Rigby, S. H. *English Society in the Later Middle Ages: Class, Status, and Gender.* New York, 1995.

Ritter, Gerhard. "Über den Quellenwert und Verfasser des sogennanten 'Heidelberger Gesprächbüchleins für Studenten' (Manuale scholarium, um 1490)." *Zeitschrift für die Geschichte des Oberrheins* N.F. 38 (1923): 4–32.

Rocke, Michael. *Forbidden Friendships: Homosexuality and Male Culture in Renaissance Florence.* New York, 1996.

Romano, Dennis. *Housecraft and Statecraft: Domestic Service in Renaissance Venice, 1400–1600.* Baltimore, 1996.

———. *Patricians and Popolani: The Social Foundations of the Venetian Renaissance State.* Baltimore, 1987.

Roper, Lyndal. *The Holy Household: Women and Morals in Reformation Augsburg.* Oxford, 1989.

Rosenwein, Barbara H., ed. *Anger's Past: The Social Uses of an Emotion in the Middle Ages.* Ithaca, N.Y., 1998.

Rosser, Gervase. "Crafts, Guilds and the Negotiation of Work in the Medieval Town." *Past and Present* 154 (1997): 1–31.

———. "Going to the Fraternity Feast: Commensality and Social Relations in Late Medieval England." *Journal of British Studies* 33 (1994): 430–46.

————. "Solidarités et changement social: Les fraternités urbaines anglaises à la fin du moyen âge." *Annales: Économies, sociétés, civilisations* 48 (1993): 1127–44.

————. "Workers' Associations in English Medieval Towns." In *Les métiers au moyen âge: Aspects économiques et sociaux,* ed. Pascale Lambrechts and Jean-Pierre Sosson, 283–305. Louvain-la-Neuve, 1994.

Rossiaud, Jacques. "Fraternités de jeunesse et niveaux de culture dans les villes du Sud-Est à la fin du moyen âge." *Cahiers d'histoire* 21 (1976): 67–102.

————. *Medieval Prostitution.* Oxford, 1988.

Rotundo, E. Anthony. *American Manhood: Transformations in Masculinity from the Revolution to the Modern Era.* New York, 1993.

Rowland, Beryl. *Blind Beasts: Chaucer's Animal World.* Kent, Ohio, 1971.

Salisbury, Joyce. *The Beast Within: Animals in the Middle Ages.* New York, 1994.

Sanday, Peggy Reeves. *Fraternity Gang Rape: Sex, Brotherhood, and Privilege on Campus.* New York, 1990.

Sanderlin, David. *The Medieval Statutes of the College of Autun in the University of Paris.* Texts and Studies in the History of Medieval Education 13. Notre Dame, Ind., 1971.

Sandoz, Edward. "Tourneys in the Arthurian Tradition." *Speculum* 19 (1944): 389–420.

Sargent-Baur, Barbara. "Promotion to Knighthood in the Romances of Chrétien de Troyes." *Romance Philology* 37 (1984): 393–408.

Saxonhouse, Arlene. *Women in the History of Political Thought, Ancient Greece to Machiavelli.* New York, 1985.

Schröder, Rainer. *Zur Arbeitsverfassung des Spätmittelalters.* Berlin, 1984.

Schultz, James A. *The Knowledge of Childhood in the German Middle Ages.* Philadelphia, 1995.

Schulz, Knut. *Handwerksgesellen und Lohnarbeiter: Untersuchungen zur oberrheinischen und oberdeutschen Stadtgeschichte des 14. bis 17. Jahrhunderts.* Sigmaringen, 1985.

————. "Die Stellung der Gesellen in der spätmittelalterlichen Stadt." In *Haus und Familie in der spätmittelalterlichen Stadt,* ed. Alfred Haverkamp, 304–26. Cologne, 1984.

Schwinges, Rainer Christoph. "Admission." In *Universities in the Middle Ages,* ed. Hilde de Ridder-Symoens, 171–94. Cambridge, 1992.

————. *Deutsche Universitätsbesucher im 14. und 15. Jahrhundert: Studien zur Sozialgeschichte des alten Reiches.* Stuttgart, 1986.

————. "Sozialgeschichtliche Aspekte spätmittelalterlicher Studentenbursen in Deutschland." In *Schulen und Studium im sozialen Wandel des hohen und späten Mittelalters,* ed. Johannes Fried, 530–44. Sigmaringen, 1986.

————. "Student Education, Student Life." In *Universities in the Middle Ages,* ed. Hilde de Ridder-Symoens, 195–243. Cambridge, 1992.

————. "Studentische Kleingruppen im späten Mittelalter: Ein Beitrag zur sozialgeschichte deutscher Universitäten." In *Politik, Gesellschaft, Geschichtsschreibung: Giessener Festgabe für František Graus zum 60. Geburtstag,* 319–61. Cologne, 1982.

————, ed. *Gelehrte im Reich: Zur Sozial- und Wirkungsgeschichte akademischer*

Eliten des 14. bis 16. Jahrhunderts. Zeitschrift für historische Forschung, Beiheft 18. Berlin, 1996.

Sears, Elizabeth. *The Ages of Man: Medieval Interpretations of the Life Cycle.* Princeton, N.J., 1986.

Shank, Michael. "A Female University Student in Late Medieval Kraków." *Signs: Journal of Women in Culture and Society* 12, (1987): 373–80.

Simon-Muscheid, Katharina. "Gewalt und Ehre im spätmittelalterlichen Handwerk am Beispiel Basels." *Zeitschrift für historische Forschung* 18 (1991): 1–31.

Solterer, Helen. "Figures of Female Militancy in Medieval France." *Signs: Journal of Women in Culture and Society* 16 (1991): 522–49.

———. *The Master and Minerva: Disputing Women in French Medieval Culture.* Berkeley, 1995.

Sosson, Jean-Pierre. "L'artisanat Bruxellois du metal: Hierarchie sociale, salaires et puissance économique (1360–1500)." *Cahiers Bruxellois* 7 (1962): 225–58.

———. "Die Körperschaften in den Niederlanden und Nordfrankreich: Neue Forschungsperspektiven." In *Gilde und Korporation in den nordeuropäischen Städten des späten Mittelalters*, ed. Klaus Friedland, 80–90. Cologne, 1984.

———. "Les métiers: Norme et réalité. L'exemple des anciens pays-bas méridionaux aux XIVe et XVe siècles." In *Le travail au moyen âge: Une approche interdisciplinaire: Actes du colloque international de Louvain-la-Neuve, 21–23 mai 1987*, ed. Jacqueline Hamesse and Colette Muraille-Samaran, 339–48. Louvain-la-Neuve, 1990.

———. "La structure sociale de la corporation médiévale: L'exemple des tonneliers de Bruges de 1350 à 1500." *Revue belge de philologie et d'histoire* 44 (1966): 457–77.

Sprandel, Rolf. "Der handwerkliche Familienbetrieb des Spätmittelalters und seine Probleme." In *Haus und Familie in der spätmittelalterlichen Stadt*, ed. Alfred Haverkamp, 327–37. Cologne, 1984.

Stanesco, Michel. "Chevalerie médiévale et symbolisme guerrier: Le bacheler 'D'Espée engendrez.' " *Littératures* 12 (spring 1985): 7–13.

———. *Jeux d'errance du chevalier médiéval: Aspects ludiques de la fonction guerrière dans la littérature du moyen âge flamboyant.* New York, 1988.

Stella, Alessandro. *La révolte des Ciompi: Les hommes, les lieux, le travail.* Paris, 1993.

Stoertz, Fiona Harris. *Adolescence in Medieval Culture: The High Medieval Transformation.* Ph.D. dissertation, University of California, Santa Barbara, 1999.

Strohm, Paul. *Theory and the Premodern Text.* Minneapolis, 2000.

Strubel, Armand. "Le pas d'armes: Le tournoi entre le romanesque et le théâtral." In *Théâtre et spectacles hier et aujourd'hui*, ed. Congrès national des sociétés savantes, 273–84. Paris, 1991.

Stuard, Susan Mosher. "Burdens of Matrimony: Husbanding and Gender in Medieval Italy." In *Medieval Masculinities: Regarding Men in the Middle Ages*, ed. Clare A. Lees, with Thelma Fenster and Jo Ann McNamara, 61–71. Minneapolis, 1994.

Svanidze, A. A. "Town Handicraft and Hired Labour in Mediaeval Sweden in the 13th to Early 15th Centuries." In *Forme ed evoluzione del lavoro in Europa: XIII–XVIII secc.*, 559–90. Prato, 1991.

Swanson, Heather. "The Illusion of Economic Structure: Craft Guilds in Late Medieval English Towns." *Past and Present*, 121 (1988): 29–48.

———. *Medieval Artisans: An Urban Class in Late Medieval England.* Oxford, 1989.

Swanson, R. N. "Angels Incarnate: Clergy and Masculinity from Gregorian Reform to Reformation." In *Masculinity in Medieval Europe*, ed. Dawn M. Hadley, 160–77. New York, 1999.

———. "Learning and Livings: University Study and Clerical Careers in Late Medieval England." *History of Universities* 6 (1987): 81–103.

Tanaka, Mineo. *La nation anglo-allemande de l'Université de Paris à la fin du moyen âge.* Paris, 1990.

Taylor, Andrew. "Chivalric Conversation and the Denial of Male Fear." In *Conflicted Identities and Multiple Masculinities: Men in the Medieval West*, ed. Jacqueline Murray, 169–88. New York, 1999.

Thrupp, Sylvia. *The Merchant Class of Medieval London 1300–1500.* Ann Arbor, 1962.

Tierney, Brian, and Sidney Painter. *Western Europe in the Middle Ages, 300–1475.* 5th ed. New York, 1992.

Trachtenberg, Joshua. *The Devil and the Jew: The Medieval Conception of the Jew and Its Relation to Modern Antisemitism.* Philadelphia, 1961.

Trexler, Richard. "La prostitution florentine au XVe siècle: Patronages et clientèles." *Annales: Economies, sociétés, civilisations* 36 (1981): 983–1015.

Truant, Cynthia Marie. *The Rites of Labor: Brotherhoods of Compagnonnage in Old and New Regime France.* Ithaca, N.Y., 1994.

Unwin, George. *The Gilds and Companies of London.* 4th ed. London, 1963.

Vale, Juliet. *Edward III and Chivalry: Chivalric Society and Its Context 1270–1350.* Woodbridge, Suffolk, 1982.

Vale, Malcolm. *War and Chivalry: Warfare and Aristocratic Culture in England, France, and Burgundy at the End of the Middle Ages.* London, 1981.

Vale, Malcolm G. A. "Warfare and the Life of the French and Burgundian Nobility in the Late Middle Ages." In *Adelige Sachkultur des Spätmittelalters: Internationaler Kongress.* Veröffentlichungen des Instituts für Mittelalterliche Realienkunde Österreichs, 169–93. Vienna, 1982.

van Werveke, Hans. "Ambachten en erfelijkheid." *Mededelingen van de Koninklijke Vlaamsche Academie voor Wetenschappen, Letteren en Schoone Kunsten van België, Klasse der Letteren* 1 (1942): 5–26.

———. "De medezeggenschap van de knapen (gezellen) in de middeleewsche ambachten." *Mededelingen van de Koninklijke Vlaamsche Academie Voor Wetenschappen, Letteren en Schoone Kunsten van België, Klasse der Letteren* 5: 3 (1943): 5–24.

Verger, Jacques. "L'histoire sociale des universités à la fin du moyen âge: Problèmes, sources, méthodes (à propos des universités du Midi de la France)." In *Die Geschichte der Universitäten und ihre Erforschung*, ed. Siegfried Hoyer and Werner Fläschendräger, 37–53. Leipzig, 1984.

———. "Teachers." In *Universities in the Middle Ages*, ed. Hilde de Ridder-Symoens, 144–68. Cambridge, 1992.

Verriest, Léo. *Les luttes sociales et le contrat d'apprentissage à Tournai jusqu'en 1424*. Brussels, 1912.

Voelkle, William M. "Moran Manuscript M. 1001: The Seven Deadly Sins and the Seven Evil Ones." In *Monsters and Demons in the Ancient and Medieval Worlds*, ed. Anne E. Farkas, Prudence O. Harper, and Evelyn B. Harrison, 101–14. Mainz, 1987.

von Staden, Heinrich. "Women and Dirt." *Helios* 19 (1992): 7–30.

Wagner, Anthony Richard. *Heralds and Heraldry in the Middle Ages: An Inquiry into the Growth of the Armorial Function of Heralds*. London, 1956.

Wehrhahn-Stauch, L. "Bock." In *Lexikon der Christlichen Ikonographie*, ed. Engelbert Kirschbaum, 314–16. Rome, 1968.

Wei, Ian P. "The Self-Image of the Masters of Theology at the University of Paris in the Late Thirteenth and Early Fourteenth Centuries." *Journal of Ecclesiastical History* 46 (1995): 398–431.

Weisheipl, J. A. "Curriculum of the Faculty of Arts at Oxford in the Early Fourteenth Century." *Mediaeval Studies* 26 (1964): 143–85.

Weissman, Ronald F. E. *Ritual Brotherhood in Renaissance Florence*. New York, 1982.

Wheeler, Bonnie, and Charles T. Wood, eds. *Fresh Verdicts on Joan of Arc*. New York, 1996.

Wiesner, Merry. "Guilds, Male Bonding, and Women's Work in Early Modern Germany." *Gender and History* 1 (1989): 125–37.

———. "*Wandervogels* and Women: Journeymen's Concepts of Masculinity in Early Modern Germany." *Journal of Social History* 24 (1991): 767–82.

Woods, Marjorie Curry. "Rape and the Pedagogical Rhetoric of Sexual Violence." In *Criticism and Dissent in the Middle Ages*, ed. Rita Copeland, 56–86. Cambridge, 1996.

Woolgar, C. M. *The Great Household in Medieval England*. New Haven, Conn., 1999.

Zotz, Thomas. "Adel, Bürgertum und Turnier in deutschen Städten vom 13. bis 15. Jahrhundert." In *Das ritterliche Turnier im Mittelalter: Beiträge zu einer vergleichenden Formen- und Verhaltensgeschichte des Rittertums*, ed. Josef Fleckenstein, 451–99. Veröffentlichungen des Max-Planck-Insituts für Geschichte. Göttingen, 1985.

———. "Die Stadtgesellschaft und ihre Feste." In *Feste und Feiern im Mittelalter: Paderborner Symposion des Mediävistenverbandes*, ed. Detlef Altenberg, Jörg Jarnut, and Hans-Hugo Steinhoff, 201–13. Sigmaringen, 1991.

Index

Acknowledgments

As my employment during the time I worked on this book spanned several institutions, I have accumulated debts in several places. Financial support was provided by Temple University in the form of a Grant in Aid of Research, a Summer Research Fellowship, and a year-long Research and Study Leave. Completion of the work was supported by the University of Minnesota in the form of a McKnight Summer Fellowship and a Summer Research Fellowship in the Humanities, research funds that allowed me to travel and to hire a research assistant, and release time from teaching. I am particularly grateful to a succession of department chairs at Temple—Jim Hilty, Morris Vogel, Margaret Marsh, and Richard Immerman—for creating an atmosphere that supports faculty research even under sometimes difficult circumstances (and David Good at Minnesota for the same, albeit under somewhat less difficult circumstances).

The bulk of the research was conducted in Van Pelt Library of the University of Pennsylvania, and I am grateful to the staff there for welcoming a scholar not connected with that institution. I am grateful also to the Bibliothèque Royale/Koninklijke Bibliotheek in Brussels, the Bibliothèque Nationale in Paris, the British Public Record Office, the Corporation of London Records Office, and the London Guildhall Library for access to manuscripts.

Various audiences heard portions of the book presented as papers, and I thank them for helpful comments: the History Department of William and Mary College; the Shelby Cullum Davis Center for Historical Study at Princeton University; the Medieval Institute at the University of Notre Dame; the Medieval Studies Program at the University of California at Santa Barbara; the "Pre-Modern Teenager" conference at the Center for Reformation and Renaissance Studies, University of Toronto; the "Queer Middle Ages" conference at the Graduate Center, City University of New York; the "Learning, Literacy, and Gender in the Middle Ages" conference at Fordham University; the International Congress on Medieval Studies at Western Michigan University; and the Comparative Women's History Workshop, Center for Advanced Feminist Studies Colloquium, and the History Department of the University of Minnesota.

Some of the material in Chapter 1 was previously published in *The Pre-modern Teenager: Youth in Society, 1150–1650,* ed. Konrad Eisenbichler (Center for Reformation and Renaissance Studies, University of Toronto, 2002), and some of the material in Chapter 2 in *Becoming Male in the Middle Ages,* ed. Jeffrey Jerome Cohen and Bonnie Wheeler (Garland, 1997), and *Conflicted Identities and Multiple Masculinities: Men in the Medieval West,* ed. Jacqueline Murray (Garland, 1999). Permission to reuse this material here is gratefully acknowledged.

I have quoted all texts in translation (in the case of English texts, in modernized form). All translations are mine unless otherwise noted. Most of the translations are from published editions accessible in most university libraries, so I have not quoted the originals in the notes.

Christopher Karras, Jo Ann McNamara, Jacqueline Murray, Jerry Singerman, and an anonymous reader were kind enough to read the entire manuscript and comment copiously. Bernard Bachrach, Judith Bennett, Rita Copeland, Richard Kaeuper, Joel Kaye, and Kathryn Reyerson read individual chapters at various stages in their development. I have taken much of their wise advice, but for that which I have not taken, and for any other errors, I alone am responsible. My research assistant Kathryn Kelsey came to the project late and did not get to do the interesting part, but she has been invaluable with the less fun but necessary process of verifying references. Martha Davis helped me with a problematic Latin passage.

My family has had to put up with more than the usual dislocation caused by an academic writing a book, and I am constantly thankful for the good grace with which they do it. Since Chris has begun to write "Needs more theory!" in the margins of my drafts, he no longer qualifies as the proverbial naïve reader, but he has made this book and, indeed, my career possible both by his moral support and by his assumption of a greater share of parenting than he ever expected. Nicola's interest in young men is a good deal less academic than mine, and Elena has little use for them at all. Nonetheless, because they are so good about understanding why Mom wants to be a historian, this book is dedicated to them.

CPSIA information can be obtained
at www.ICGtesting.com
Printed in the USA
JSHW011732100120
3508JS00001B/66